Management Consultancy

Management Consultancy

Boundaries and Knowledge in Action

Andrew Sturdy, Karen Handley, Timothy Clark,
and Robin Fincham

COVENTRY UNIVERSITY LONDON CAMPUS
East India House,
109-117 Middlesex Street, London, E1 7JF
Tel: 020 7247 3666 | Fax: 020 7375 3048
www.coventry.ac.uk/londoncampus

OXFORD
UNIVERSITY PRESS

OXFORD

UNIVERSITY PRESS

Great Clarendon Street, Oxford OX2 6DP
United Kingdom

Oxford University Press is a department of the University of Oxford.
It furthers the University's objective of excellence in research, scholarship,
and education by publishing worldwide. Oxford is a registered trade mark of
Oxford University Press in the UK and in certain other countries

First published 2009
First published in paperback 2010
Reprinted 2013

Published in the United States of America by Oxford University Press
198 Madison Avenue, New York, NY 10016, United States of America

British Library Cataloguing in Publication Data
Data available

Library of Congress Cataloging in Publication Data
Data available

ISBN 978-0-19-959375-0

Acknowledgements

We gratefully acknowledge the support of the following: Calvert Markham, Fiona Czerniawska, and Kimball Bailey for their early and continuing encouragement for our research; Stephanos Avakian, David Greatbatch, and Stefan Heusinkveld for their helpful comments on earlier versions of the manuscript; the Management Consultancies Association for their support and the opportunity to test out ideas; all the research participants for granting us access and for their patience and goodwill during our fieldwork; and Matthew Derbyshire and David Musson of Oxford University Press for their even greater patience in the production of this volume. Finally, we thank the ESRC for their financial support for the project titled 'Knowledge Evolution in Action: Consultancy–Client Relationships' (RES-334-25-0004), under the auspices of the Evolution of Business Knowledge ('EBK') Research Programme. Parts of Chapter 4 are developed in Sturdy et al. (2009).

Contents

List of Tables

List of Abbreviations

AIM	Advanced Institute of Management
ATM	automatic telling machine
EBK	Evolution of Business Knowledge
ESRC	Economic and Social Research Council
FSA	Financial Services Authority
KIF	knowledge intensive firm
KFI	key facts illustration
MBA	Master of Business Administration
MCA	Management Consultancies Association
MPA	Master of Public Administration
NAO	National Audit Office
NIH	not invented here
OD	organization development
OGC	Office of Government Commerce
PBL	project-based learning
POA	Prison Officers' Association
PTB	performance test bid
TCE	transaction cost economics
TPM	Techno project manager

The Authors

Andrew Sturdy is Professor of Organizational Behaviour and Head of Department at the Department of Management, University of Bristol, U.K. He was previously Professor of Organizational Behaviour at Warwick Business School, University of Warwick. His research is focused on the global and local flow of management ideas and is widely cited in academic and popular media. In addition to his research with diverse client and consulting organizations, he advises various government agencies on the use of management consultancy. He is currently leading a research project on internal consultancy in the UK funded by Economic and Social Research Council (ESRC).

Karen Handley is Senior Lecturer in HRM and Organizational Behaviour at Oxford Brookes University Business School. Before entering academia, she worked as a Principal Consultant in two management consultancy organizations. Her previous research investigated workplace learning in management consultancy organizations and she is currently Assistant Director of a research project, Engaging Students with Assessment Feedback, funded by the Higher Education Academy.

Timothy Clark is Professor of Organizational Behaviour at Durham Business School, Durham University. He has conducted a series of research projects into different aspects of consultancy work and more recently has focused on the role of management gurus. These projects have resulted in a number of publications, including *Managing Consultants* (Open University Press, 1995), *Critical Consulting: New Perspectives on the Management Advice Industry* (2002, Blackwell, with R. Fincham) and *Management Speak* (2005, Routledge, with David Greatbatch).

Robin Fincham is Professor of Organizational Behaviour in the School of Management, University of Stirling. His research interests have focused on innovation, particularly the strategic use of IT and, more recently, the role of management knowledge and ideas in organizational change and expert labour. His published work includes a co-authored book, *Expertise and Innovation* (1994, Oxford University Press) and a collection (co-edited with T. Clark), *Critical Consulting: New Perspectives on the Management Advice Industry* (2002, Blackwell).

1

Consultancy, knowledge, and boundaries

Introduction

Few people will have avoided encountering either directly or indirectly the outcome of some kind of management consultancy intervention in organizations and societies. And yet, except for those directly involved, very little is known about what actually happens in one of the core consultancy activities—projects with clients. This is not to say that the wide and growing academic and practitioner literature on consultancy has nothing to say about client–consultant relations in general. Here, a core concept is that of boundaries and, in particular, knowledge and organizational boundaries. More specifically, it is widely held that the client–consultant relationship is primarily one of expert organizational *outsiders* (consultants) bringing outside knowledge or legitimation to organizational *insiders*—clients.[1] This view has become a largely taken-for-granted assumption about client–consultant relationships and, combined with the empirical neglect of management consultancy projects in action, is the starting point of this book. In particular, we seek to begin to fill the empirical space in the study of this aspect of consultancy and to examine in depth and unpack the nature and boundaries of management consultancy projects. Such a task is important in at least three respects.

- First, if management consultancy is as significant as it is claimed, then furthering our understanding can help in the development of critique and/or practical/policy prescriptions. For example, if consultancy

[1] Internal consultants are not considered in this study nor are consultants on secondment, interim managers, or specialist contract staff (see Barley and Kunda 2004; Garsten 2003; Sturdy and Wright 2008). The very distinction made between external and internal consultants reinforces the primary image of the former as expert 'outsiders'.

projects are revealed as not *necessarily* being a key site for the flow of new management ideas, then appropriate steps can be taken to address this or focus on other empirical domains.

- Second, it is important because consultancy is illustrative of a wide range of other activities and areas of interest and significance. Exploring client–consultant relations in action can, for example, shed light on topics such as inter-organizational relations; project working, organizational change, and management innovation; expert labour; professional services; and, more generally, upon management and knowledge in society.

- Third and finally, challenging taken-for-granted assumptions is potentially of value more generally. Following sociological traditions (e.g. Berger 1963) and a broad notion of critical thinking, it can serve to denaturalize phenomena or 'world views'. For example, debates about knowledge-intensive firms and societies raise questions about who is seen as 'expert' and therefore privileged in relation to others (Starbuck 1992). Although this is not our main objective, we hope that our analysis contributes to such concerns.

Our account is based primarily on the findings of a three-year study funded by UK government's Economic and Social Research Council (ESRC) and conducted within a broader programme of research on the 'Evolution of Business Knowledge' (EBK) (www.esrcsocietytoday.ac.uk; see also Scarbrough 2008; Sturdy et al. 2008). Mostly using observation and interview methods, four management consultancy projects were studied in depth and over time. The main focus was on how client–consultant relationships and interactions in the formal project meetings appeared to affect flows of management knowledge. Clearly, such a focus represents only a part of what might be considered as the work of management consultants and clients. However, and as we shall see shortly, many other consultancy activities have been explored elsewhere. What has been notably lacking in research on consultancy is longitudinal studies which examine clients and consultants working together in action. Primarily because of the great difficulties in gaining access as 'non-participants', such research is very rare indeed. Other than accounts by consultants themselves, almost all published research on consultancy relies on public sources or post hoc accounts from interviews and surveys. This literature has generated considerable insight and carries other advantages which in-depth studies lack. We hope, however, that the necessarily selective account of management consultancy in the following chapters goes some way in beginning to shed light on an otherwise largely hidden and yet important aspect of contemporary management practice.

In this chapter, we begin to set out the framing and rationale for our subsequent analysis. First, we introduce the various literatures which attribute a significance to management consultancy, moving towards more focused studies on consultancy and then, our particular areas of interest, knowledge flow in client–consultant relationships. Building on this, an alternative framework is developed as a basis for beginning to assess the complex, varied, and dynamic structural dimensions of insider–outsider relations in consulting projects. This chapter concludes with a brief overview of the structure of this book and of the following chapters.

The Field of Management Consultancy

As is now quite well known, management consultancy has seen a remarkable and largely continuous growth in the last twenty years, especially in the USA and much of western Europe (see Kennedy Information 2004). While definitional lines are notoriously vague in relation to consultancy, some of this growth can be attributed to the increasing scope of the activities of large consulting firms to encompass areas beyond those of traditional consulting. Here, 'independent expert advice' or 'change facilitation' is complemented by outsourcing and the implementation of organizational and technological change. At the same time, however, other professional and IT firms have developed their advisory activities and the number of small or niche consulting firms has also grown (Management Consultancies Association 2007). Overall, the growth in management consultancy has led to increased attention to the sector and its activities.

The Importance of Management Consultancy in Society

Before exploring academic studies which engage with management consultancy both indirectly and directly, it is important to recognize that the growth of consulting has prompted or re-ignited a number of public or, at least, policy concerns as well as a general business discourse around management consultancy. These wider issues are often neglected in academic research as they lack sufficient novelty or are difficult to access, but are often a key point of reference in some of the more popular texts. First, questions have been raised about the impact of consultancy usage on the

3

role of organizational management (i.e. 'make' or buy-in management) and, in the public sector, on civil servants and politicians—democracy versus 'consultocracy' (National Audit Office 2006; Saint-Martin 2000: 20). Related to this, particularly post-Enron, is the question of accountability for decisions and actions, especially given that management consultancy is often seen as a shadowy and costly activity that is associated with radical organizational change, including various forms of rationalization (Born 2004; Brockhaus 1977; Macdonald 2004; Mickhail and Ostrovsky 2007). At the same time, the expansion of the sector and its discourses, combined with its association with those in visible positions of power in organizations and governments, has, arguably, led to a growth in the status of the occupation or, at least, its desirability as a career option for graduates for example (see Armbrüster 2006; Karreman and Rylander 2008).

Certainly, management consultancy maintains a high presence in the various business media. This reinforces a combination of controversy and prestige around consultancy, resulting in a particular discourse of consulting jokes for example (see also Sturdy et al. 2007). This polarity is also reflected in the expansion of prescriptive guides setting out how to do, manage, and use management consultancy (e.g. Czerniawska 2002; Lippitt and Lippitt 1986; Maister 1993) alongside, often sensationalist, insider or journalist exposés of consulting sharp practices at the expense of clients, employees, and taxpayers (e.g. Craig 2005, 2006; O'Shea and Madigan 1997; Pinault 2001). Both types of publication are typically dismissed or ignored in academic research. This is short-sighted, for although the authors of such books almost certainly have very different agendas from those of researchers, they are also likely to have had access to and/or direct experience of the day-to-day practices of consultancy, including those which largely remain hidden from the academic gaze (e.g. Moore 1984). As we shall see shortly, prescriptive texts contain some valuable insights into the nature of consultancy project work.

The growing presence or shadow of management consultancy in organizations and society is reflected in academic studies focusing on other fields of enquiry. In particular, in the UK especially, but also in western and 'emerging' economies, consultants are seen as key agents and symbols of broader social changes. For example, in Thrift's account of 'soft' or 'knowing capitalism', management consultancy is a key 'generator and distributor of new knowledge ... a vital part of the cultural circuit of capital' and of a hegemony of new managerialism (2005: 35–6).

This cultural circuit of capital is able to produce constant discursive-cum-practical change with considerable power to mould the content of people's work lives and, it might be added, to produce more general cultural models that affect the rest of people's lives as well . . . capitalism's commissars. (2005: 93)

Similarly, for Sennett (2006), consultants are both symptomatic and agents of 'the culture of the new capitalism'. In particular, familiar criticisms of consultants being used to rationalize human processes without accountability, responsibility, or local knowledge are located within the context of short-term financialization, change at any cost and a broader growth of 'social distance', and 'divorce between command and accountability' in organizations (2006: 57, 70; see also Froud et al. 2000).

The view of consultants as agents of new management knowledge and organizational change is more or less explicit in much research from within organization studies where consultancy features, but not as the principal focus. This covers a wide spectrum of activities such as small firms (e.g. Christensen and Klyver 2006) and inter-organizational relations (e.g. Nooteboom 2004), but is most evident in four related areas of study and debate. First, consultancy is seen as a part of the broader field of professional and business services (e.g. Furusten and Werr 2005; Karantinou and Hogg 2001; Miozzo and Grimshaw 2006; Muzio et al. 2008) where emphasis varies between debates over the notion of professions and elites in contemporary society and the nature of service processes (see also Williams and Savage 2008). Second, while consultants are typically seen to lie on the periphery of the professions, they are regarded as central to, if not emblematic of, knowledge work and associated debates around the organization of knowledge-intensive firms (KIFs), knowledge workers, and associated knowledge management processes (e.g. Alvesson 2004; Alvesson and Karreman 2007; Kinnie et al. 2006; Robertson and Swan 2003). Third, and more conventionally, a number of studies of organizational change, particularly ethnographic accounts, have pointed to the often crucial and controversial role played by management consultants in various rationalization and strategy processes for example (e.g. Born 2004; Czarniawska and Sevon 1996; Jackall 1986; Pettigrew 1985) although, surprisingly perhaps, labour process research has rarely focused on this. Fourth, and of particular relevance to our study, research on the diffusion or translation of management ideas, practices, and innovations echoes the views of Thrift (2005) in seeing consultancy as a key element or mediator in the management knowledge industry or system, alongside business schools, management gurus, and the business media for example (e.g. Abrahamson 1996; Birkinshaw et al. 2008; Clark 2004; Sahlin-Andersson and Engwall 2002*a*; Suddaby and Greenwood 2001).

Management Consultancy Research

Throughout the following chapters, we shall be drawing on what has become a substantial body of research focusing more directly on management consultancy. This can be understood in a number of different ways such as in terms of debates, perspectives, levels of analysis, and empirical foci (see Table 1.1; Armbrüster 2006). Engwall and Kipping (2002) for example distinguish industry-, firm-, and project-level analysis, but as we shall see, although most research discusses projects, especially in terms of the client–consultant relationship, very little examines them directly. In addition, a number of studies seek an overview, addressing a wide range of themes and levels of analysis (e.g. Armbrüster 2006; Buono 2001, 2002; Clark and Fincham 2002), including through historical work (e.g. Kipping 2002; Marsh 2008; McKenna 2006). Of the more focused studies, some address broader themes such as identity (Alvesson and Robertson 2006; Meriläinen et al. 2004; O'Mahoney 2007; Whittle 2005), innovation and organizational development (Argyris 1970; Argyris and Schön 1996; Bessant and Rush1995; Schein 1969; Wood 2001), and the 'knowledge industry' (Kipping and Engwall 2002). Relatively little work has been done on particular types of consultancy such as internal consulting (cf. Lacey 1995; Wright 2008) or on consulting sectors such as the public sector (Hughes et al. 2007; Saint-Martin 2000) or international development (Wood 1998). Similarly, although consultancy has been explored in particular national contexts (see Kipping and Engwall 2002), there is little comparative work or exploration of contexts where consultancy is not highly utilized (cf. Mohe 2008; Saint-Martin 2000; Wright and Kwon 2006).

The majority of research, and that which is of particular relevance to our interests, focuses on consultancy practices or, rather, those of consultants. Here, studies range from the organization and globalization of firms (Jones 2003; Morgan et al. 2006); product development (Anand et al. 2007; Heusinkveld and Benders 2005) and, relatedly, consulting methods (Werr 1999; Werr et al. 1997); knowledge management (Bogenrieder and Nooteboom 2004; Hansen et al. 1999; Morris 2001; Sarvary 1999); and forms of consulting knowledge. In the latter case, for example, Werr and Stjernberg (2003) set out three core types of varying levels of tacitness/explicitness and specificity to context—experience, methods

Table 1.1. A classification of selected books and reports on management consultancy

Type/focus	Examples
Research/policy reports	NAO (2006); MCA (2007); Kennedy Information (2004)
Prescriptive guides and textbooks	Maister (1993); Lippitt and Lippitt (1986); Markham (1997); Czerniawska (2002)
Journalistic/insider exposés	Craig (2005, 2006); O'Shea and Madigan (1997); Pinault (2001)
Related fields (e.g. social change; organizational change and relationships; professional services; knowledge workers/firms; and mediation)	Thrift (2005); Sahlin-Andersson and Engwall (2002a); Alvesson (2004); Furusten and Werr (2005); Born (2004); Jackall (1986)
Overviews/general	Armbrüster (2006); Clark and Fincham (2002); Buono (2002)
Historical studies	McKenna (2006); Marsh (2008)
Management innovation and OD	Schein (1969); Wood (2001)
Knowledge industry/mediation	Kipping and Engwall (2002)
Role in public sector	Saint-Martin (2000)
Organization and management of firms/staff	Jones (2003)
Consulting methods	Werr (1999)
Rhetoric/promotion	Clark (1995)
Selection and evaluation	Deelmann and Mohe (2006)
Consulting projects	[current volume]

(abstract 'road maps'), and cases (see also Werr 1999)—while others also point to analytical expertise or 'objectivity' derived specifically from an outsider status or distance (Semadeni 2001). Alongside such work, given the ambiguity of much consulting knowledge, considerable attention has been given to consulting rhetoric and promotion activities (Berglund and Werr 2000; Bloomfield and Danieli 1995; Clark and Salaman 1998; Fincham 2002; Kieser 1997). There has been much less focus on client activities (Hislop 2002; Macdonald 2006) except, perhaps, in relation to their consulting selection and evaluation practices (Gluckler and Armbrüster 2003). Indeed, as clients have become more experienced and as purchasing has become more centralized or professionalized in many contexts, this subject has become a growing area of interest (Deelmann and Mohe 2006; Werr and Pemer 2007).

While both consulting and client practices have received some attention, joint activities have been neglected, much as day-to-day managerial work once was (Mintzberg 1973). This is almost certainly a consequence of the difficulties of research access as well as, perhaps, the resource (time) implications of departing from conventional interview and survey methods. There are some exceptions however. In particular, a little known or cited study by De Jong and van Eekelen (1999) details and quantifies the precise practices involved in consulting projects, such as the number of meetings and telephone conversations. Similarly, Sturdy et al. (2006) explored some of the less formal, backstage joint practices of clients and consultants and emerging research is beginning to address this method-ological neglect (e.g. Smith 2008; Whittle 2008). Furthermore, and as we shall see, some of the prescriptive literature, written by practicing or former consultants, contains important insights into a world that has otherwise remained largely invisible to all but the participants. In other words, Engwall and Kipping's assessment that 'the interaction process between consultants and their clients is still poorly understood' (2002: 8) still largely holds.

Despite the continued neglect of interaction, the client–consultant rela-tionship is a focus of much research (e.g. Fincham 1999; Fullerton and West 1996; Kitay and Wright 2003, 2004; McGivern 1983; Nikolova 2007; Sturdy 1997a; Werr and Styhre 2003). Here, as we shall argue, although there is an increasing recognition of varying dimensions to the relation-ship, most research gives primacy to its contractual or organizational basis. In particular, it is seen, first and foremost, as an insider–outsider relationship. This is particularly evident in studies which connect the client–consultant relationship to what is typically deemed to be the pri-mary function of consultancy—knowledge flow or mediation. However, again, relatively few studies focus specifically on the role of consultants in knowledge flow within client organizations (Antal and Krebsbach-Gnath 2001; Lahti and Beyerlein 2000). As Semadeni put it, 'one area that has yet to be explored is the knowledge arbitrage function performed by management consultants' (2001: 53). Rather, it almost seems that the assumption is that because consultants actively promote new manage-ment approaches and are widely used, they do indeed perform this role. We now examine this literature further.

Towards a View of Client–Consultancy Relationships as Complex, Varied, and Dynamic

There is now a substantial and continuing literature on the economic importance of knowledge to organizations and ('knowledge') societies (e.g. see Argote et al. 2003). Much of this emphasizes the role of those involved in bringing new knowledge into organizations from the outside either as some form of knowledge transfer or as part of the process of helping firms to create new knowledge themselves (Anand et al. 2002; Birkinshaw et al. 2008; Burt 1992; Haas 2006; Hargadon 1998). As already noted above, management consultants are often placed at the forefront of these activities, not least because of the scale, profile, and growth of their activities in many western economies in recent years (Engwall and Kipping 2002; Suddaby and Greenwood 2001). Such a view echoes the traditional notion and definition of consultants as independent experts, that is, as outsiders with new knowledge. As McKenna argues:

Whether in computer systems, strategic counsel, organizational design, or corporate acquisitions, management consulting firms have become, and continue to be, a crucial institutional solution to executives' ongoing need for outside information. (2006: 78)

Indeed, McKenna describes consultants as 'pre-eminent knowledge brokers' on the basis of their 'status as outsiders' and the 'economies of knowledge' this brings compared to insiders—they 'have flourished primarily because they have remained outside the traditional boundaries of the firm' (2006: 12–16; see also Sorge and Van Witteloostuijn 2004). Such a view is founded on transaction cost economics whereby 'the very reason why clients hire consulting firms is the fact that consultants have the ability to gain experience, expertise, methods and tools in one industry or organization and then apply them in another, thereby saving the client the costs of developing them in-house' (Armbrüster 2006: 54). But this view is also evident more generally. Consultants are seen to bring either technical or process expertise *from the outside* (see Kieser 2002a; Schein 1969; Werr et al. 1997). For example, Armbrüster notes how 'the work of consultants is based on experience and accumulated expertise, albeit in other types of expertise than clients' (2006: 52). Likewise, Gammelsaeter (2002: 222) suggests that

consultants as carriers of knowledge are generally embedded in contexts that are external to the organization, whereas the management they interact with is embedded in internal organization.

Here, it is fellow consultants or other external centres of expertise such as elite universities who are seen as a key source of learning (Bogenrieder and Nooteboom 2004; Werr and Stjernberg 2003). Clients meanwhile are, according to this view, seen as being mostly concerned with internal, 'operational' knowledge directed towards 'regulating' day-to-day activities of their organization (Armbrüster and Kipping 2002), in Gouldner's (1957) terms, as 'locals' (cf. Haas 2006). It is thus also the more ambiguous 'external' nature of a consultant's perspective, which is valued by client management (Semadeni 2001) although this is less often acknowledged in comparison to the value perceived in specific knowledge and its association with successful 'progressive' firms or nations or the brand of the consulting firm itself (see Chapter 2).

The dominance of this expert outsider view is partially acknowledged elsewhere. For example, Armbrüster's review of the consulting literature identifies two broad perspectives—the 'functionalist' and the 'critical'— whereby the former views consultants as 'carriers and transmitters of management knowledge' (2006: 2). He suggests that the 'critical' literature has a much broader view of what consultancy is all about, pointing, for example, to a few studies of organizational change and management consultancy which adopt a more 'micro-political' tradition where legitimation or status as much as new knowledge is key (e.g. Bloomfield and Best 1992; Bloomfield and Danieli 1995; Jackall 1986; Moore 1984). This is true and we adopt a similar position here, in relation to knowledge flow. But many critical studies also subscribe to the conventional view of consultants as outsiders bringing new knowledge. For example, we have already seen how Thrift ascribes consultancy with a central role in 'knowing capitalism', indeed as being 'responsible for producing the bulk of management knowledge' (2005: 37). Similarly, and more directly, Clegg et al. see management consultants as especially innovative, introducing 'new ways of thinking, seeing and being in the world' (2004: 35–6). But even in less general accounts and ones which are sceptical of the robustness of consulting knowledge in effecting change, consultancy is seen as a largely effective system of persuasion or as emblematic of 'knowledge intensiveness' (Alvesson 2004; Clark 1995), providing a measure of reassurance to individual clients (Kieser 2002a; Sturdy 1997a). Despite such claims and as we have already noted, there has been very little research conducted as to exactly whether, when, or how knowledge flow occurs between clients and consultants. Indeed, this neglect applies more generally, beyond the context of consultancy. As Tagliaventi and Mattarelli noted, 'one particularly important topic which has as yet to be explored empirically is knowledge flow between the heterogeneous communities and networks that cut across an organization' (2006: 292).

Those few studies which do examine knowledge flow at the level of the client–consultant relationship are largely consistent in reproducing the conventional and common-sense view of consultants—as expert and 'objective outsiders' (e.g. Semadeni 2001: 55). This is reflected in the high degree of consensus over the inherently problematic nature of the knowledge 'transfer' process—the use of consultants is a double-edged sword. First, consultants' value is again seen as being based on their outsider status, in being able to bring new and potentially valuable knowledge to clients. They are not immersed in the day-to-day operational world of organizations, but are relative cosmopolitans who can draw on a range of, often privileged, sources, including innovative clients, and their own specialist skills in knowledge development or translation. For example, Antal and Krebsbach-Gnath (2001), like McKenna above, see consultants' outsider status, their 'marginality', as the necessary contribution they bring to organizational learning in terms of new knowledge—the *strength of weak ties* (cf. Anand et al. 2002; Granovetter 1985). In addition, their outsider status is viewed as providing them with a privileged insight into client knowledge 'which may not be readily perceptible to the client organization' (Semadeni 2001: 55).

However, and second, others draw attention to the problems that consultants' outsider status brings for knowledge flow (e.g. Engwall and Kipping 2002; see also Ginsberg and Abrahamson 1991). Kipping and Armbrüster (2002) in particular, and following Meyer (1996), focus on what they describe as the *burden of otherness* faced by consultants. They document historical cases of client resistance towards outsiders, and such accounts continue to be reported (e.g. Czerniawska and May 2004). Although we shall argue that resistance derives from a number of other sources, including group identity dynamics and control issues, here, contrasting or alien knowledge bases are seen as 'primary' in explaining the consultants' 'burden' and their failure to communicate meaningfully with clients and effect lasting change. Their knowledge is *too new* (Armbrüster and Kipping 2002: 108; Kipping and Armbrüster 2002: 221; see also Schön 1983: 296) and/or they lack a shared frame of reference, a common language, or, what Nonaka (1994) describes as, *redundant knowledge* (Lahti and Beyerlein 2000; Semadeni 2001: 48).

Such studies provide a useful starting point for our own research. In particular, the emphasis on outsider status points to the importance, primacy even, of boundaries—organizational and knowledge (understanding) boundaries—in helping to make sense both of client–consultant relations and of knowledge flow in this context. Indeed, the view of consultants as outsiders clearly has some validity. For example, it is evident in each of, what Werr and Styhre (2003) identified as, the three core perspectives on consultant–client relationships—helper–recipient, manipulator–victim, and a contingent view of power/dependency relations between the two parties. Aside from the issue of outside knowledge/perspective outlined above, what lies at its heart is formal organizational attachment—a contractual/legal boundary. Here, despite some common goals, conflicts arise in pursuing organizational objectives and responsibilities, in terms of consultants selling on further business as opposed to long-term problem resolution for example (e.g. Moore 1984; Sturdy 1997*a*).

There are other dimensions to consultants' apparent outsider status too, although these are rarely the focus of research. For example, consultants and clients sometimes inhabit different social and occupational worlds, spending relatively little time with each other and, in some cases, segregated from each other's day-to-day activities (De Jong and van Eekelen 1999). Even the closer relations, often associated with senior levels, may be becoming more distant as clients become more 'rational' or transactional (i.e. organizational) in their dealings with consultants such as through professionalized purchasing departments and tendering (Kennedy Information 2004: 4; also Czerniawska 2002; Werr and Pemer 2007). However, and as already intimated, other studies suggest that the client–consultant relationship is more complex, contingent, diverse, and dynamic than general accounts and those of knowledge flow in consultancy suggest. We now examine this literature further in order to develop a more nuanced basis for understanding consultancy relations before turning to a broader literature on boundaries and inter-organizational knowledge flow in the following chapter.

Consultants as Insiders and/or Outsiders—Towards Socio-Spatial Embeddedness and Inter-Project Diversity

In keeping with a growing recognition of the fluidity and permeability of organizational boundaries and a longer-standing tradition of (intra-)organizational heterogeneity (e.g. Gouldner 1957), a number of recent studies of consultancy have begun to challenge the dominant 'outsider' view and its universality, highlighting diversity *between* client–consultancy assignments. Three studies are of particular note although they do not address or focus on the implications for knowledge flow.

First, Czarniawska and Mazza (2003) develop Kipping and Armbrüster's (2002) notion of consultants' 'otherness' (cf. Meyer 1996) by reference to liminality—a transitional 'condition where usual practice and order are suspended' (2003: 267; see also Chapters 2 and 7). They apply this to consulting project teams where clients and consultants are both located outside of their respective organizational contexts in joint activity, working alongside each other or in constant contact, often in a segregated space—in operational proximity (also Clegg et al. 2004; De Jong and van Eekelen 1999; Werr et al. 1997). Here then, a new boundary is introduced such that the participants may become neither insiders nor outsiders in the traditional (i.e. organizational) sense, but in between or in transition. In terms of physical space and shared practices, they might both be seen as (project) insiders and may come to identify emotionally with the project team, structures, and activity in addition to, or even more than, their respective organization, occupation, or role for the period of the project at least (Czarniawska and Mazza 2003). Of course, the new set of boundaries does not necessarily or constantly undermine completely organizational or employer-defined roles (Sturdy et al. 2006). As Christensen and Klyver (2006: 311) note from their study of consulting in small firms:

... [the client is] highly focused on the specific [project] output that may be anticipated. This forces the consultant to be very specific and concept oriented. On the other hand, the consultants are highly focused on the budgets available and thus the time limits set. This may hamper time for joint reflection and situational as well as contextual translation processes.

Related to the issue of liminality is the second study of note, by Werr and Styhre (2003). Here, the authors challenge the dominant view by pointing to recently emerging partnership contracts and discourses of the client–consultant relationship (also Karantinou and Hogg 2001) where greater attention is given to consultants' implementation responsibilities and their long-term relations with clients, such as through a 'preferred supplier' status or as part of a retainer contract (see also Czerniawska and May 2004; Kennedy Information 2004). They cite the case of a 'house consultant', contracted on an almost permanent basis with a client and, despite the consultant's formal employment status, seemingly more of an organizational insider than many client staff (Werr and Styhre 2003: 62). This has parallels with studies of temporary workers or interim managers (e.g. Garsten 1999, 2003), but in this case, the role remains that of advice giving.

Third, Kitay and Wright (2003) present a more contingent than historical and generalized view. Informed partly by a recognition of different forms of consultancy such as Schein's (1969) classic distinction between process (facilitative) and resource (expert) consulting, they point to more persistent variations *between* consulting assignments. In particular, by drawing on Granovetter's (1985) seminal insights on embeddedness, they show how consultants (and, to an extent, their firms) can be seen as either 'insiders' or 'outsiders' according to the presence/absence of personal and social ties, beyond a market transaction. For example, they identify two particular 'insider' roles—partner and implementer. 'Partnership' is not so much associated with an emerging relationship discourse (as above), as with the practice of maintaining close extra-project ties with clients over time. Indeed, contrary to recent claims mentioned above of the demise of such links, other studies confirm the continued salience and, even, centrality of personal relationships and shared social characteristics (e.g. Gluckler and Armbrüster 2003; Jones 2003; Sturdy et al. 2006). At the same time, 'implementers' may be *organizationally* close, junior consultants on secondment or 'in house' for example, but not especially close in terms of personal ties or organizational identification (also Garsten 2003; Kitay and Wright 2004). Once again, this suggests that the purely organizational dimension of the insider–outsider relationship cannot be taken for granted as primary and that other boundary dimensions, in this case social and temporal boundaries, need to be made explicit.

Knowledge Boundaries—Consultants as Knowledge Insiders?

Together, the above three studies present an important challenge to universalist 'outsider' notions of consultancy by starting to move and expand the relationship boundary towards a more ambiguous, shifting, or liminal quality and beyond organizational attachment towards other bases such as (*a*) spatial activity, (*b*) emerging partnership discourses/contracts, and (*c*) personal relations. However, and importantly for our area of interest, they do not address a fundamental aspect of the dominant view— the characterization of consultants as *knowledge* outsiders. Indeed, they reinforce this view and that of studies of knowledge flow through consultancy in that the consultant remains the expert, bringing outside (e.g. 'technical' or 'esoteric') knowledge (Kitay and Wright 2003) to the client or 'reformee' (Czarniawska and Mazza 2003: 281). This too needs to be challenged as a general characteristic if a more nuanced understanding of the client–consultant relationship and its potential for knowledge flow is to be developed.

The assumption that consultants are knowledge outsiders is most clearly problematic in cases where consultants are deployed, not to bring new knowledge to the client, but to confirm or legitimate existing client understandings. This is a familiar, long-standing, and popular criticism of consultants (O'Shea and Madigan 1997), but can also be seen as a form of 'management audit' to lessen exposure to corporate liability claims. As McKenna observes, 'from the late 1980s onward, consultants increasingly found themselves selling legitimacy, not simply knowledge transfer' (2006: 230). More generally, however, the legitimating role of consultancy usage serves organizational politics to help ensure change projects and other management agendas are supported or progressed (Semadeni 2001; Sturdy 1997a) and a signalling function to financial and other stakeholders and their agents (Armbrüster 2006; Froud et al. 2000). In all these senses, consultants can be seen as *fundamentally conservative* in terms of the knowledge they bring or present (mirror) to clients (Clegg et al. 2004; cf. Sturdy et al. 2004), at least those whom they are dealing with directly, a point to which we shall return.

The view of management consultants as knowledge outsiders is also partially undermined by the fact that their knowledge base is significantly derived from the practices of other, especially 'leading', clients rather than fellow consultants or research institutes as suggested earlier (Armbrüster and Kipping 2002). Indeed, this is often a key reason for their appointment by clients—their mediating role as knowledge arbitragers (conduits) and arbiters (judges) of other clients' knowledge (Semadeni 2001). This view is more evident in the literature on business services than consultancy specifically, and reflected in supplier preferences for 'interesting' (i.e. innovative) clients (Fosstenlokken et al. 2003; cf. Werr and Stjernberg 2003). Indeed, clients have been characterized as effectively partial employees of professional service firms in terms of their joint participation in 'product' development (Mills and Morris 1986). Of course, when such products are subsequently marketed to new clients, they then take the form of outside knowledge. However, and as we shall argue in more detail in the following chapters, even here, the process of translating such products or ideas can be seen as the co-production of knowledge (Christensen and Klyver 2006). At a general level then, much consulting knowledge is not so much outside knowledge as (other) client or shared knowledge.

Clearly, despite such challenges, in some cases, the dominant view will indeed hold, when consultants bring knowledge which is new or unfamiliar to a particular client in the form of methods, case studies, and broader experience for example (Werr and Stjernberg 2003). Furthermore, even in cases where consultants have appeared simply to legitimate or rubber-stamp client-based ideas, this may, in fact, reflect sophisticated idea/issue-selling techniques by the consultants. Here, consultants seek to persuade clients that they were the originator of the consultant-led idea or method, either directly (Dutton et al. 2001; Sturdy 1997a) or

15

through the use of client middle managers for example (Craig 2005; Sturdy et al. 2006). The important point here, however, is that the role of consultants as outsiders *cannot be assumed and certainly should not form the basis of general conceptions of consultancy, especially in relation to knowledge flow.* Moreover, in many situations and, arguably, increasingly, clients and consultants may share a wide range of other forms of knowledge or knowledge domains.

A key domain in which clients and consultants may share some knowledge is that of the client organization and/or its individual personnel. This can be assumed, given that most consulting work (ca. 60–70%) is based on repeat business (File et al. 1994; Karantinou and Hogg 2001) and that, as we have seen, personal relations are often deemed important. Likewise, and as we explore in detail in Chapter 5, sector knowledge is often shared, not least because many consulting firms recruit on the basis of experience in particular client sectors, and/or structure their activities in this way to help develop sector expertise (Kennedy Information 2004). The same is true with regard to management functions and specialisms where clients and consultants from similar functional backgrounds (e.g. strategy, marketing, and production) may work alongside each other in project teams.

The extent to which clients and consultants share knowledge domains partly reflects an increasing sophistication and/or scepticism among many clients and consulting firms' responses to this (Hislop 2002; Macdonald 2006; Sturdy 1997a). Indeed, in recent years, the traditional view of consultants as carriers of alien knowledge to clients has become even less tenable. This is linked to a number of factors. For example, very many more managers have been exposed to management tools and frameworks (e.g. organizational change, strategy, and project management models) through either formal (e.g. MBA) education (Czerniawska and May 2004; Kitay and Wright 2004), the wider media (Furusten 1999), internal change programmes, or even the use of external consultants, which has become almost habitual in some sectors (cf. Armbrüster and Kipping 2002; Czerniawska and Mazza 2003). Similarly, consultancy users are less likely to have spent all their careers in one organization (Webb 2004) and there is evidence of career cross-overs whereby former consultants assume senior positions in client firms (Sturdy and Wright 2008; Wright 2008).

Such developments, combined with the cases where consultants have come to acquire an intimate knowledge of the client organization and sector, may also undermine the second dimension of their knowledge outsider status, that of offering an external perspective regardless of any particular technical expertise, for they may 'go native' (Nooteboom 2004). Overall, however, the important thing to emphasize is that consultants can be seen as *knowledge* insiders with their clients with respect to a wide range of domains (e.g. organizational, personal, sectoral, and functional), including, in the case of legitimation, that which is at the core of the dominant view. Thus, the view expressed earlier that clients and consultants lack a shared or 'redundant' knowledge also cannot be assumed. Indeed, as we shall see, this may form the basis of a bridge, spanning other knowledge boundaries.

Boundary Complexity and Dynamics within Projects—Interests, Roles, and Phases

In addition to challenging the dominant 'outsider' view of consultancy, the above discussion undermines its universality. In short, it highlights the variability which may exist between consulting projects and calls for greater diversity and precision in terms of boundary bases or continua of client–consultant relations. In other words, we should ask the question *insider/outsider with respect to what—the project team, the contract, personal networks, and knowledge domains?* However, our account has not yet considered diversity *within* projects in terms of interests and roles for example—the question of *insider/outsider with respect to whom?*

We have noted how organization-centric views present consultants as outsiders in terms of conflicting organizational interests. While this view might be questioned by those who see consultants as simply helping to address organizational interests, through partnerships for example, it is more convincingly undermined through a pluralist perspective. Here, and as we saw in relation to the role of consultants in legitimating client knowledge, they are seen as allies of management and/or the owners of organizations, as *political* insiders (e.g. Saint-Martin 2000; Sturdy 1997b; cf. Werr and Styhre 2003). It is also implied in accounts of resistance to consultants from disparate client groups such as middle management and others whose identities and even jobs may be threatened (Jackall 1986; Moore 1984). In other words and in contrast to studies of knowledge flow in consultancy, it is not simply the boundaries of outsider status or alien knowledge—'the burden of otherness'—which explain why consultants might fail to achieve 'solutions acceptable to all involved' (cf. Kipping and Armbrüster 2002: 204) for this suggests a unitary view of organizational interests.

Such political dynamics may seem unsurprising. Indeed, they are recognized in the consulting practice of 'power mapping'. Here, consultants seek to establish, monitor, and influence (e.g. include/exclude) the interests of key individuals or groups in the client organization in terms of their likely support for effecting change and/or generating future income (Buchanan and Badham 1999; Hagan and Smail 1997). However, such dynamics are important to highlight for they draw attention not only to another important basis for boundary relations—political interests—but also to relations *within* client firms and projects more generally. Indeed, many of the more prescriptive accounts point to relationship diversity within consulting projects. For example, Arnaud suggests that 'the word client only rarely designates a single unique person' (1998: 470) and Schein (1997: 202) categorizes clients from the main 'contact' client and 'primary' owner of the problem to 'intermediate' clients who work in the project team and 'unwitting'/'indirect' clients who are unaware/aware of the effects of the consultancy alongside 'ultimate' clients such as customers. On the consulting side too there is often similar, even parallel, complexity. For example, one can distinguish between the roles of 'finders' or 'hunters' who develop and maintain client relations (relationship managers), 'minders' who manage projects, and, the more junior consultant, 'grinders' who carry out the specific service (*Fortune Magazine*, 14 October 1996; see also Karantinou and Hogg 2001). Also, consulting roles or styles (e.g. coach, facilitator, catalyst, reflector, and extra) may vary within projects, performed by the same or different consultants (see also Lippitt and Lippitt 1986; Moore 1984; Tisdall 1982).

Thus, a much more complex picture is emerging on which to assess insider–outsider or boundary relations in consultancy. Again, this is supported by studies of business services generally where relations have been described as 'a network of inter-organizational contacts, joint working and interpersonal and group exchanges ... which embraces many functional areas and hierarchical levels within the supplier and client companies' (O'Farrell and Moffat 1991: 215). However, such distinctions remain almost invisible in consultancy research in organizational theory which either generalizes from an organization-centric or unitary perspective (where consultants are seen as outsiders) or focuses on *inter*-project diversity. While the latter helps to address the question of insider/outsider with respect to *what*, a recognition of *intra*-project diversity in terms of political interests and associated roles and actors extends analysis further, towards the question of insider/outsider with respect to *whom*?

The next important dimension of our analysis is a consideration of relationship *dynamics* or the 'when?' question. Some reference has been made to debates over broad trends in client–consultant relationships, towards partnerships or greater client sophistication for example (cf. Werr and Styhre 2003). Similarly, it was noted how repeat business or a 'lengthy courtship' might lead to the development of closer relations and the reduced salience of personal and organizational knowledge boundaries (Kitay and Wright 2003: 36). However, little attention has been given to changes *within* consulting projects. Here, again, the prescriptive literature is of some, albeit limited, help. It recognizes project dynamism, but largely in terms of linear and rational phases (e.g. Markham 1997) with an additional recognition of the early need to establish the client relationship (and contract) effectively (e.g. Cockman et al. 1999; Lippitt and Lippitt 1986; O'Farrell and Moffat 1991). For example, Mulligan and Barber set out a progression for consultants from being initially client-centred to becoming problem-, strategy (implementation)-, and finally quality/evaluation-centred (2001: 94).

Notwithstanding the fact that relationships are of ongoing importance and that projects do not typically follow linear phases neatly (Gluckler and Armbrüster 2003; Whittle 2008), such models are useful as a starting point for assessing the ways in which insider–outsider boundaries may change over time and, even, how hybrid internal–external roles are performed (Birkinshaw et al. 2008). For example, in keeping with the transitional (temporary) nature of liminality, those physical boundaries between the project team and its members' organizations are likely to be greater both before and after joint problem solving and shared implementation work (cf. Czarniawska and Mazza 2003). Likewise, in terms of knowledge boundaries, consultants' organizational knowledge is likely to increase during a project, as is the clients' level of understanding of any consulting tools in use, thus reducing boundaries and producing specific forms of insider/outsider relations. Similarly, in terms of political interests, these may well diverge as project objectives are seen as having been addressed and consultants begin to focus more on generating future business. However, and once again, the frameworks remain at the level of the consulting project and do not differentiate between different client/consultant actors or roles. Here, for example, we might see more junior consultants disengage from personal client relationships as the project comes to a conclusion. Similarly, functional knowledge boundaries are likely to intensify as consultants engage in an expert role and lessen during more facilitative or process-oriented periods. Such possibilities begin to highlight the potential analytical value of combining project dynamics with different and multiple bases for boundary relations and the various actors and roles involved in consultancy.

Discussion and Conclusion

We have argued that studies of knowledge flow through consultancy draw on the common-sense, dominant, and persistent view of consultants as organizational and knowledge outsiders with respect to their clients. By drawing on and developing both recent and more prescriptive studies of consultancy we have challenged the universality and simplicity of this outsider view by pointing to

- spatial aspects of joint project working
- emerging trends towards partnership contracts
- personal relationships between clients and consultants

At the same time, the generalized image of consultants as outsiders in terms of being carriers of new knowledge to client learners was questioned with respect to

- the legitimatory role of consultants
- structural and emerging features which bring various client and consultant knowledge domains closer (e.g. repeat business, career interplay, education)

Finally, attention was drawn to variability *within* consulting projects in terms of

- political interests
- the roles of the different client and consultant actors, including the project team
- how boundaries might change over time as the project progresses (e.g. phases)

Although these specific elements are not exhaustive, the overall aim here is to begin to recognize and organize relationship boundary complexity, intra- as well as inter-project diversity, and relationship dynamics. In the most basic of terms, we have raised three questions in response to the dominant view—insider/outsider with respect to what, whom, and when? (See Table 1.2.)

Table 1.2. Micro-structural boundary relations in consultancy projects—an initial framework from studies of consultancy relationships

Boundary bases (what?)
- Space/activity (e.g. liminality of joint working and communication)
- Contract (e.g. partnership vs. transaction)
- Personal/social ties
- Knowledge domains (e.g. shared/contrasting personal, general management, functional, organizational, and sector knowledge)
- Political interests (e.g. project objectives, sell on, job loss, and legitimation)

Actors (who?)
- Organization (i.e. dominant view)
- Project team (cf. others)
- Individuals and/or roles (e.g. client types, consulting roles, and hierarchical levels)

Dynamics (when?)
- Project phases and other (e.g. non-linear) changes (e.g. from repeat business and liminal transitions)

However, from the above discussion it is clear that such distinctions are not always easy to draw—they are an assertion of what are, in practice, both permeable and fluid conceptual boundaries. In addition, our account so far has been based largely on studies of management consultancy where boundaries are typically used in a common-sense or un-theorized way, particularly in the context of knowledge flow. This has helped to generate empirical insight and, as we have seen, to challenge dominant and universalist views of consultancy. But in order to develop our understanding further, particularly in terms of the implications for knowledge flow, we need to examine boundaries and knowledge in a broader context and with a firmer theoretical base. This is the aim of the following chapter. First, however, we shall briefly outline the structure of this book as a whole.

We have seen how management consultancy has become significant across a wide range of domains in business, organizations, and society, particularly in relation to its apparent role in the generation and use of various forms of management knowledge, ideas, and practices. Here, a traditional view of the importance of management consultants as being concerned with their expert and (knowledge and organizational) outsider status remains dominant both generally and in studies of consultancy specifically. In the specific literature on knowledge flow in consultancy, for example, the view is that consultants face a dilemma based primarily on the attractiveness and incompatibility of the new knowledge they bring to clients. And yet, there is very little research about this process in the context of client–consultant relationships and practices in consultancy projects. For this reason, our research can be seen as exploratory in nature. This, combined with our in-depth methodological approach and a concern to reveal something of the interaction and micro practices involved in consultancy projects, means that our analysis is necessarily selective in its areas of focus. However, and as we shall see, we pursue a common theme throughout.

This Book's Structure

The overall structure of this book is largely conventional in that after setting out and reviewing relevant literature and our research approach and contexts, we then present our empirical analysis. This takes the form of four chapters. Each of these addresses a particular boundary–knowledge issue and, to an extent, can be read as a distinct analysis. However, together they progressively develop a broader account which begins with setting out an overview of the structural complexity of boundary–knowledge relations (Chapter 4) and then takes one aspect of those relations (sector knowledge) and explores it in detail across the different consultancy projects (Chapter 5). The account then shifts its focus of analysis towards interactive practices of clients and consultants. Here, we take two specific examples, one, a practice typically associated with consultancy and learning, that of challenge (Chapter 6), the other is less conventional, but one which we found to be especially revealing of client–consultant project relations in action, the use of humour (Chapter 7). These two chapters give particular emphasis to the dynamic nature of boundaries, how they are reproduced, negotiated, and transformed, both over the course of the projects and in the moment, through micro-interactions. Thus, rather than seek to provide a general account, these chapters highlight selected instances and extracts from particular projects. They are followed by a short conclusion (Chapter 8) which highlights our central argument and points to various areas where further research is needed.

2

Boundaries and knowledge flow

Introduction

Theoretically, the consultancy literature spans a range of perspectives, often mirroring those in the study of management idea adoption more generally (see Sturdy 2004 for a review). Given a rather prescriptive bias in much of the literature and/or a sense that consultancy is, in itself, a field of study, theoretical positions are often more or less implicit. Nevertheless, certain perspectives are clearly evident. In particular and as we have noted, much of the prescriptive literature reflects some of the assumptions of transaction cost economics. It also tends to adopt a view of knowledge as object-like which is transferred, rather than translated (cf. Latour 1986). Less prescriptive approaches often draw on dominant perspectives in organization studies more generally, neo-institutionalism and social embeddedness in particular (e.g. Armbrüster 2006; Kipping and Engwall 2002; Saint-Martin 2000). Other perspectives are also evident, often in combination, such as psychodynamics, actor–network theory, dramaturgy, identity theory, and, to a lesser extent, labour process theory (Alvesson 2004; Bloomfield and Best 1992; Clark 1995; Jackall 1986; Sturdy 1997*b*).

Our own analysis of consultancy is informed by a range of broadly sociological interests and influences which, hopefully, shed light on our object and subject of enquiry. These include situated learning theory, dramaturgy, critical theory, and concerns with power, knowledge, and identity more generally, and each is more or less evident in the following chapters. Clearly, notwithstanding debates around paradigm (in)commensurability (Willmott 1993), this represents quite a mixture. Overall, however, our approach is a dynamic structural one. Following traditions of critical realism and structuration in particular, we see a structural analysis, whereby social structures are not wholly determining, but simultaneously reproduced and transformed through social (inter)action (e.g. Giddens 1984; Whittington 1992) as one (not the only) useful way of making sense of the phenomena under consideration. As we hope to demonstrate, this view of structuring as 'loose', negotiated, and dynamic helps makes sense of broad and largely expected patterns of behaviour at the same time as their local reproduction and deviations from what one might expect from a more determinist approach.

Given such a perspective, it is, perhaps, unsurprising that we have a particular interest in boundaries for they can be seen as demarcations of social structure in action—social *structuring* (Santos and Eisenhardt 2005). But before going on to explore boundaries in more detail, it is important to note that the concept has a much broader resonance and relevance to our study. First, it is evident in everyday 'insider–outsider' discourses and experiences of consultancy and, as we shall see, in the context of knowledge flow, in terms of prescriptions centred on breaking down or spanning boundaries (Tushman and Scanlan 1981). More generally, boundaries have received renewed attention in recent years from the apparent prospect of their demise into 'boundarylessness' or their becoming increasingly fluid, elusive, shifting, and porous with the advent of post-bureaucracy, post-modernity, and globalization for example. Here, art, fashion, politics, management, markets, organizations, and geography are said to become less bounded and distinct. However, such epochalism, as Hernes and Paulsen point out, is countered by the fact that boundaries have long 'been elusive and complex phenomena' (2003: 8; also Marshall 2003). Instead, such developments are better seen in terms of our coming to understand things in more processual ways—a world of flux and flow rather than stability and order (e.g. knowledge as a process rather than an object). In addition, they reflect empirical changes in what (and, perhaps, how many) boundaries are *felt* as important—the organization or nation as no longer a core source of identity for example, but one of a number of shifting identities. In short, the confusion arises from seeing boundaries simply as things rather than as more or less conscious structuring *processes*.

We now explore boundaries in three specific contexts relevant to our study—social science, organizations, and knowledge flow with a particular emphasis on the latter. Here, we draw on a range of studies to develop a simple framing of interconnected physical, cultural/knowledge, and political boundaries and begin to develop a more contextual understanding of these in terms of liminality and project working before developing this further in subsequent chapters in the specific context of consulting projects.

Boundaries, Social Science, and the Sociology of Knowledge

A useful starting point for our discussion of boundaries is Lamont and Molnar's review (2002) of the concept. For them, 'boundaries are part of the classical conceptual toolkit of the social sciences' because the idea 'captures a fundamental social process, that of relationality' (2002: 167, 169). For example, the authors outline a range of different fields of enquiry associated with concerns to create, maintain, contest, or dissolve institutionalized social differences such as class, gender, race, and territorial inequality—'us and them' or 'insiders and outsiders' (ibid. 168). But boundaries are not simply an analytical tool for social scientists. Lamont and Molnar (2002) draw a conceptual distinction between two types of interrelated and 'equally real' boundaries—symbolic and social.

Symbolic boundaries are 'conceptual distinctions made by social actors to categorize objects, people, practices, and even time and space' (ibid. 168), but they are also inter-subjective or experienced. They emotionally separate and unite people and are contested in struggles over reality, resources, and status. For example, the organizational boundary is important to the extent to which, or when, actors identify with the organization. Such a view is similar to Wenger's notion of boundaries as *discontinuities* defined by practice, made visible when trying to cross them (1998). Thus, boundaries are a way of expressing the constructions, labels, and experiences produced through a combination of perceiving *identity* (what something is), *difference* (from something else), and some *intention* (desire or thought) of reducing or maintaining that difference.[1] For example, a wall becomes a boundary with the awareness that the land either side of it is different in some way and/or with a desire to retain/change that difference or move from one side to the other, with national or property borders for instance. An important point to note here is that a symbolic boundary might be experienced or felt without necessarily expressing it as assuming a particular form—it is only *partially*

[1] This connects to notions of identity such as Gouldner's (1957) 'manifest' identity such as that of elder, as opposed to the 'latent' identity of cosmopolitan/local and to the experienced, 'emic', occupational identity outlined by Zabusky and Barley (1997) as opposed to an ascribed or 'etic' identity.

discursive. This is evident in the more explicitly experiential notion of insiders and outsiders from the traditions of alienation or deviance—a sense of belonging or otherness (Becker 1963; Camus 1946).

Social boundaries, according to Lamont and Molnar, are akin to conventional social structures. They arise when 'symbolic boundaries are widely agreed upon' and take a constraining (and enabling) character. In other words, they are 'objectified forms of social differences manifested in unequal access to and unequal distribution of resources and social opportunities' (2002: 168). Here then, the organization boundary can be important regardless of whether actors identify with it or its other(s). This view is closer to the, somewhat problematic, Parsonian notion of boundary maintenance and systemic order and ordering. However, the concept of social boundary can be sustained in a more dynamic, socially constructed sense by regarding any order and disorder as the outcome of ongoing negotiation or social action—the continuous interplay between structure and action (Giddens 1984; see also Heracleous 2004; Hernes 2004; Nippert-Eng 2003). Furthermore, dynamism is also condition and consequence of structural multiplicity and complexity in most social contexts (Whittington 1992). This point is illustrated in an essay by Merton (1972) on insiders and outsiders and the sociology of knowledge (see also Merton 1968: 338–54, 405–7). Given its relevance to our own concerns with boundary relations and knowledge, we briefly consider this study before exploring boundaries in the context of organizational knowledge specifically.

Merton was concerned with a specific political and epistemological debate within sociology at the time of writing about whether one can only claim legitimate knowledge of a cultural context from the inside (as a member) or from the outside, as a 'stranger who moves on'—the 'insider and outsider doctrines' (1972: 32). However, the debate had a much broader sociological significance and, for our purposes, clearly has implications not only for an understanding of the knowledge of external management consultants and their clients, but also for our own position as 'outsider' researchers—'observers as participants' (see Chapter 3).

In short, Merton rejected the extreme versions of both doctrines in favour of the view that both insiders and outsiders have 'distinctive assets and liabilities' (1972: 33). For example, he cites Simmel's view of the outsider role and its epistemological assets which, incidentally, parallel contemporary claims of many consultants as well as academic researchers.

He [sic] is freer, practically and theoretically ... he surveys conditions with less prejudice ... he is not tied down in his action by habit, piety, and precedent [but the objectivity of the stranger] does not simply involve passivity and detachment; it is a particular structure composed of distance and nearness, indifference and involvement.

(1950: 404–5, cited in Merton 1972; see also Marsh 2008; Smith 2008)

Merton goes on to point out that, given the highly socially differentiated nature of most societies (e.g. age, gender, race, and occupation), *we are all both insiders and outsiders* in a dynamic way, according to context. However, this multiplicity and dynamism was not acknowledged in the extreme doctrines which located people in terms of a single social category. As Merton stated:

This neglects the crucial fact of social structure that individuals have not a single status but a status set: a complement of variously interrelated statuses which interact to affect both their behavior and perspectives. The structural fact of status sets ... introduces severe theoretical problems for total Insider (and Outsider) doctrines of social epistemology ... [for] aggregates of individuals share some statuses and not others; or, to put this in context, that they typically confront one another simultaneously as Insiders and Outsiders. (ibid. 22)

The implication of this heterogeneity for Merton is that 'the boundaries between Insiders and Outsiders' are relatively permeable—'with or without intent, the process of intellectual exchange takes place precisely because the conflicting groups are in interaction' (pp. 37–8). He does not elaborate on this potential—as we will do—but points to the barrier presented to this process by the insider and outsider doctrines themselves which contribute to a form of groupthink—'perspectives become self-confirming as both Insiders and Outsiders tend to shut themselves off from ideas and information at odds with their own conceptions' (p. 40). In other words, the view that either cultural insiders or outsiders have a superior knowledge impedes the very flow of knowledge between parties—that is, symbolic boundaries become social boundaries in constraining interaction. This is clearly significant in the context of our study given what we said in the previous chapter of the dominant view of consultants as outsider experts. If either clients or consultants are seen as having a monopoly on legitimate knowledge by virtue of their insider/outsider status, learning is precluded.

We shall return to these issues at various points in our analysis, but for the moment, we shall simply draw some contemporary parallels with Merton's position. For example, one need not take such a strong and traditional structural perspective in order to relate to Merton's image of multiple positions. For example, status sets can be readily compared to identity sets. Indeed, many recent observers have described work organizations in a similar way, particularly with regard to different, and sometimes conflicting, social systems (Whittington 1992), social identities (Parker 1995; Trice and Beyer 1993), or, from a post-structural perspective, fragmented and 'overdetermined' selves (Laclau and Mouffe 1985). Furthermore, at an empirical level, in the current late modern context of seeing bureaucratic distinctions between (paid) work and non-work and temporally stable senses of self as less viable, such heterogeneity and dynamism should be unsurprising (Hochschild 1997; Webb 2004). However, within organization studies, the proclivity to give primacy to a single social category—in this case organizational employee—persists. For example, in a review of studies of inter-organizational relationships, Marchington and Vincent bemoan the neglect of what they call inter-personal (as well as institutional) factors in arguing that

there has typically been a tendency to treat organizations as homogeneous and cohesive agents ... as the principal (and often sole) level of analysis, so ignoring influences both beyond and within the organization. (2004: 1030–1)

As we saw in the last chapter, this tendency is also reflected in accounts of knowledge flow in client–consultancy relations where the *organizational* form of the insider–outsider relation is dominant and the consultant's (organizational) outsider status is seen as the basis of his or her expertise and its legitimacy in relation to the client. The limitations or partiality of this view became evident in our discussion of more complex boundaries in consulting projects and this is supported by specific studies of boundaries within organizational studies more generally, to which we now turn.

Boundaries and Organizations

We have noted how boundaries have received growing attention across disciplines. This is also evident in organization studies in the form of economic, strategic, and organizational approaches (*Human Relations* 2004; *Long Range Planning* 2004). Indeed, more generally, boundaries and boundary setting can be seen as 'intrinsic to the very process of organizing' (Hernes 2004: 10). More specifically, however, boundaries are a particular contemporary concern in relation to three broad areas: variations of the 'make or buy' decision inherent in transaction cost economics

(TCE); the flow of knowledge within and between organizations in terms of resource-based and learning/knowledge-intensive organizations; and changes in the structure of organizations and relations between work and 'everyday life' (see Hancock and Tyler 2009; Hernes and Paulsen 2003 for a review).

In an assessment of theoretical perspectives, Santos and Eisenhardt are critical of the dominance of a legal or contractual view of organizations and TCE in particular, which emphasize concerns with efficiency (2005). They point to a range of other perspectives and construct a typology of boundary forms on this basis. Here, the contractual view is complemented by boundaries associated with organizational competence (or knowledge), identity (cognition/emotion), and power, in the rather limited sense of a sphere of organizational influence. Similarly, but from a slightly broader focus, Hernes (2004) uses Lefebvre's work (1991) on space to develop a framework comprising 'physical' boundaries in terms of 'physical' structures such as electronic communications as well as formal rules; 'social' boundaries of identity and belonging; and 'mental' boundaries in the sense of ideas and concepts which are important to particular groups.

Such typologies are useful in representing (and, indeed, *drawing*) boundaries which are seen to have analytical relevance. But they also present problems. For example, they were devised for different purposes and so are not directly comparable. Neither locates particular boundaries within the classic social/symbolic distinction. In fact, Hernes' terms may even confuse the issue in that his social boundaries appear similar to Lamont and Molnar's 'symbolic' view (2002), while his mental boundaries appear akin to their notion of 'social' boundaries or structures. Furthermore, in each case, the different boundaries are clearly closely related or overlapping. This is, in fact, partially addressed in both studies. For example, the physical boundary also has social and mental characteristics (Lefebvre 1991). Similarly, but more importantly, in Santos and Eisenhardt's case (2005), power is inherent in each of the other forms of boundary—competence, identity, and contract. Indeed, it is also a necessary effect of the act of drawing a boundary itself—who and what is included and excluded (Hacking 1999). Despite such problems, as the saying goes, 'you have to draw the line (boundary) somewhere!' We have attempted this by adapting the models of Hernes (2004) and Santos and Eisenhardt (2005) for our own specific purpose and context into a 'loose' framework of interrelated physical, cultural, and political boundaries (see Table 2.1).

Before turning to this development in detail through a consideration of boundaries and knowledge flow, it is important to highlight boundary

Table 2.1. Classifications of primary boundaries (without consideration of process)

Santos and Eisenhardt (2005)	Hernes (2004) (after Lefebvre 1991)	This study
Contractual[a]/legal (efficiency)	Physical (e.g. electronic) and formal rules	Physical
Identity	Social—identity/bonding (emotional)	Cultural[b] (cognitive/emotional)
Power.(sphere of influence)		Political (interests, rules, contracts[a], exclusion)
Competence[b]	Mental (central ideas and concepts in group)[b]	

[a/b] Highlight related phenomena in different rows.

processes. As noted above, in order to avoid overly deterministic analysis and an undue emphasis on order, our approach follows that of Hernes (2004) and others (e.g. Hacking 1999; Nippert-Eng 2003) in their attention to the role of actors in negotiating, reproducing, challenging, and deconstructing boundaries and the enabling and constraining consequences of this 'boundary work' (see Chapters 6 and 7 in particular). Here, in contrast to our own and others' basic classifications of boundaries and, in keeping with Merton's view above, diversity and complexity are key features. Boundaries become composite (i.e. multiple sets of varying strength, substance, and form) and 'are constantly subject to construction and reconstruction ... [but this] does not prevent some boundaries from being relatively stable' in a given historical context (Hernes 2004: 10). In other words, the social and/or symbolic nature of boundaries is specific to context.

Boundaries and Knowledge Flow

As we have seen, all social interaction can be seen as an apparent movement of knowledge across boundaries, between simultaneous insiders and outsiders. However, attention tends to focus on what is deemed by particular actors as special knowledge or particularly salient boundaries. Thus, in the context of technological 'development' and cultural change, for example, anthropologists have long been concerned with studying the 'spread' of knowledge between disparate groups of people. Likewise, Christian missionaries seeking to spread the word of God found that even this relatively 'dogmatic' form of knowledge was adapted or translated as it 'travelled' (Huczynski 1993). Similarly, there are numerous classic historical cases of technical innovations or discoveries which failed to travel across geographical (and other) boundaries or over time (see Rogers 1995).

In the current context of 'knowing capitalism' and 'knowledge-intensive' organizations and societies, management, as well as technological, innovation and best practice lie at its rhetorical core. Here, aside from the issue of protecting intellectual property, huge emphasis is placed on *breaking down* national, sectoral, departmental, and, especially, organizational boundaries to allow knowledge to flow so as to be 'exploited' or used to 'explore' and create new knowledge (March 1991). There are two key assumptions here. The first is that the knowledge in question is unambiguously positive in its outcomes—pro-innovation bias (cf. Rogers 1995). This is rarely challenged in organizational research, even that which focuses on knowledge and learning (cf. Contu et al. 2003; O'Neil et al. 1998; Semadeni 2001). Second, and of particular relevance to our concerns, is the view that boundaries are synonymous with barriers—that they are dysfunctional.

In fact and following our earlier discussion of Merton (1972), boundaries are a *necessary condition for knowledge flow and learning*—a means of communication (Lamont and Molnar 2002: 177). Even at the common-sense level of boundaries in knowledge flow, where else would new knowledge come from? But this is only part of the story, of course. The notion of knowledge as socially embedded—how it is either rooted in specific contexts or constituted by those contexts—suggests that boundaries are important. In the first, more structural and static view, the embedded nature of knowledge, its 'stickiness', makes it difficult to tease out and travel to new contexts, but it can be done (e.g. Szulanski 2003). In the second, more action-oriented and dynamic view (e.g. Orlikowski 2002), knowledge is not *in* context but made by the context (as words constitute a sentence) so knowledge cannot be transferred or moved. Rather, new contexts (and knowledge) are constructed through interaction or practice and knowledge is translated or, in a metaphorical sense, it *flows* (also Czarniawska and Joerges 1996; Sahlin-Andersson and Engwall 2002b). Practice is structured by boundaries, which are themselves simultaneously experienced, reproduced, negotiated, and/or transformed through it. Thus, boundaries become both a condition and/or barrier to learning *according to context/s*. They serve to represent the shifting contours of embeddedness.

These issues and perspectives lie at the heart of what has become a huge field of study—inter-organizational learning or knowledge transfer—

although studies 'seldom explicitly take the nature of boundaries into consideration' (Easterby-Smith et al. 2008: 685). Again, notwithstanding concerns with context or the situational specificity of knowledge,[2] emphasis is typically placed on generating universal approaches to 'freeing up' knowledge on the assumption that this is a good thing whether in terms of spanning boundaries or removing them (re-/dis-embedding). In setting out what are considered key boundaries and issues in the field, we now briefly explore this literature selectively, with a particular emphasis on work which connects with our own concerns with knowledge flow in consultancy (e.g. Nooteboom 2004; Orlikowski 2002; Szulanski 2003; Wenger 1998). In particular, we discuss *physical*, *cultural*, and *political* boundaries which approximately correspond to those identified by Carlile (2004) in his study of managing knowledge across boundaries. We point to some of the interrelationships between these boundary classifications and, importantly, to the notions of shades of grey or relativity and temporality in boundary phenomena, through the concepts of optimum cognitive distance and liminality.

Physical Boundaries

It is self-evident that knowledge flow is enabled or constrained by physical arrangements which allow or present a barrier to interaction and communication (Szulanski 2003). For example, the classic form of training through 'sitting next to Nellie' is now conceived more in terms of 'operational proximity' (e.g. Tagliaventi and Mattarelli 2006). The physical boundary is not, of course, restricted to such co-presence or face-to-face contact, but relates to various forms of information and communication technology as well as architecture and ergonomics (e.g. Duffy 1997; Edenius and Yakhlef 2007) which both facilitate, but also shape, the nature and form of interaction and knowledge flow—in effect, boundary objects (Star 1989). Similarly, it might be extended to broader conditions which affect the traditional sociometric dimensions of relationships in terms of the frequency, duration, stability, and direction of interactions (Inkpen and Tsang 2005; Scott 2000).

This physical dimension compares to what Carlile (2004) describes as a 'syntactic' boundary which he associates with basic knowledge, or information 'transfer' in that, on its own, it is insufficient to facilitate

---

[2] Clearly, not only boundaries are context specific, but so are understandings of them. For example, an organizational boundary has different meanings in different cultural contexts (see Meyer and Lu 2004).

other knowledge processes such as those based in practice or the co-production of knowledge (Scarbrough et al. 2004). In addition, and as with all boundaries, attention should be given to power—in this case, those who are physically included/excluded from interaction (Ebers and Grandori 1997; Lave and Wenger 1991). This is most evident in the case of project working, including consultancy, where close interaction can create a new boundary for knowledge flow—to and from project team members' respective departments or organizations (Tempest and Starkey 2004). It is also important to highlight that physical boundaries are not simply an objective or object-like phenomenon. Space and objects should also be seen as social and emotional—cultural; understood by actors in different ways for example (Lefebvre 1991; Wilson et al. 2008). This means that 'operational proximity' by no means guarantees knowledge flow, in a co-located project team for example, but it can help generate socio-emotional identification and dis-identification, to which we now turn.

Cultural (Cognitive/Emotional) Boundaries

In keeping with the breadth of the concept of culture, cultural boundaries are complex phenomena.[3] In the context of knowledge flow however, two key dimensions are evident—cognitive and emotional (see Sturdy 2004 for a discussion of their intimate interrelationship). Crudely, this concerns boundaries of understanding and motivation—how people cannot or will not understand each other. In more sophisticated terms, it can be seen through the notions of *optimum cognitive distance* (Nooteboom et al. 2007) and what Wenger (1998) describes as *'economies of meaning'*— the sense of ownership or identity that individuals attach to knowledge. The following shows how this relates to the two features which we described earlier as the 'burden of otherness' in consultancy—alien knowledge and outsider status.

OPTIMUM COGNITIVE DISTANCE

Cultural boundaries lie at the heart of what Carlile (2004) terms semantic boundaries or conflicting languages or meanings such as different knowledge domains. A key concept here is that of the 'cognitive distance' between parties (Bogenrieder and Nooteboom 2004). Here, wholly shared knowledge bases (i.e. too little cognitive distance) implies that

[3] For example, although relevant in a wider context, we shall not explore the issue of cultural variations in cognitive and learning styles (e.g. Bhagat et al. 2002; Warner 1991).

there is no boundary and therefore no potential for learning, while too great a distance presents a barrier to shared understanding as any sense of resonance is lacking. In other words, it is not simply a question of knowledge differences being both a strength and a burden, as is evident in the dominant view of knowledge flow in consultancy. Rather, the situation is more nuanced—some 'otherness' is essential for learning, but not too much. This optimum balance of newness and resonance is a long-standing theme (e.g. Simmel 1950), in rhetoric for example, and has come to be associated with 'absorptive capacity' in the sense of having a 'stock of prior-related knowledge' as a prerequisite for using 'outside sources of knowledge' (Szulanski 2003: 29).

However, others point not only to the importance of a balance in cultural (i.e. cognitive) boundaries, but also to variations based on the type of knowledge or process in question (e.g. Hansen 1999; Holmqvist 2003). In particular, a distinction is drawn between the *exploration*, or the development of new knowledge and ideas, and the use or *exploitation* of existing knowledge (March 1991). Here, the weak ties and alien knowledge associated with the traditional 'consultant as outsider' view potentially facilitate innovation or 'exploration' (as well as allowing the exchange of explicit or simple knowledge). But, this does not simply bring a simultaneous dilemma or 'burden' of knowledge transfer problems as the conventional view suggests. Rather, the limitations are more specific in terms of 'otherness' hindering the exchange of more embedded/tacit/complex knowledge and exploiting existing knowledge. For these processes, less cognitive distance (i.e. more cultural closeness) is needed (also Hagedoorn and Duysters 2002; Sorenson et al. 2006).

Thus, we are now able to construct a more developed view of learning potential through boundaries, moving away from the simple tension of the simultaneous strength and burden of otherness towards the notion of an optimum level of cognitive distance and one which itself varies depending on the type of knowledge/process involved (see Table 2.2).

Table 2.2. Cognitive distance and knowledge processes

Level of 'otherness'	Knowledge relationship potential
Relatively high cognitive distance	• Exploration (and exchange of explicit or simple knowledge)
Relatively low cognitive distance	• Exploitation (and exchange of both explicit/simple and embedded/tacit knowledge)

Adapted from Hansen (1999), Holmqvist (2003), Nooteboom (2004).

PERSONAL RELATIONSHIPS—'REDUNDANT KNOWLEDGE' AND SHARED CHARACTERISTICS AS BRIDGES

Further complexity can be added to the above view by considering the role claimed for personal relationships in overcoming knowledge boundaries or sub-optimal cognitive distance. Here, shared understandings or weak semantic boundaries in one domain may serve as a resource or learning bridge in other knowledge domains by virtue of helping establish an emotional connection or 'intimacy' in personal relationships (Szulanski 2003). Inkpen and Tsang (2005), for example, identify actors' shared norms as a key 'relational' element in the social capital which aids knowledge flow in inter-organizational networks. These shared characteristics refer not only to common or 'redundant' knowledge (i.e. low cognitive closeness) (Nonaka 1994), but also to broader, albeit related, social similarities such as those which might arise from common social and cultural backgrounds (e.g. education, gender, class, ethnicity, and lifestyles) or develop over time such as from joint working in project teams. For example, Zucker (1986) refers to 'characteristic-based' trust which may develop 'freely' and help overcome or lessen other boundaries such as contrasting knowledge domains and, even, conflicting interests. Clearly, in the context of consultancy, this translates directly to the importance of personal relations, shared social characteristics, and the instrumental tactics of consultants ('relationship managers') in seeking to establish close personal relations with clients, particularly those at, or likely to achieve, senior positions (Sturdy et al. 2006).

THE REPULSION AND ATTRACTION OF OUTSIDER KNOWLEDGE

The potential for shared social characteristics and understandings to facilitate the flow of (not too) new knowledge is clearly more than a purely cognitive issue. Following long traditions in social identity theory and inter-group behaviour, it relates to the emotions of belonging and in/out-group identification. Here, crudely speaking, the value and knowledge of the in-group are elevated while those of the out-group/s are denigrated and blocked (see Paulsen 2003 for a discussion of these issues). In organizational contexts, this has been referred to as the 'not invented here' (NIH) syndrome (Katz and Allen 1982) of valuing only that which is associated with the in-group and recoiling from outsider-sourced knowledge. Thus, a cognitive boundary (different understandings or knowledge) can become an emotional barrier and vice versa. This can be particularly acute in the context of external competition or perceived power inequalities such as the neo-imperialism of particular countries (Chanlat 1996), multinationals' joint ventures with small firms (Child and Rodrigues 1996) and, as we shall see, management consultants. Here, there can be an inclination to reject knowledge associated not just with outsiders, but with powerful ones especially.

Some caution is needed here however. In particular, how can we explain the attractiveness of knowledge specifically on the basis of its association with outsiders, including powerful ones? This was the focus of Menon and Pfeffer (2003) who cited the examples of a preference for 'Japanese' manufacturing ideas in the USA in the 1980s and for the ideas of external consultants over insider knowledge. They highlight how concerns in the literature with knowledge *transfer* detract from the related process of knowledge *valuation*. Clearly, outsider knowledge can be seen as valuable through its association with economically successful users such as economies or firms—the 'dominance effect' (Smith and Meiksins 1995). But Menon and Pfeffer's argument adds to this. In particular, 'while outsiders face social, physical, and legal obstacles that inhibit knowledge transfer' (2003: 498) (i.e. the 'burden of otherness'), they have two advantages.

First, especially in conditions of *intra*-organization competitiveness, insider knowledge represents competition for status and advancement to all but those associated with it, while outsider-sourced knowledge is less easily dismissed. Indeed, it can be used as a political tool for legitimation. Thus, 'although organizational boundaries promote identification, they also demarcate an arena within which competition for promotion, status, and salaries occurs' (2003: 498). In other words, and as we have already noted, in most organizational contexts, multiple or hybrid boundaries and identities prevail. These can vary in significance and strength according to time, place, and individual—once again, we are all insiders and outsiders simultaneously.

The second advantage noted for outsiders is that internal knowledge is relatively accessible and therefore assessable for flaws and does not have the same scarcity or uniqueness value of outsider knowledge, like fine art. As a result, while internal knowledge may be (cognitively and culturally) easier to transfer (as well as often being cheaper), this is hindered by undervaluing it in comparison to knowledge from extra-organizational competitors and other external sources. Furthermore, although Menon and Pfeffer do not discuss this, the phenomenon is strengthened by the branding activities and pricing strategies of outside actors such as consulting firms.

Overall then, and contrary to the dominant view of outsider knowledge being attractive for its newness, but difficult to adopt for the same reason, we find that not only is an *optimum* cognitive distance necessary for learning, but that in certain contexts at least, the attractiveness of outsider knowledge is based on its relative political legitimacy within internal boundaries, its scarcity, and the relative un-testability or opaqueness of its economic value. This brings us to the importance of political boundaries and highlights the very loose distinctions between our three conceptual boundaries.

Political Boundaries—Beyond 'Knowledge at Stake'

Communication or contact, optimal knowledge boundaries, close personal relations, and shared characteristics by no means guarantee knowledge flow. Political relations are crucial. These relate to Carlile's (2004) third key boundary after syntactic and semantic—the 'pragmatic' boundary in the adoption of new knowledge. Here, knowledge needs not only to be communicated (syntactic boundaries) and translated (semantic boundaries), but also to be transformed into something else. For Carlile, the key issue seems to be the existential (i.e. cognitive/emotional) threat posed to recipients' prior knowledge—their knowledge 'at stake'—or what Szulanski (2003) refers to as overcoming the motivation to unlearn. This relates to the motivation we have seen linked to group identity for example (cf. Brown et al. 2005). However and once again, there is an implicit assumption of a single or primary source of identity or, at least, that the knowledge in question is tied to one important identity. Even if this is the case, it is entirely possible to understand, and even promote, an idea or concept and maintain an attachment to contradictory ideas and concepts (e.g. Festinger 1957; cf. Whittle 2005). In other words, knowledge is not always at stake.

More importantly, the approach reflects a somewhat limited view of politics (as well as motivation). Other studies of knowledge flow have pointed to a broader, more material notion of power and interests (e.g. Orlikowski 2002) such as the dependency relations involved in joint ventures or the subsidiaries of multinationals for example. Here, new practices (and their associated knowledge bases) may be imposed on subordinate units, with failure to adopt them being penalized (Child and Rodrigues 1996; Kostova and Roth 2002). Similarly, at the level of the individual employee, there may be little choice but to adopt and adapt a new practice, whether or not any prior knowledge 'at stake' is discarded. For

37

example, critiques of cultural theories of the flow of management ideas across geographical boundaries suggest that the employment relationship, in the form of the dependence of labour on capital, can significantly counter the hindering effects of any culture clash presented by a new knowledge (Sturdy 2001; Wilkinson 1996). Thus, knowledge flow is not primarily a question of establishing shared interests, as many commentators suggest (Inkpen and Tsang 2005), at least not with all parties concerned. Rather, the form of adoption is shaped by power relations varying between commitment and, in the most dependent/subordinate cases, behavioural compliance for example (Child and Rodrigues 1996). In this way, the legal/contractual form of the organizational boundary, as owners of subsidiaries or joint ventures and labour, is as much a political boundary as one associated simply with efficiency (cf. Santos and Eisenhardt 2005).

Other Boundaries

We have given primacy to what we describe as physical, cultural, and political dynamic boundaries. It is important to note that doing so is effectively an assertion that these are important phenomena and perspectives, given our focus of study and theoretical position. For, as we have seen, boundaries are concerned with structuring and, in their 'symbolic' form at least, are almost infinite in number. Orlikowski (2002), for example, sought to identify and classify numerous boundaries that the employees in her study actually felt routinely 'shaped and challenged their everyday work' (2002: 255). We share an interest in consciously experienced or articulated boundaries, but given our more structural view, we are also concerned with 'social' boundaries which may have become so institutionalized as to become less visible to actors, except in their effects, the employment relationship for example.

But our prioritization is also pragmatic in that an aim of this chapter was to introduce some of the key concepts which inform our subsequent analysis. Accordingly, two often cited boundaries are important to mention here, albeit briefly. The first is personal boundaries such as those which might be associated with personality or personal styles which can create barriers to communication and meaning construction. To a large extent, given our sociological position, they can also be seen as cultural boundaries in that individual differences are socially mediated. Nevertheless, individual dynamics, processes, and styles are important as will become evident in our empirical analysis. For example, when examining the role of humour in boundary dynamics, it is clear that some individuals are more adept than others and that this is not solely a consequence of shared identities or common or 'redundant knowledge'.

The second boundary, which is especially common in studies of knowledge flow, is the knowledge boundary. We have already seen this as part of cultural boundaries, in the sense of contrasting knowledge bases of actors. But more commonly, it has a different meaning—demarcations between *types of knowledge* (notably tacit and explicit, simple and complex), which are revealed when seeking to convert one to the other (Nonaka and Takeuchi 1995; Wenger 1998). Clearly, and as we have already shown in relation to the idea of optimum cognitive distance, forms of knowledge are important to its flow. Even at a common-sense level, the idea of 'acquiring' knowledge associated with, say, a precise, mathematical technique seems very different from engaging with a 'quality culture' for example (Lillrank 1995). However, this depends crucially on context. Moreover, following others (e.g. Blackler 1995), and given our focus on the conditions and nature of knowledge in flow, we are sceptical of views of knowledge as having an objective and object-like quality, even if such a discourse is often difficult to avoid in practice. At the same time of course, we are conscious that our choice of particular boundaries and what is meant by them effectively 'valorizes some point of view and silences another' (Bowker and Star 1999: 5).

Boundary Contexts—Liminality and Projects

Another area which we have not explored in any detail is that of generic prescriptions of managing or, in practice, spanning boundaries for knowledge flow. There are numerous such accounts, many of which are helpful in pointing to likely areas of importance in understanding knowledge flow (e.g. see Anand et al. 2002; Hargadon 1998; Lahti and Beyerlein 2000; Tushman and Scanlan 1981). For example, practices such as joint working; networking; the use of boundary spanners, and objects; facilitating communities of practice; the development of trust and shared values; interpersonal styles and many others are presented as at least partial solutions to knowledge 'stickiness' or production. However, as Orlikowski (2002) points out, such boundary-spanning activities are double-edged and can have unintended 'negative' consequences:

... sharing identity becomes organizational groupthink, interacting face to face leads to burn out, aligning effort discourages improvisation, learning by doing is lost through [staff] turnover, and supporting participation is immobilizing because of conflicts and time delays. (2002: 257)

In effect, context is all important. The idea that there are universal, 'checklist', solutions to these issues is not tenable. This is not to say that prescriptive accounts have no analytical or pragmatic value, for many tend to be based on similar broad (e.g. western, 'knowledge-intensive') contexts. With this in mind, we shall now briefly explore literature which relates to two related contexts of particular empirical relevance to our study—*liminality* and *project* working. Indeed, liminality is also of conceptual or general relevance for it draws our attention to the relativity or shades of grey of boundary relations as well as to that of temporality and dynamism.

Liminality is an anthropological term referring to a social space that is 'betwixt and between the original positions arrayed by law, custom, convention and ceremony' (Turner 1977: 95, 1987). In other words, it refers to a space that is between boundaries, often in a dynamic sense of being in transition such as that between childhood and adulthood. Given recent attention to the idea that boundaries are becoming more fluid, some have argued that liminality is particularly apposite or common in late modernity—constantly betwixt and between (Barley and Kunda 2004; Czarniawska and Mazza 2003; Sennett 2006). However, this is questionable as we suggested earlier in relation to boundaries in general. What is important about the concept for our purposes is that it highlights how boundaries are not always clear cut—insider or outsider—but can be graduated and dynamic in the sense of moving between seemingly bounded states. This is in keeping with Wenger's (1998) notion of 'boundaries of practice' which

... are not simple lines of demarcation between inside and outside, but form a complex social landscape of boundaries and peripheries that open and close various forms of participation. (www.ewenger.com)

Liminality is also of particular relevance for its claimed experiential consequences and creative/learning potential. Finding oneself in a liminal space is seen as an uncomfortable and potentially disturbing experience. This is because the relatively settled identities, routines, and rules disappear. At the same time, this means that liminality may also be a creative, liberating, productive, and even desirable place by virtue of its location beyond 'normal' practices (Garsten 1999). In particular, the usual physical, cultural, and political boundaries, which may impede learning and knowledge flow, are suspended. At the same time, however, this potential can be exaggerated, especially if liminality is becoming more habitual, for new identities, routines, and norms are opened up—new structures and boundaries between those within and those beyond the liminal space (Sturdy et al. 2006).

In organizational contexts, liminality has received growing research attention. Here, it is typically the regular, traditional routines and iden-tifications of the formal organization which are suspended. Examples of those who dwell in liminal organizational spaces include temporary employees, not quite part of one organization or another (Garsten 1999), professionals who identify with neither their organization nor their occu-pational group (Zabusky and Barley 1997), and those engaged in inter-organizational networks and joint ventures for example. In addition, and as we noted in Chapter 1, the focus of our study—project working, including inter-organizational projects such as consultancy—has been identified as an important liminal space (Czarniawska and Mazza 2003) particularly with regard to its potential for knowledge creation and flow across boundaries (Clegg et al. 2004; Tempest and Starkey 2004). Indeed, in the case of projects more generally, a sub-field of study, project-based learning (PBL), has emerged to which we now briefly turn.

Projects are an important and growing organizational form in many industries and typically share certain characteristics—a finite duration (ranging from a few weeks to several years), a specific task, and the engage-ment of project members with differentiated expertise. These characteris-tics are often positioned as creating organizational advantages not only in terms of flexibility, but also in terms of the potential for learning. First, by bringing together people with different experience they are seen to draw on the 'strength of weak ties' and support tacit learning (Granovetter 1973; Schindler and Eppler 2003). Second, by working together towards a typically explicit goal, project members are deemed to learn in a way which is more difficult to achieve in functionally structured arrange-ments where relationships and knowledge are often more segregated or bounded—through *learning-by-absorption* and *learning-by-reflection* (Ford and Randolph 1992; Scarbrough et al. 2004). Third, and echoing the arguments of Menon and Pfeffer (2003) about outsider knowledge noted earlier, the relatively transient nature of projects can mean that the knowl-edge they produce poses a lesser threat to vested organizational interests than that arising from individual departments (Sydow et al. 2004).

However, counter-arguments can be put forward. For example, it can be argued that a neutral (liminal) project status in the organization can diminish the legitimacy and credibility of knowledge produced in the project team. At the same time, even if the project members are able to discard or suspend their other (e.g. departmental or organizational) identities and learn within the apparent liminality of the project team, a new boundary can develop around the team (Tempest and Starkey 2004). Furthermore, project working has its own structures and norms which may not always facilitate learning or innovation (Keegan and Turner 2002). For example, the demands of the immediate task—of doing— may take priority over or inhibit reflection and deeper understanding (Sweller 1988; Sydow et al. 2004; also Christensen and Klyver 2006). Similarly, some have argued that 'the one-off and non-recurring nature of project activities' provide limited scope for drawing out any generalized principles (Hobday 2000) which can be systematically applied and tested in new projects (Gann and Salter 2000). Finally, and echoing the view that is dominant in studies of knowledge flow in consultancy, there is an assumption that bringing together diverse knowledge bases is beneficial for learning. But as we have seen with regard to the notion of optimum cognitive distance, new ideas may be too different and challenging to foster acceptance or even understanding (Bogenrieder and Nooteboom 2004; Chinn and Brewer 1993).

Thus, and as in the case of universalistic prescriptions more generally, these polar arguments suggest that projects are by no means a panacea for encouraging knowledge flow or generation among members, let alone beyond project boundaries. Rather, and once again, knowledge flow is seen to be more complex and contingent. At the same time, however, there are common structural conditions to project working including that of management consultancy projects. We shall examine these along with the specific conditions of particular projects in the following chapters.

Conclusion

This chapter explored the nature of boundaries, particularly in the context of knowledge flow. We have seen how boundaries imply a dynamic, structural view, concerned with relationality and lie at the heart of social scientific analysis and, increasingly, organizational studies. Here, we introduced the distinction and relationship between social and symbolic boundaries and the importance of recognizing multiplicity, complexity, and dynamism such that, following Merton, we typically *'confront one another simultaneously as Insiders and Outsiders'* (1972: 22) through multiple status or identity sets. This was linked to those organizational studies which depart from tradition and do not assume a single or primary boundary or identity associated with the contractual limits of the organization. Rather, by developing the analysis of Santos and Eisenhardt (2005) and Hernes (2004), we constructed a typology of three core and intimately related boundary types or characteristics—physical, cultural, and political—and associated processes of negotiation, transformation, and reproduction.

In the context of knowledge flow, these processes can be seen as central to the different conceptions of knowledge as embedded in, or by, contexts (e.g. Orlikowski 2002; Szulanski 2003). This idea was then developed further by exploring physical, cultural, and political boundaries in relation to studies of knowledge (e.g. Carlile 2004). Here, attention was drawn to the simultaneous social, cognitive, and emotional character of cultural boundaries—cannot learn, will not learn—and a more materialist notion of political boundaries whereby knowledge can flow regardless of cultural clashes, through behavioural compliance for example. Related to this, we discussed Menon and Pfeffer's study (2003) which revealed how concerns with the problems of 'transferring' knowledge because it is alien sometimes mask its legitimatory value and attraction, especially in contexts of intra-organizational competition—an outside source can attract as well as repel. In addition, and importantly, a more nuanced

Table 2.3. Summary of a composite and dynamic approach to boundaries and knowledge flow

Dynamism—social-symbolic boundary interplay as enabling and constraining	
Physical	• Operational proximity; technologies; architecture; (boundary) objects; sociometrics
Cultural (cognitive/emotional)	• Multiple knowledge domains and identity sets; optimum cognitive distance for knowledge types/processes; 'redundant knowledge' and personal characteristics; belonging ('economies of meaning'; NIH) and attraction of outsider knowledge
Political	• Knowledge at stake; structured interests (e.g. contractual/dependency relations); inclusion/exclusion
Generic context—for example, multiplicity and gradations of insider/outsider relations or identity sets, including liminality	

43

and contingent view of boundaries than that of the 'black and white', insider–outsider notion was developed, first, through a recognition of the context-specific nature of boundaries and PBL and therefore, the problematic nature of a universalist, 'checklist' approach to managing them. Second, we introduced the notion of a graduated boundary or optimum cognitive distance for knowledge flow (Nooteboom 2004) according to particular knowledge types (e.g. tacit/explicit) and knowledge processes (exploration/exploitation). This countered the simplistic view of knowledge being either outside/new or inside/already known. Third, and of particular relevance to consultancy projects, we explored the concept of liminality—where actors dwell between boundaries, as neither insider nor outsider, but in transition—and of constructing new boundaries and dynamics, such as that between the project team and others.

The themes and concepts explored in this chapter are summarized in Table 2.3. This provides conceptual reference points for much of our subsequent discussion and analysis of boundaries in context. We shall draw selectively on the generic notions of cultural, physical, and political boundaries as well as those of cognitive distance and liminality as a way of organizing our understanding of consultancy projects in action.

For example, following a brief account of our research methods and descriptions of the case studies in the next chapter, our analysis begins with an attempt to illustrate the complexity and dynamism of multiple and simultaneous boundaries through an overview of knowledge flow potential in the consultancy projects which formed the focus of our research.

3

The research—case studies and research methods

Introduction

One of the key motivators in conducting the research reported here was a recognition that, despite receiving growing attention, the world of client–consultant relations was poorly understood and largely hidden to all but those directly involved in it—consultancy insiders. As outlined in Chapter 1, the vast majority of research conducted is cross-sectional and based on interviews, mostly with consultants. This and other research has been extremely valuable, but, like all research, is necessarily partial. In particular, in addition to mostly emphasizing the active role of consultants over clients, post hoc 'snapshot' interview accounts tend to obscure normal, day-to-day interactions—relationships and knowledge *in action*. As Mintzberg (1973) highlighted over thirty years ago in relation to managerial work generally, observation is a necessary supplement to interview methods if we are to understand *practices*. Furthermore, if relationships, knowledge, and boundaries are all seen as dynamic in quality, then longitudinal research should help to shed light on this characteristic. The research reported here begins to address both these issues in the context of consultancy and the related domains of professional services, 'knowledge work', and inter-organizational relations/learning. However, it is necessarily selective. For example and as we shall see, observational access was restricted in one of the cases, and in the other cases was mostly limited to that most formal of work practices—the meeting. Our observations, interviews, and analysis were also selective, but necessarily so especially given the breadth and ambiguous nature of our research focus— knowledge flow—and the exploratory nature of the research project overall. Nevertheless, it is hoped that the following chapters provide some new insight into the nature of consultancy relations and some inspiration to others to develop research further.

In order to make sense of and assess our analysis and claims, it is important to have some understanding of our research assumptions and practices as well as the contexts in which the research was conducted. This chapter seeks to provide such an account and provide a reference point of information about the case study projects (although contextual detail is also provided and sometimes repeated, for ease of understanding, in the following analytical chapters). Indeed, given the paucity of data available on consulting projects more generally, the account of them may be of interest and use in its own right. First, we introduce the case studies by giving a chronology of the main events as well as a brief portrayal of the main organizational and individual characters—the 'insiders and outsiders'—involved. We also identify a broad and emblematic theme which characterizes each case. We then briefly discuss our research methods.

The Case Studies

A case study methodology was chosen for its suitability for the study of complex, processual phenomena such as relationship development/management and knowledge flow (Stake 1995). More specifically, our research design was established to allow a focus on *client–consultant relationships* and *processes of knowledge transfer* (or translation) as units of analysis. The design was informed by a range of theoretical interests such as a situated, practice-based view of knowledge which acknowledges the negotiated, provisional, and mediated nature of 'knowing' (Blackler 1995) within structured power dynamics of participation and exclusion (Fox 2000; Lave and Wenger 1991; Wenger 1998).

The chosen research settings were consultancy projects on the assumption that they encapsulate important dynamics of client–consultant relationships and their management, and of knowledge flow. Clearly, formal projects are not the only site of client–consultant relationships or knowledge flow—pre-project and other promotional activities and channels, including informal and backstage interactions, are also important. However, all are under-researched, and projects are probably the most important in terms of their share of client–consultant joint activity.

Selection of the projects was influenced by a desire to maximize the degree of difference. An alternative approach would have been to select similar cases. Each approach presents different opportunities for comparative analysis. Our focus on difference was informed by a recognition that consultancy practice is considered to be highly variable (Sadler 2001), involving differences in project objectives, functional area (e.g. IT implementation vs. strategy), and, in particular, between sole practitioner consultants and multinational firms, in/experienced clients, and public and private sectors. Despite this, much research makes general claims about consultancy on the basis of data from only one of its particular forms. While our approach precludes any claim to representativeness, we were keen to ensure that some of this variability was incorporated into our design, even if this did bring some disadvantages in terms of comparability. We also hoped to cover the projects throughout their development moving from the enquiry phase, through project implementation, and finally to post-project reviews six and twelve months after completion.

To a large extent our selection objectives were achieved such that the final dataset reflects some variability across dimensions such as sector; project type; firm size and geographical scope; project duration and size; and client experience. However, each project is not necessarily typical of its particular categories. Nevertheless, the characteristics are important to note and some are shown in Table 3.1 together with the pseudonyms used for the project organizations in order to ensure their anonymity.

Research Access

Before describing the case study projects, it is important to mention the nature and process of achieving research access. The problems of obtaining and maintaining research access are general and well known, but particularly acute in contexts where participants are likely to feel especially sensitive about being questioned, observed, scrutinized. Management consultancy is such a context and the difficulties of achieving research access are an important factor in the relative lack of existing data and research which we have already noted, especially beyond that obtained through interviews. The following are important factors hindering access to client–consultant relations in situ:

- Consultancy projects very often address politically or commercially sensitive topics such as rationalization or strategic change.

Table 3.1. Characteristics of the four project case studies

Project organizations Client (sector/type) Consultancy (sector/type)	Project type (% UK market, 2005)[a]	Consultant roles Primary Secondary	Project length	Consultant numbers
Global (private sector, multinational) StratCo (US/global strategy house)	Strategy analysis and advice (5%)	• Experts/extras • Legitimators	9 months	9
Prison (public sector) Network (two local consultants from a network of associates)	Project management advice and quality assurance (11%)	• Experts • Facilitators/legitimators	6 months	2
Imperial (private sector, mutual, retail financial services) Techno (UK-based IT consultancy)	IT development and implementation (11%)	• Experts/extras/implementers • Legitimators	2 years	6
Borough (public sector, local authority) OpsCo (global IT/general consultancy)	Operations advice (eprocurement) (5%)	• Experts • Legitimators	2 years; including mini project of 4 months	4

[a] Market figures from MCA 2006.

- Projects are also often sensitive in their own right in terms of the financial cost to the client. The explicit association of consultants' time with a financial value is also important.
- Consultant and client identities as experts are central to the project and vulnerable to being exposed to others as wanting.
- Access is required from both organizations and the parties to a relationship which is typically one of relatively low familiarity.

Aware of such factors, we sought access primarily through potential clients on the assumption that consultants, however positive towards the research, would be more wary of requesting the participation of the other party. Clients, in their formal structural location as customers, would be in a stronger position to do so—consultants would want to please their clients, especially pre-project, and would not want to be seen as having anything to hide. However, this presented the practical problem of identifying organizations which were about to commission consultants.

In the event, obtaining access proved exceedingly difficult, despite having experience of research in this area, a 'legitimate', funded project and attempting various ways of gaining access over a number of months. There was considerable interest, 'in principle', but access was finally achieved only through existing contacts (peers and students for example), indirectly. This mirrors the nature of consultancy business itself which is rarely achieved through the 'cold call' (Gluckler and Armbrüster 2003) and also confirmed our assumptions about the client's role in brokering the process with the other party. It is highly unlikely that the consultants in all four of our cases would have agreed to participate by requesting the consent of their clients if we had approached them directly. We recognized this issue and sought to reassure both parties of individual and organizational confidentiality/anonymity, and we offered feedback to both parties. Our stated interests to participants were to understand the client–consultant consultancy process—interactions, knowledge, and relationships—rather than investigate the substantive focus of the project or evaluate its outcomes. In order not to act overtly as agents for either party, our feedback in terms of formal reports and meetings as well as questions in the field tended to be tentative and generic in nature. This helped to preclude distrust developing in a political sense, but marked us out as professional/occupational and project outsiders. Clearly, this shaped the nature of our research, data, and therefore analysis. Before outlining these research activities in more detail, we turn to the projects themselves and how they were organized.

As is common in consulting projects of any significant size and was evident in the three largest of our cases, projects are typically organized in the following way. As we saw in Chapter 1, on the client side, there are a number of key roles (Schein 1997). First, the most senior individual or 'contact client' has overall responsibility and, usually, 'signs off' for the project. She or he tends to be more actively involved in the initial and final stages than regular project meetings, but oversees the work of the client project manager or 'primary' client. This is a key role which typically involves regular liaison with the senior consulting staff on the project and a range of client employees as well as direct supervision of the project and its consulting and ('intermediate') client team members. In the former case, supervision would be shared with, or achieved through, his or her counterpart on the consulting side—the consultant project manager or 'minder'. This consulting role lies between the more senior roles and one or more junior consultant levels—the 'grinders'. The consultant project manager has a primary responsibility for the success of the project and typically has some responsibility and incentive for the development of new business ('sell on'). The latter role may be less significant in cases where a separate client relationship manager—or 'finder'—is present who tends to be more senior, often at Partnership level.

Case 1: Global *and* StratCo—*'Consultants on Trial'*

The first case study was a strategy portfolio analysis conducted by the Group strategy department of a large multinational company, *Global*,[1] and a US-based strategy consulting firm, *StratCo*. The project involved data modelling and analysis with the aim of producing recommendations for investment or divestment for inclusion in the client's annual planning decisions and ongoing strategy formulation. The project consisted of two phases of three and six months.

Global was a sophisticated and experienced user of consultancy services, especially in its Group strategy department where it maintained a long-standing relationship with two leading strategy consulting firms—*StratCo* and *Insight*. To consolidate and formalize these relationships, *Global* had recently granted both firms 'preferred partner' status. However, in the most sensitive and critical strategy projects, *Insight* was positioned as the lead consultancy firm relative to *StratCo*. Indeed, at the time of this case study, *Insight* was completing a project relating to *Global's*

---

[1] In order to maintain the anonymity of *Global*, we cannot discuss its sector in detail.

annual strategic planning process. Despite its central position and close relationships at senior levels, when the need for a related project arose and went out to tender, *StratCo*, not *Insight*, won the work. *Global*'s decision was premised on the belief that *StratCo* could provide a valuable 'second' or 'fresh' opinion on the strategy and, in effect, their competitor's work. Their ability to work at this senior level was to a significant extent 'on trial', and the consultants were acutely aware of the negative power dynamics which that position implied. Nevertheless, the project was also seen as a welcome opportunity for *StratCo* to demonstrate its competence and capabilities at this level and to secure future business of a similar type. This was consultancy at its highest status level in a high-profile global client company.

In the first stage of the project, which lasted three months, *StratCo* brought a team of eight consultants and analysts, managed by a senior partner with responsibility for all projects undertaken globally for this client (of which there were many) but no other clients at this level. The consultancy team worked mainly at their own offices, and liaised by phone, email, or in person with *Global*'s project team of six individuals working in the Group strategy department at the client's head office. At this stage, there was minimal input from *Global*'s operational units, most of whom were kept unaware of the project's existence. The individuals involved retained many of their existing corporate responsibilities and so had limited time to brief and guide the consultants. *StratCo* were tasked with identifying strategic development opportunities—'good ideas'—for *Global* given specific financial constraints and using as a baseline the financial and operational models developed earlier by *Insight*.

The access limitations as well as the density and non-completeness of some of the financial data presented *StratCo* with considerable difficulties in the first weeks of the project. However, as they made sense of the data with the help of the client, they began to develop new perspectives on the data leading to the identification of new strategic opportunities which they sounded out or 'validated' with the few operational managers who were informed of the project. Through an iterative process of informal meetings and formal presentations and workshops these opportunities were presented to—and discussed with—senior executives. At the end of stage 1, a list of analytical lenses or metrics and of associated investment and divestment opportunities had been agreed.

With some reservations, *Global*'s overall satisfaction with *StratCo*'s work led them to extend the project to a second stage to deepen the analysis of strategic opportunities, and to develop scenarios to help the executive decide whether the opportunities were worth pursuing. This second stage lasted a further six months, and involved a smaller *StratCo* team drawn from the prior team, but additionally with a new project manager. In addition to these full-time members of the team, the same *StratCo* senior partner oversaw the stage 2 project, and became involved in internal reviews as well as client–consultant meetings. During this stage, the project relied on a larger client team which drew more explicitly and widely on the expertise of operational managers, and attracted the visible support and directional guidance of the Divisional Director which had been largely absent for most of stage 1. The institutionalization of the fortnightly meetings of the 'Core Team' (client managers plus supporting consultants) provided an impetus resulting in fully researched investment and divestment recommendations for the Executive Board.

The project was politically and commercially highly sensitive—it had the potential to impact the size and future of *Global*'s various operations throughout the world—'if we invest in X, then we need to divest in Y' where X and Y relate to organizational fiefdoms and, potentially, the jobs of large numbers of people. The initial exclusion of representatives from operational units and the secrecy around the exercise illustrates the sensitivity. It was also reflected in the extent of research access we were granted which mainly involved interviews and some observation of project review meetings rather than observation of the substantive discussion and decision-making meetings. Nevertheless, this was partly compensated for by the longitudinal nature of our access to participants, in that we were able to interview them a number of times over the duration of the two phases of the project and in some cases in follow-ups after its completion. This enabled us to clarify information and obtain multiple perspectives on the progress of the project and the possibilities and difficulties experienced by participants in relation to the project dynamics. (see Table 3.2.)

Case 2: Prison *and* Network—'*Gentle and Persistent Persuasion of Client'*

The second case provides a stark contrast with the first in many respects. It was located in the public sector, a prison, and involved two consultants from a network-based consulting organization providing project and financial management advice to a client team preparing a 'performance test bid' (PTB) for a small 'failing' prison ('*Prison*'). The duration of the project was approximately six months.

Table 3.2. Key characters in Case 1

Global	
Ray (contact client)	• Vice President of strategy and planning who regularly commissioned consultants. Ray brought a vital element of continuity to this unit, which was to some extent used as a training and development ground for potential senior managers.
Mick (primary client)	• Client project manager in phase 1 of the project. A supportive manager who was frustrated with the lack of direction from senior management about the strategic direction of the business, and therefore the aims of the project during the first phase.
Chloe (primary client)	• Client project manager in phase 2 of the project. A strong and well-organized project manager who had worked in strategy roles at *Global* for several years. Chloe talked of her frustration at seeing strategy consultancy projects re-inventing the wheel every couple of years because (in her view) the methodologies and tools used previously were not well documented, and because there was inadequate knowledge transfer.
John (intermediate client)	• Strategic Planning Analyst in the division. A bright analyst and modeller who had worked at the World Bank before joining *Global* in the last three years.
StratCo	
Victor (finder)	• Vice President at *StratCo*—a very senior level, above 'Partner'—and the relationship manager for *Global*, giving him a peripheral involvement in all *Global* projects and ongoing relationships with senior *Global* executives. Victor had worked with *Global* for seven years and said that his role meant he carried 'a lot of the memory of the [client] organization'.
Julian (minder)	• Consultant project manager in phase 1 of the project. Julian had been at *StratCo* for many years, and did a 'similar' strategy portfolio project at *Global* five years previously. He knew several of the key players in the *Global* team and looked forward to promotion through working on this project.
Ralph (minder)	• Consultant project manager in phase 2 of the project. Ralph had worked in the engineering business and had been at *StratCo* for six years. He often talked about loving the intellectual challenge of the *Global* work.

The consultancy project emerged as a possibility when *Prison* received a particularly poor Home Office inspection report and was subsequently required to submit a PTB showing how it could implement a set of sustainable service-level agreements. Failure to receive a satisfactory evaluation of the bid would have potentially serious consequences for all the prison employees and their trade union, the Prison Officers' Association (POA), in that it could lead to its management being put out to tender to private contractors. *Prison* was given four months to prepare and submit the PTB and was allocated two fast-track civil servants to (project) manage this process—Martin and Cara—and a limited budget for consultancy support. On the basis of word-of-mouth recommendation and prior experience of efficiency programmes elsewhere in the public sector, the more senior client, Martin, approached a small firm, *Network*. *Network* proposed two consultants: James, who was a Director of *Network* and was to provide financial management advice; and Stuart, an associate, who also worked as an independent consultant, who could provide project management expertise. After a business case was approved (which mentioned our research project), a contract was drawn up. This provided for two/three consulting days for project management awareness training for the whole bid team; two/three days to scope financial management aspects of the bid; followed by ten to twelve days for ongoing project and financial management support. In the event, almost all this time was allocated to project rather than financial management and was translated as weekly or fortnightly meetings between Martin and Stuart. James was only marginally involved.

Thus, there were two related projects—the PTB and the supporting consultancy project. The PTB team worked in an off-site training centre near the prison gate. It comprised Martin and Cara plus six to eight full- or part-time prison service staff who led different 'strands' of the bid, such as 'Safety'. In terms of the supporting consultancy work, this was almost exclusively in the form of Stuart meeting with Martin—a process of gentle and persistent persuasion and support of the client to become more project management oriented. Cara would sometimes join these meetings and there were some group meetings and occasional one-to-one meetings between Stuart and other PTB team members and the Prison Governor. Almost all these client–consultant meetings were observed and recorded using either taped audio recordings and/or detailed contemporaneous notes. Many of the meetings lasted several hours and often involved joint working as well as formal 'review-type' meetings. Thus, we were able to observe in detail the type of coaching and mentoring activities which characterize the 'supportive/enabling' form of consultancy. There was almost no consultancy work conducted off-site, except for occasional phone calls and emails between Martin and Stuart. (see Table 3.3.)

Table 3.3. Key characters in Case 2

Prison	
Martin (contact and primary client)	• The client and PTB project manager and principal client was seconded from the Prison Service and had just completed a Masters degree in Public Administration. He had no previous experience of working with management consultants.
Cara (intermediate client)	• The deputy PTB project manager and responsible for one of its 'strands'. Also seconded from the Prison Service and completing an MBA at the time of the project.
Tony (intermediate client)	• Prison Governor and member of the local PTB project board. Recruited eight months previously to lead the response to the prison inspectors in terms of immediate improvements.
Lesley (intermediate client)	• A prison officer at *Prison* and POA representative working with Tony on one of the PTB project strands. Lesley was critical as a boundary spanner between the PTB team and the prison staff, enjoying the experience of learning about project and team management from Stuart.
Network	
Stuart (minder and grinder)	• An experienced engineer and project manager who was recruited to provide project management advice to the PTB project team. Stuart had relatively little public sector experience and his 'alien language' was initially a barrier to his relationship with the clients.
James (finder and grinder)	• A Director of *Network* who was commissioned to provide financial management advice to the PTB team. James had much less involvement with the clients than did Stuart and, perhaps for this reason, did not develop a deep understanding of their particular culture and difficulties faced.

Case 3: Imperial *and* Techno—*'Performance Pressure with Sociability'*

The third project involved the implementation of a core IT system in a retail financial services company, a mutual building society.[2] The main parties were a medium-sized IT-consulting firm that specialized in the banking sector, *Techno*, and a medium-sized regional mutual building society that has been in existence for over 150 years, *Imperial*. The project duration was around two years.

[2] Building societies are UK financial institutions which primarily provide savings/investments and mortgages to personal customers. Some have mutual status which means that they are formally owned by their members rather than shareholders.

The decision by *Imperial* to replace its IT infrastructure was taken in response to a realization that the existing system and IT department were unable to deliver, particularly in relation to a shift from self-regulation to statutory regulation of mortgage sales. This involved a significant modification in the information systems that were needed to conduct business with customers. For example, one area that was the source of much discussion during the project related to the content of a key facts illustration (KFI) which was prescribed within the new regulations. As a consequence, the new IT system had to be able to produce KFIs that were fully statutorily compliant. In addition, the system needed to produce accurate monthly and quarterly electronic financial reports that were in the format mandated by the regulatory body, the Financial Services Authority (FSA).

Following a competitive tender, *Imperial* selected *Techno* for a contract worth just under £2m to implement a new IT system to support delivery of all its core products (mortgages, savings, and investments). The main attraction of *Techno*'s system and service offer was its flexibility, broad base (full mortgage application processing and post-completion administration), and the fact that it provided compliance with the future system of mortgage regulation (although this proved not to be the case). In addition, the system was used by a large proportion of UK building societies. As a result, *Imperial* would be able to benefit by sharing the costs of the future development of the software with other *Techno* customers in the sector who were also members of the 'user group'. It was thus regarded as a relatively safe investment. This was important as the project represented a very significant investment for *Imperial* and a high-risk and high-profile one in that any system failure could adversely affect service delivery and reputation with customers and regulators.

The core coordination process of the project was the monthly Change Board meetings. These involved key *Imperial* managers and executives (see below), the on-site *Techno* project manager, Julian, the *Techno* client or relationship manager, Gordon, and, occasionally, other consultants of varying seniority who were based at the head office. These meetings provided a regular and formal channel for discussing and reviewing the progress of the project, and presented an opportunity for the client and consultants to come together as a group. They would start at 10.30 am and would last around two hours followed by a self-service lunch in the directors' dining room for all those in attendance. A typical meeting began with a review of the actions since the previous meeting followed by a series of reports from the consultants (Project Board Monthly Report,

Project Workplan, Technical Issues Log, and Risk Log). Julian spoke to these latter reports and presented a summary of the main issues and identified those that had been addressed, those that had not, and their level of importance. These reports were often very detailed and discussion would ensue around the length of account numbers, transferring names on accounts following an account holder's death, the interface with other programs used by the Society and its automatic telling machine (ATM) system, and so forth.

There was also a review of the implementation timetable, project costs, and discussion of specific issues and problems arising from the installation of different versions of the software. These latter discussions included such issues as the failure of new versions of the system to 'fix' problems within the prior version, concerns about the number of workarounds, specific issues with the system such as its inability to produce personalized letters or deal with different accounts and very small balances. It was at these points that Gordon would contribute with information on the expected release dates of new versions of the software, how they were working in pre-release tests, and how other societies were dealing with similar issues. Following the formal business in relation to the IT system there would be a short break where the *Techno* staff left and the *Imperial* staff then discussed the related change management programme within the Society.

These meetings were the focus of our research observations although a range of other ad hoc meetings, including business lunches and a dinner, were also observed. Indeed, this project was characterized by greater closeness or sociability than the others, akin to an *extended family*. In addition, client and consultant members of the project team were interviewed formally and informally (i.e. on a regular ad hoc basis after meetings and during site visits), and a range of project documentation (briefing documents, all Change Board papers, and related material presented in other settings) was collated. Detailed contemporaneous notes were taken at the Change Board meetings and audio recordings of all interviews were also made. (See Table 3.4.)

Case 4: Borough *and* OpsCo—'Going through the Motions—the Tail End of a Failed Partnership'

The fourth project involved the purchasing department of an urban local authority, *Borough*, and a global generalist consultancy firm, *OpsCo*. Like the third case, the project was, initially at least, involved with an IT

Table 3.4. Key characters in Case 3

Imperial

Paul (contact client)
- Managing Director and long-standing employee with previous experience and connections across the sector, regionally and nationally. He chaired the Change Board meetings and had general experience with consultants in other parts of the business.

Duncan (contact client)
- General Manager and Director with over 30 years' building society experience and day-to-day managerial responsibility for the success of the IT project, meeting the Special Projects Manager and *Techno* project manager weekly. He had previously worked with *Techno* as a client at a competitor building society.

Des (intermediate client)
- Society Secretary, Director, and long-standing *Imperial* employee with responsibility for its IT Department. He had previously worked with consultants in both IT and other parts of the organization.

Belinda (primary client)
- Special Projects Manager with 25 years at *Imperial* and day-to-day responsibility for liaising with the consultants to ensure the successful implementation of the system. Worked in an open plan office with the consulting team. This was her first major project and she had no previous experience of working with consultants.

Joyce
- With over 30 years at *Imperial*, worked closely with Duncan in her responsibilities for quality assurance, compliance with regulations as well as system training at branch level.

Techno

Gordon (finder)
- Client (relationship) Manager who had worked for *Techno* for ten years after an earlier career in the building society sector. He had a dual role with *Techno* as he was responsible for the overall client relationship but this included a sales target too. He had a number of banking clients, including building societies, based throughout the UK.

Julian (minder)
- Project Manager. Qualified in PRINCE2 project management methodology, his main responsibility was to ensure that *Techno* delivered the software in accordance with the project plan. He was also running a smaller project with another building society. Replaced by Martin when he left *Techno* towards the end of the project.

Lucy (finder)
- Sales Director. Lucy was a senior UK director of *Techno* and was their second in command. She was called in at times of crisis. Normally Lucy would have delegated such tasks to her manager who was responsible for managing both Gordon and Julian. However, Duncan had known Lucy for over 20 years when they both occupied more junior positions in their respective firms so this personal relationship was used, if required.

implementation and product development (in e-procurement), but in this instance the consulting firm was considerably larger and more generalist, with a broader base of IT experience. *OpsCo* had been involved with *Borough* for a number of years before embarking on two small-scale spending-review projects which formed the focus of our research. However, these emerged from a much broader historical context which is important to the unfolding client–consultant relationship we observed.

Like other 'innovative' local councils, *Borough* had embarked on what it called a 'strategic partnership' arrangement some three years earlier with an IT conglomerate we have called *SystemsCo*. The five-year contract comprised three tiers: (1) outsourcing the IT department; (2) identifying opportunities to improve IT; (3) implementing strategic projects identified in the previous tier. Tier one was carried out immediately. Tier two was started and involved *OpsCo* only as a junior partner in the contract. One of the projects identified from Tier two was the scoping and implementation of a new e-procurement process and system. Following a number of delays, the project was finally approved by *Borough* and it was at this point that our research began. It would involve reviewing council spending of £150m, with estimated annual ongoing savings of between £2.5m and £4.5m and represented a major investment of almost £4m. The initiative was an important and high-profile part of *Borough*'s overall efficiency programme, launched in response to a UK government public spending review. However, it was not to be.

Protracted negotiations ensued between the three parties—*Borough, SystemsCo*, and *OpsCo*—regarding implementation and procedures for sharing risks and rewards and for dealing with disputes. There was also a growing concern among some senior managers at *Borough* about cost-effectiveness. Eventually, the project was shelved and *OpsCo* was commissioned instead to conduct two procurement reviews with the aim of identifying potential cost efficiencies from agency staff (relating to Council spending worth over £10m) and a related category of 'consultancy' expenditure which included a range of professional activities of which only a small part related to management consultancy. These reviews comprised information and data gathering from relevant *Borough* employees by a junior consultant. This information was analysed through various templates and spreadsheets devised and adapted by *OpsCo* and then presented and discussed at project meetings. Here, another key issue concerned change management—ways of securing the buy-in of *Borough* departments to a more 'professional' (and hopefully cost-effective) approach to purchasing. These project meetings were

Table 3.5. Key characters in Case 4

Borough	
Dennis (contact client)	• Director of Resources who had recently arrived from another local authority and had some reservations about the efficacy of using external management consultants, a concern shared by his Chief Executive.
Damon (primary client)	• Head of Procurement and a key sponsor for the tier 2/3 modernization programme and the UK government's e-procurement initiative. Damon had a good and relatively long-standing relationship with the client manager at *OpsCo*.
Terry (intermediate client)	• Senior manager with responsibility for human resource management strategy and policymaking.
OpsCo	
Colin (finder)	• Client (relationship) manager for *Borough* who also became the manager of procurement consultancy services at *OpsCo* during the term of the project. Colin had worked with *Borough* and other councils for many years and had a breadth of sector knowledge which he was always ready to display.
Derek (minder)	• Project manager with broad knowledge of public sector procurement based on industry as well as consultancy experience.
Andrew (grinder)	• Junior consultant, new to consultancy, who conducted most of the stakeholder interviews and presented data at meetings.

observed as the key part of our research. Almost all of them were recorded and/or detailed contemporaneous notes were taken. In addition, a sample fact-finding interview with a client as well as some informal 'backstage' exchanges was observed and client and consultant members of the project team were interviewed periodically, both formally and informally. A range of project documentation was also collected. (See Table 3.5.)

Research Methods

Having described the empirical aims of the research and the selection and some of the characteristics of the case study consulting projects, we now turn to a more detailed explication of our research methods—the collection and analysis of data. These have already been introduced briefly in discussing their specific form in the individual cases. However, here we discuss them collectively to facilitate a more contextualized understanding of our subsequent analysis of the research.

Data Collection

The data collection methodology was informed by our research questions, which in turn reflected our theoretical orientations and understanding of existing literature such as that described in Chapters 1 and 2. In addition, and throughout this project, data collection for the four cases was informed by our continual engagement with consultancy organizations and user groups such as the Office of Government Commerce (OGC) and the Management Consultancies Association (MCA). Engagement with these groups sensitized us to practices, issues, and debates relevant to the consultancy sector as a whole, and provided a forum in which to test our initial ideas and findings. In addition, we conducted a questionnaire of consultants and their clients who had submitted a short case study as an entry for the MCA's annual awards. This was carried out opportunistically and was not fully under our control. As a consequence, it is not reported here. Nevertheless the shared focus on relationships and learning through projects helped inform our case study research and data analysis. For example, it helped draw our attention to the idea that much client and consultant learning experienced in project teams relates as much to project practices as to the content or discipline of the project itself (see Handley et al. 2006; Sturdy et al. 2008).

Our main concern was to provide insights into the consultant–client relationship by providing a window onto real-time client–consultant interactions as well as participants' accounts of those interactions and of the broader project context. As we have already outlined, we were able to observe meetings over the duration of the four projects. We also gathered a broad range of other data to enable us to build a comprehensive picture of the project interactions, drawing for example on pre- and post-meeting semi-structured interviews, on informal discussions with project participants over lunch or as they travelled to and from meetings, and on supporting documentation such as project plans, terms-of-reference, and meeting minutes. In each of the cases, at least two of the research team were involved in data collection and two of the team were involved in three cases. Table 3.6 shows the approximate total number of interviews and observations for each case study.

Table 3.6. Approximate number of interviews and observations in each project case study

	Interviews	Observed meetings
1 Global	51	4
2 Prison	12	9
3 Imperial	9	14
4 Borough	13	8

RESEARCH FOCUS

The two areas of focus for our research and data collection were the client–consultant 'relationship' and 'knowledge flow'. These are complex constructs and processes which cannot easily be translated into measurable units of analysis in the positivist tradition. Nevertheless, in an effort to sharpen our empirical gaze, we developed a research framework which identified particular aspects of 'relationships' and 'knowledge flow' which would be important to our research.

The first area of focus was 'relationships' which, as we have already seen, are considered of primary importance in the consultancy literature, but which clearly are of much more general significance, even within the limited realm of organization studies. For example, relationships have been variously described in terms of sociometrics, attribute data, practices, evaluations/sentiments as well as their contractual, idealized, and practised manifestations (see Grey and Sturdy 2007; Scott 2000; Uzzi 1997). Our analytical method was informed by some of these wide-ranging approaches, but was shaped and focused by our theoretical assumptions about social structuring or boundaries which, as we saw in Chapter 2, are centrally concerned with relationality. In particular, our preliminary reading of some of the literature on inter-organizational learning and of our early data drew our attention to various meaningful separations and connections between consultants and clients and their construction as *'insiders'* and/or *'outsiders' to each other*. In other words, as the research progressed, it quickly became apparent that *'client' and 'consultant' should not be seen as unitary bodies* in relation to one another. We therefore refined our research agenda and focus to examine relationships through their boundary dynamics.

The second area of focus was knowledge transfer or, to highlight its dynamic and fluid nature, 'flow'. Here, we initially developed a conceptualframework informed by situated learning theory (Lave and Wenger

1991) and a practice-based view of knowledge (Orlikowski 2002). The focus here on participation, identity, and practice (see Handley et al. 2007 for further details) resonated with the investigation of boundary relations and insider/outsider positions. For example, one aspect explored as part of the research was the role of participation in humour in bridging or disguising the structured tensions between clients and consultants (see Chapter 7). Likewise, the question arose of who can become a full participant in a community, and who remains a marginal participant or is excluded and how is this achieved? Our focus on relationships and knowledge therefore converged into an emphasis on the boundaries between different forms of knowledgeable practice.

OBSERVATIONAL DATA

We have already outlined the empirical value of observation to our research given its prior neglect in studies of consultancy. The method chosen was *'observer as participant'* (i.e. 'sitting in'). This term highlights how participation cannot be avoided, but is distinct from that of *'participant as observer'* which is common in consultants' and academic-consultants' accounts of their own work, either in the form of prescription or in the form of revelation. As we saw in the previous chapter in relation to Simmel's and Merton's views on insider and outsider accounts more generally, this is not to argue that one approach is inherently superior to another. Rather, each has different characteristics and gives rise to different types of data and insight. Furthermore, differences arise from varying interests or perceived interests. For example, much of the academic literature either neglects or dismisses consultant accounts, presumably on the grounds that it tends towards prescription rather than analysis, lacks objectivity, and is likely to favour or, at least, not be critical of consultancy. Such assumptions are not without substance, but not only can interests of some kind never be excluded, but insider accounts are likely to contain meanings which are less accessible to those of non-consulting academics. Here, however, a potential strength is the possibility of revealing and questioning that which is taken for granted by practitioners.

One of the decisions for observational research is where to direct the researcher's gaze. Constructs such as 'relationship' cannot be simply identified let alone measured, except in terms of basic sociometrics. Nevertheless, there needs to be some clarity over what researchers are looking *for* if only to avoid the accumulation of a mass of untargeted fieldnotes. To avoid this, and following Robson (1993), we began with our research questions and theoretical orientations, and then identified the types of events, activities, actors, interactions, and emotional behaviours which might reveal insights into the phenomena of interest. For example, to investigate the nature of consultant 'challenges' to their client (and vice versa), we identified the different behaviours which might reflect a form of challenge (such as 'confrontation' and 'facilitation', following Heron 1990). In particular, we paid attention to the phenomena mentioned earlier such as 'forms of participation', identity-construction, and portrayal of insider/outsider positions. More generally, observation as a method exposed the frequent uncertainty and fluidity of knowledge in use (see also Chapter 5).

While not developing an observational schedule to measure and count specific phenomena or types of interaction, our prior theoretical discussions and conceptual frameworks sensitized us to the type of observational data we should look for. In addition to our fieldnotes, we were usually able to record the conversations which occurred during meetings. The recordings were fully transcribed. Where meetings were not recorded, detailed notes were taken describing the nature and flow of the conversation, non-verbal behaviours, especially unusual ones such as smiling or laughter, and the use of artefacts such as presentation materials. A form of conversation analysis technique was also used to record some interactions at one of the case study sites, *Imperial* (see Chapter 7).

INTERVIEW DATA

Observational methods provide a window onto the physical interactions between case study participants, such as turn-taking and non-verbal behaviours, as well as the substantive conversations which unfold between them. However, such methods come with their own difficulties and limitations. For example, informal meetings and other communications may not be readily accessible to researchers, especially if such conversations are dealing with highly confidential matters. Even the more accessible meetings pose problems, especially in the context of business norms of formality and the suppression of emotion, if not feelings. Indeed, many of our observations revealed more about meetings than the nature of the relationships or knowledge flows (see Schwartzman 1986). Likewise, observational methods are not helpful in exploring non- or partly interactive processes such as report/presentation writing, email correspondence, and 'backstage' activities. Another limitation is that observation gives insights only on *observable* behaviours, to the neglect of the motivations, intentions, reflections, sentiments, and contexts behind those behaviours.

For each case study, interviewees were selected using a purposive sampling strategy, aimed at interviewing all project members (clients and consultants) at least once over the duration of the client project, and in most cases two or more times. In addition, and where feasible, we also interviewed the sponsors and other stakeholders from the client and consultant organizations in order to ask broader questions concerning the project context, background, progress, and outcomes.

Interviews were semi-structured, lasted between 45 and 90 minutes, and were recorded and fully transcribed. (Some informal meetings, over lunch, on the train, and in the pub, for example, were not recorded.) The flow of the conversation allowed for a balance between interviewer-initiated questions on the one hand, and unprompted comments initiated by the interviewee on the other. Choice of questions was informed by a previously developed interview schedule which translated the research questions of the funded project into a set of optional interview questions (see Sturdy et al. 2008). The schedule was accompanied by guidance notes to the interviewer. During the course of our research, the initial schedule was reviewed and amended following discussion among the research team about our practical experiences in using it, and suggestions for its improvement and amendment according to emerging research foci, such as boundaries.

DOCUMENTARY DATA

To provide some context for interviews and observation, and as an aid in the analysis, we collected a variety of documentary data over the course of the client projects. This included minutes of meetings, Gantt charts representing planned project events, analysis (i.e. output) templates, presentation materials, background documentation (such as public sector policy papers), and other project documents such as 'business cases' outlining the rationale for the client–consultancy projects. Such documentation set out the more formal, technical, legal, and contractual aspects of the project which become 'taken for granted' or more opaque during client–consultant interactions. They therefore provided an effective counterpoint to the visible and immediately accessible data that was obtained through interviews and observations. Documents such as presentation materials and Gantt charts provided a visual summary of progress (or intended progress) and were useful prompts during interviews with informed participants. Unfortunately, email correspondence, which would provide a valuable insight on project dynamics, was not made available to us (see Whittle 2008 for an example of its use in a consulting context).

Data Analysis

We have previously referred to the theoretically informed nature of our research and of our research focus. This meant that our analytical approach was already sensitized to look for phenomena such as multiple and dynamic structures and processes of exclusion and inclusion in relationships, and to explain observed phenomena in terms of situated learning, knowledgeable practice, power relations, and so on. Nevertheless, we sought to remain alert to emerging themes arising from a more inductive analysis of the data. Clearly, there is an ongoing tension here in that explicit prior theory will influence data interpretation to varying degrees. However, by using inductive qualitative techniques to analyse data at a micro level of interaction, we were able to remain relatively open to unexpected insights which might challenge existing theoretical assumptions or prior empirical research. Moreover, much of the data was in a transcribed form so that it could be examined at a later date for a more careful and sensitized analysis.

The process of analysis broadly followed what Kvale (1996) calls 'categorizing' and 'condensing'. Our strategy was therefore twofold. The first element was to summarize and *condense* entire texts (e.g. interviews, observation fieldnotes, or project meeting transcripts) keeping intact some quotations but maintaining the narrative thread. The second element was thematically to *categorize* discrete segments of interview text and observation fieldnotes using open coding techniques, and then to compare and contrast those segments in order to reveal nuances of meaning.

The second element—that of 'coding'—is potentially problematic because it requires a preliminary interpretation and judgement about the meaning of the text even before a broader understanding of the research data is obtained. There is a need to avoid 'swift' and superficial coding. Furthermore it is important to revisit initial coding efforts as the researchers develop their understanding of the themes in the data. To achieve this, our research adopted a number of strategies, including the development of a 'code-book'; the use of software to manage and facilitate re-analysis of the data and codes; and regular discussion among the research team about the validity of data interpretation and 'coding'.

CODE-BOOK

The code-book documented the development of theoretically informed and inductively developed 'codes' used in our research to label segments of text. The format followed Boyatzis's recommendations (1998) and included, for each of the main codes, three elements: code name (i.e. the descriptive label); definition or guidance on how to know when the code occurs plus description of any qualifications or exclusions; and (where possible) examples, both positive and negative, to eliminate possible confusion when looking for the code. The code-book documented approximately eighty primary codes and provided a comprehensive resource which was augmented and elaborated (e.g. with more examples from the data) through regular discussion among the research team. Codes documented in this way included, for example, 'insider/outsider dynamics', 'humour', 'sector knowledge', 'self-confidence', 'hoping-to-learn', 'project roles and responsibilities', and 'project background'. Any substantial revisions to code-book entries precipitated a re-analysis and re-coding of relevant texts—a time-consuming procedure.

To support the process of data management, coding, and analysis, we used the proprietary software package NUD*IST NVivo. This was initially set up with a number of *a priori* codes, such as 'relationships', and these were then added to after our preliminary reading of the data. Eventually, about 130 primary and low-level codes were listed and organized under 20 categories such as 'identity' and 'participation'. The work of coding the data using the code-book and NVivo software constituted only one part of our preliminary data analysis. We were acutely aware of the dangers of what has been called 'coding fetishism' (Delaney 2000; see also Marshall 2000)—the desire to continue labelling discrete segments of texts as though the reduction of data and its separation into piles of coded segments were an end in itself. We were also cognizant of the distorting effect of working only with extracts of text divorced from the context in which the text was spoken.

'Condensing' allowed us to retain an understanding of the narrative of each interview or meeting, and facilitated iteration between 'in detail' and 'in context' levels of analysis. The 'condensed' versions of our data were accumulated in the form of 'case packs'—one for each case study. These contained documentation of the background, events, personalities, and narratives, including summaries of all interviews and observed meetings; profiles of all personalities; Gantt charts of the projects (where available); selected consultants' presentation materials; and a timeline of key events.

These outputs from the preliminary analysis—the case packs and the coded data within NVivo—were complementary in many ways, and provided a basic set of materials which could be discussed and shared within the research team. This activity was occasionally facilitated by the use of various display techniques, such as mind-mapping and the use of 'tabulations' (Miles and Huberman 1994). For example, following a preliminary reading of the data, it became apparent that a useful lens with which to review relationships and knowledge processes might be to consider consultants dynamically as 'insiders' and/or 'outsiders' to the client. Therefore, in the first instance, the data across all four cases were first coded in NVivo for its relevance to 'insider/outsider'; second, the coded text was tabulated to distinguish between different qualities of being an insider or outsider (i.e. in respect to 'what'). By doing this, we were able to distinguish between a variety of dimensions or structures, including social background; type of knowledge or expertise; and personal relationships. Having distinguished these dimensions, we were then able to investigate how different insider/outsider configurations impacted on or conditioned the potential for knowledge flows between consultant and client.

Having explored the data using lenses previously identified through a review of the consultancy literature (e.g. on the nature of 'insider/outsider' positions), we began our second phase of analysis. This phase was more inductively driven, with the aim of looking primarily at instances of knowledge flow (or its failure) between client and consultant, and seeking insights which might explain these processes. Here, we relied on a re-reading of the case pack material and of all data coded under the NVivo categories relating to learning and knowledge. By focusing on each example, comparing it with others, and investigating apparent 'deviances' we were able to clarify research themes and refine our interpretation of the case studies (see also Sturdy et al. 2008).

Analysis 'Testing'

Throughout this period, we sought to sound out some of our interpretations, analysis, and findings with research participants and other interested parties. In all four case studies, for example, we conducted feedback meetings, at least once, in which we tentatively discussed our initial interpretations and ideas with the participants, obtained clarification of missing or ambiguous data, and asked for participants' reactions to our analysis. In all cases, these sessions appeared to be well-received and also provided additional data which enriched our understanding. However, such activities were not wholly productive, especially where our relationship with the participants was more formal, less relaxed and where both clients and consultants were present, as this was most likely to bring out some of the sensitivities discussed earlier in relation to securing research access. This had implications for our research focus on learning as well of course. Indeed, we also experienced what many consultants may feel projected from their clients—an expectation or hope that we would reveal a profound and/or immediately useful insight or technique in return for their cooperation. From our perspective, whether or not this would ever be possible, it was certainly not realistic at such an early stage of analysis. As our research developed, however, we talked to a wider audience in user groups in business, policymaking, and media communities, and again sought to sound out our initial interpretations while seeking to challenge existing views of client–consultant relationships and knowledge. For example, seminars were given to the Richmond Group of consultants and to the Management Consultancies Association as well as more diverse audiences such as those hosted by the ESRC's Advanced Institute of Management and Evolution of Business Knowledge initiatives. Finally, we presented our work at a number of academic conferences and seminars and submitted it for review and publication in journals and books. Such processes do not guarantee an improvement of quality—respondents and reviewers may be misguided or ignored. However, they did prompt continued reflection and development of ideas, which remains ongoing.

Conclusion—Towards Selectivity

In this chapter, we have sought to outline some of the contexts of our research, setting out the overall rationale for exploring consultancy projects in action and a brief narrative of each of the case studies and their key actors (see Table 3.7 for a summary). We then discussed the approach we adopted in terms of securing access and the research methods, data, and analytical techniques used in order to help the reader assess and make sense of our arguments more generally. But how did these research activities translate into the following chapters of this book? How have our data and analysis developed into specific themes and their empirical illustration and elaboration? In short, beyond a pragmatic need for some degree of focus, how has over three years of research been reduced to four substantive empirical themes, and why these particular themes? The remainder of this chapter sets out briefly some of the rationale for selectivity in terms of both the core topics—boundary complexity, sector knowledge, challenge, and humour—and the data used to develop them.

Table 3.7. Summary of cases

Client	Domain	Theme	Key consultants	Key clients
Global	Strategy	'Consultants on trial'	Ray Mick/Chloe John	Victor Julian Ralph
Prison	Project management	'Gentle and persistent persuasion of client'	Stuart James	Martin Cara Tony Lesley
Imperial	IT implementation	'Performance pressure with sociability'	Gordon Julian/ Martin Lucy	Paul Duncan Des Belinda
Borough	Procurement	'Going through the motions—the tail end of a failed partnership'	Colin Derek Andrew	Dennis Damon Terry

The focus of our original research questions was on the conditions which enable and constrain knowledge flow in the context of client–consultant project relations. This remained a core research question throughout the research project and has been discussed in detail elsewhere (Sturdy et al. 2008). Here, it is important to note that even where 'knowledge transfer' was a formal consideration of the project (e.g. *Prison* and *Global*), it soon gave way to other, more concrete or operational objectives as resources became stretched and priorities shifted. However, we revealed a range of conditions which partly matched those identified by others who have sought to generate prescriptive guidelines to facilitate knowledge flow, such as motivation, planning, resources, and 'operational proximity' (e.g. Szulanski 2003). In addition, our attention was drawn to two areas of particular interest. First, knowledge flow appeared to occur in multiple directions rather than primarily from consultant to client. Second, actors often appeared to find learning about the project or client/consultant management process—what they were doing—more meaningful than the ostensible knowledge domain of the particular project (e.g. strategy or procurement). However, it soon became clear that, given our view of knowledge as predominantly embedded and processual, and given the exploratory and in-depth nature of our research, seeking to draw out generalizable conditions for knowledge flow was highly problematic. Not only is knowledge as an identifiable object necessarily elusive, but also particular conditions—say 'working in close proximity'—have varying meanings (and therefore outcomes) according to context. In addition, the dynamics of relations, such as the development of trust, indifference, or closeness over time, are neglected. Finally, and as Orlikowski (2002) also points out in relation to 'boundary spanning activities', such practices can also have unintended 'negative' consequences. In short, a checklist approach is of only limited usefulness as a guide to predicting knowledge flow outcomes. Rather, attention is required to specific contexts and negotiated processes and this implies a different and more selective focus in data collection.

The themes which we have chosen to focus on emerged on the basis of a range of interrelated factors. First, and as outlined in Chapters 1 and 2, they were informed by our various prior interests and understandings of different literatures such as that on consultancy and inter-organizational knowledge processes. These shaped our theoretical lenses on the data and its collection and our recognition of empirical gaps which needed to be addressed. Second and relatedly, through these lenses as well as other less explicitly theoretical perceptions, the themes emerged 'from the data' and its initial analysis—what we saw, read and heard, and found interesting through reflection and discussion.

Thus, in terms of our overall focus on boundary relations, it very quickly became clear that, at the level of the consulting project at least, the formal organizational boundary and differences in knowledge did not match the prevailing view in the literature on consultancy and elsewhere in (inter-)organizational studies, but that boundaries, actors, and relations were multiple and complex (Chapter 4). But this largely structural overview perspective also raised new questions, about detail and dynamics for example. Here, we found from our observations that sector knowledge was frequently shared, ambiguous, and negotiated. It was also largely neglected in the literature as a form of consulting expertise and potential boundary spanner (Chapter 5).

As has already been emphasized, we were also concerned for theoretical and empirical reasons with relationship dynamics in action and here, we were particularly drawn to the more visible *processes* of negotiation and the management of tensions which arose during encounters. This is a potentially very broad area of investigation, encompassing almost all forms of human interaction. Two processes which emerged as areas of particular interest were those of challenge (Chapter 6) and humour (Chapter 7). Challenge is a core element of conventional understandings of both learning and consulting interventions and yet neglected, especially in relation to recent literature on consultancy (cf. Smith 2008). We also found that its experience by actors varied as individual relationships and trust developed over the course of the projects although its situated nature meant that its effectiveness could not be taken for granted.

The emergence of humour as an area of focus is, perhaps, less transparent. Indeed, for those who have observed or participated in consultancy and business meetings more generally, it may seem surprising, for the typical formality of such events would suggest that politeness or emotional restraint is the norm. This was the case in our projects as well, and these characteristics would warrant further valuable research. However, in such contexts, humour is especially visible through the contrast to regular interactions it presents. Also, studies of humour in other contexts have shown how it can serve as a medium and outcome of tensions and boundary relations—it can unite and divide and express, defer, and suppress conflicts and tensions. Thus it provided an important window on some of the boundary relations and tensions we were concerned with. In particular, it opened up an opportunity to study some of the micro-dynamics of consultancy and boundary negotiation which, again, have rarely been explored. Furthermore, and as we have discussed elsewhere, humour is an important element in a broader business discourse of consultancy where consultants are the butt of jokes (an issue we address in Sturdy et al. 2007).

Overall then, in keeping with the exploratory nature of our research, our analysis is selective in terms of particular perspectives and dimensions of knowledge flow and boundary relations. In addition, selectivity is evident empirically as analysis moves through the chapters to a more micro level. Thus, in considering boundary multiplicity and complexity (Chapter 4) and the specific case of sector knowledge (Chapter 5), we are better able to incorporate and compare all the case studies. However, as attention is focused more on the negotiation and construction of boundary relations through relationship dynamics and immediate interactions, a further degree of selectivity is required. In particular, in our analysis of challenge (Chapter 6) and humour (Chapter 7), there is some discussion of these phenomena in the cases overall, but emphasis is placed on particular cases. This is not to say that humour or challenge was absent in the other cases, although its presence or visibility did vary. Rather, it is a question of our chosen level of analysis and focus in that our concern here is with specific contexts. This raises a broader methodological question about carrying out micro-level analysis of multiple cases whereby the process of comparison can serve both to simplify or reduce situational specificity and to reveal its importance. There is not the scope here to resolve this issue, but we hope that our approach provides some useful insight into what are largely unknown processes.

4

Re-thinking potentials for knowledge flow

Introduction

Having introduced the conceptual, methodological, and empirical contexts of our study, this chapter begins our analysis of the consultancy project cases. In particular, it leads directly on from Chapters 1 and 2 where the dominant view of knowledge flow in consultancy—expert outsiders bringing new knowledge—was presented against more nuanced positions of the client–consultant relationship from studies of consultancy in general and then, in Chapter 2, wider research on knowledge flow and boundaries specifically. In particular, it seeks first to illustrate empirically the complexity and dynamism of client–consultant project boundary relations, presenting a rhetorical challenge to the dominant organization-centric view of consultant as outsider bringing new expertise. Second, with reference to some of the concepts introduced in Chapter 2, especially that of cognitive distance, it sets out to explore the implications of boundary complexity for knowledge flow potential through consultancy.

To recapitulate briefly, in Chapter 1 attention was drawn to the multiple possible bases for relationship boundaries. These broadly correspond to what were described in Chapter 2 as physical, cultural (cognitive/emotional), and political boundaries. For example, joint working in project teams relates to the idea of operational proximity and communication technologies. Likewise, personal ties and shared/contrasting knowledge domains (e.g. organizational and sector knowledge) parallel concerns with optimum cognitive distance and shared or 'redundant knowledge'. Similarly, political boundaries in consultancy around conflicting objectives and legitimation form part of what was seen more

Table 4.1. Composite map of boundaries/knowledge and consultancy projects

Specific context of actors—organization, project team, individuals, and/or roles (e.g. client types, consulting roles, and hierarchical levels)

Physical boundaries	• Operational proximity; technologies; architecture; (boundary) objects; sociometrics.
	• Space/activity (e.g. liminality of joint working and communication).
Cultural (cognitive/emotional) boundaries	• Multiple knowledge domains and identity sets; optimum cognitive distance for knowledge types/processes; 'redundant knowledge' and personal characteristics; belonging (NIH); and outsider attraction.
	• Personal/social ties. Knowledge domains (e.g. shared/ contrasting personal, general management, functional, organizational, and sector knowledge).
Political boundaries	• Knowledge at stake; structured interests (e.g. contractual/ dependency relations); inclusion/exclusion.
	• Political interests (e.g. project objectives, sell on, job loss, and legitimation).

generally in terms of structured interests and patterns of inclusion/ exclusion. In addition to the core boundary bases, Chapter 1 pointed to a variety of actors in the relationship, apart from the organization and this was, following Merton (1972), developed further in Chapter 2 in terms of the multiplicity and gradations (e.g. liminality) of simultaneous insider/outsider relations or identity sets. Finally, we introduced the importance of dynamism in the crude terms of consultancy project phases and other relationship dynamics (e.g. from repeat business) in Chapter 1, and then in a more conceptual sense in Chapter 2 through processes of negotiation, transformation, and reproduction and the transitional nature of liminality (see Table 4.1).

At the same time, the importance of context was emphasized in both chapters in terms of the situational specificity and valence of particular boundaries (Orlikowski 2002) and of management consultancy projects, both generally and in their various forms.

We now seek to address this empirically, through an introductory analysis of boundary multiplicity, complexity, and dynamism or, more specifically, multiple insider–outsider relations. We hope to show how, in the context of specific consultancy interactions, individuals may 'confront one another simultaneously as Insiders and Outsiders' (Merton 1972: 22) in what Wenger described as a complex social landscape of changing boundaries and peripheries (1998). Given the large number of possible boundaries to consider, for rhetorical reasons we shall focus on those which present a counter view to the idea of consultants as outsiders.

This chapter is organized as follows. First, we examine the core issue, for our purposes, of knowledge domains before examining the related cultural boundary associated with personal relations alongside the physical dimension of shared social space. From these boundary *bases*, we move to a consideration of the different *actors* involved and their varying roles. This raises the question of relationship *dynamics* and the negotiation of boundaries through various practices (see also Chapters 6 and 7). Finally, we turn to boundary politics, with a particular emphasis on patterns of inclusion/exclusion and an alternative conception to the dominant view of consultants as outsiders. The concluding discussion points to some of the implications of the analysis particularly for evaluating likely barriers and bridges to knowledge flow to and from clients. Overall, we argue that the dominant assumption in accounts of learning from management consultants both over- and underestimates the micro-structural potentials for knowledge flow.

The Cases—Consultants as Insiders?

The client–consultant relationship in the case study projects can be readily classified in the traditional, organization-centric way as that of an organizational outsider bringing external expertise (e.g. strategy, IT, procurement, and project management) to the client in terms of advice and/or implementation. However, our empirical focus on relationships within the confines of specific projects immediately raises the issue of liminality, although for some clients, at *Global* and the main clients at *Prison* for example, such activity was more the norm than an uncomfortable, transitional space. Likewise, two of the projects, *Borough* and *Global*, were, at times, explicitly located within the partnership discourse outlined by Werr and Styhre (2003), the former emerging out of a failed 'partnership' initiative and the latter leading to the discussion of a longer-term relationship although in both cases this relates solely to the formal, organizational relationship. Finally, the projects might be classified under Kitay and Wright's framework (2003) based on personal relations and expertise. Here again, the consultants can be seen as 'outsiders' in the sense of being 'advisers', providing esoteric knowledge with negligible relationship history and, in the case of *Global*, moving towards the development of a 'partner' role, albeit in a formal sense. However, even a limited knowledge of the projects soon reveals limitations in such models in that *Borough* and *Imperial*, in particular, involved elements of another, 'insider implementer', role in assisting with IT implementations. Not only did roles change within projects, but while some consultants saw or presented themselves as insiders, this view was not always shared by their clients. We now explore some of these complexities, first in relation to the various knowledge domains as cultural bases for insider/outsider relations or 'cognitive distance'.

Knowledge Domains/Experience

Far from bringing new outside knowledge to their clients, the case study consultants were sometimes reluctant to do so and typically shared and/or produced common knowledge with their clients. The former was most evident at *Global* who explicitly requested the consultants to challenge them with new insights, but felt that they had been politically cautious (see Chapter 6). Indeed, the consultants' contribution was considered as almost purely 'inside' knowledge such that *Global* managers rejected a non-expert self-identity, seeing themselves effectively re-purchasing their own expertise, albeit in a more accessible or commodified form.

All the ideas we have in here, we [Global strategy staff] came up with most of them. I have a file that's three years old—it was done earlier [before] ... why Stratco can make so much money off of us, is we don't embed things. We almost rely on consultants to be kind of our library. (Global Project Manager)

This is not to say that consultants should be seen as entirely passive or simply commodifiers and custodians of shared knowledge, but as co-producers. However, this also demonstrates that what some clients and others might see as external consulting expertise is, in part, client-based knowledge. In two of the other cases as well, *Prison* and *Borough*, clients were effectively 'partial employees' of the consultancy in that the consultants saw their projects as a form of product development for future projects:

We've been involved in similar ... [projects with other councils] but this is the first—which is why it is so important for us really—what I would call full transformation of procurement.... And that's why I've forced my company to be patient around it coming through. Because I think that once we've worked with [Borough] and got the approach right, I think it will then be something that other councils . . . well. There's a way of taking this and then scaling it, yeah, elsewhere across the country. (Senior OpsCo consultant)

More generally, we can see how consultants often shared common knowledge domains with many of their clients. This is perhaps unsurprising, for, as we noted in Chapter 1, many consulting firms recruit on the basis of experience in their client sectors. *Techno*, for example, recruited its consultants heavily from the building society sector where the firm had a large market share. Similarly, *Stratco* selected a number of consultants for the *Global* project team, precisely for their experience in the relevant sector. Even in the *Prison* case, where the consultant lacked specific (prison) sector experience, he was appointed specifically on the basis of his public sector background compared to other short-listed firms. In this albeit limited sense, then, even he was a comparative insider. Here, we can begin to see a particular insider/outsider boundary (sector knowledge) in relative terms and better characterized as a continuum (see Chapter 5).

We noted in Chapter 1 how a core assumption of the view of consultants as outsiders is that they do not share *organizational* knowledge with clients. However, we have also suggested that this might be tempered by the frequency of repeat business in consulting. Thus, consultants and clients may come to share knowledge of the client organization's personnel, power dynamics, and decision-making and communication norms. This was indeed evident at *Stratco* who had a number of other long-term *Global* projects ongoing elsewhere. Indeed, given the *Global* practice of regularly transferring its senior staff, it was reported that it was sometimes easier to contact the consultants for their knowledge of *Global* than it was employees, although this depends upon different consulting roles. The Senior Partner at *Stratco*, whose responsibility had been to manage these relations for the previous seven years, boasted about having a *Global* identity badge and inside knowledge, joking with *Global* staff that he was *'more Global than they are'* and, when his opposite number at *Global* was appointed, that he could *'tell him some things about his [new] job'*. However and once again, the (organizational knowledge) insider status is relative and tactical, but not simply compared to clients in this instance. It was felt by many at *Global* that *Stratco*'s key competitor, *Elite* consulting, had more strategic projects and history than *Stratco* and as a result had greater internal strategic knowledge even than the *Global* Strategy Department itself.

Elite are so inside Global. . . . I wouldn't say insidious but they have projects in various parts so they can reflect more on the Global Group context than we [the Strategy Department] can.

In addition to shared/appropriated sector and organizational knowledge, we saw in Chapter 1 how the progressive spread of management discourses in the media and the 'professionalization' of management knowledge and education have made the notion of consultants as knowledge outsiders or 'cosmopolitans' even less tenable. This was certainly the case with the main clients at *Global* and *Prison*. Indeed, *Global* managers also included some former *Stratco* consultants and even Partners. Moreover, as consultants move into implementation projects, as at *Borough* and *Imperial*, their expertise mirrors that of many more managers (see also Czerniawska 2002). The Deputy MD at *Imperial* for example had considerable experience of similar IT implementations, including working with *Techno* at another Society. More generally, a common functional knowledge base between client and consultant project members has long been the case in certain fields such as strategy in large firms like *Global*. Moreover, in this area they also share a relative lack of operational responsibility in their work and, in this case at least, even share similar work-/ lifestyles or tacit knowledge.

The folks here at the Global strategy I mean they work almost like consultants. They work long hours, very data-driven you know they work weekends, they work very, very hard and you know tackle and think about a lot of similar issues (as consultants). (Stratco consultant)

These parallels are perhaps unsurprising and both clients and consultants shared relatively elite occupational and international educational backgrounds, including US MBAs for example. However, even in the seemingly less glamorous and specialized context of the *Prison* case, clients and consultant shared some common (e.g. project management) discourses and work-styles.

Personal Relations and Shared Social Space

In Chapter 1, we argued that the 'consultant as outsider' view places consultants as inhabiting different worlds and having internal reference groups. This has been reinforced recently by increasingly formalized practices of consultant selection. However, we have also seen how some regard extra-project personal relationships, especially at senior levels, as crucial in helping to generate and sustain business. The case studies generally reinforce the latter view, strengthening the case against an assumption of cultural (cognitive/emotional) distance. As the *Global* Senior Project Manager noted:

When you can connect with somebody on the consulting side you somehow feel they are not a consultant, because you can develop a relationship with them and an understanding of them.

However, the cases also point to variations and to the more ritualistic and mutually instrumental nature of social relations, especially beyond immediate project activity. Echoing the work of Jones (2003) in a similar field of consulting, the *Stratco* Partner emphasized the importance of individual over corporate relationships/reputation and encouraged his senior subordinates to cultivate these for their own, and the firm's longer-term interests as careers developed and crossed. Given this, one needs to be cautious of the 'insider' claims made by senior consultants. However, instrumentality works both ways as client executives use the relationships too, as a source of 'off the record' information (see also Sturdy et al. 2006). Here, for example, *Stratco*'s relative disadvantage compared to *Elite* in terms of consultants' organizational knowledge can be linked to a long-standing and sustained personal relationship at the most senior (CEO/Partner) levels—'... they speak together every Saturday, I mean they just call each other up and talk business' (*Stratco* manager).

At *Imperial*, there was not the same sort of relationship history but, close, or at least, sociable and informal, relations were more evident *during* the project. Here, a traditional use of informal spaces such as post-meeting lunches was made by the client (i.e. *Techno* relationship) manager to socialize informally, especially over local sports and the local and national building society sectors they were all steeped in. This developed into visits to the theatre and football matches and playing golf together. In the much smaller *Prison* project, the consultant had a lot to achieve interpersonally with the client, who initially described him as somewhat 'difficult to love'. Also, time, resources, and scope for operational proximity were more limited, such that the consultant's relationship-building techniques were pursued intermittently, during coffee breaks for example, and appeared less ambitious and more like the everyday informal exchanges of a workplace such as discussions about the weather, TV programmes, and traffic problems.

The *Prison* case reflects Czarniawska and Mazza's (2003) image of consultancy as a liminal activity in that client/s and consultant/s worked closely together, face to face, in a shared, often segregated space. Here, even without extensive extra-project social relations, a shared sense of 'project team' identity in relation to others—*project* outsiders—can develop. For example, the main client at *Prison* favourably compared the intensity of this face-to-face working with the relationship with his boss. It was also evident in the comment of a *Stratco* consultant:

It is a far more fluid relationship in terms of you don't have to have formal phone calls or emails... it's very natural and very dynamic... you basically become part of the team to the point that they [clients] sort of forget that you are actually consulting.

However, consulting does not always take such a liminal form. In the *Global* project, while senior consultants talked a lot about close personal relations, there was little collective work activity, particularly early on, rendering junior consultants, especially, outsiders in this physical sense. Moreover, the length of time spent working with clients does not necessarily reduce the sense of boundary. Parity in status and background or social characteristics is important too. For example, at *Imperial*, the *Techno* Project Manager was on-site during the length of the project, but he remained a cultural (emotional) outsider to senior clients as he was mostly engaging with relatively junior *Imperial* employees. Indeed, in contrast to the partnership view of consulting (Werr and Styhre 2003), as consultants become more involved in implementation work and therefore in contact with a greater diversity of client employees, beyond the project team, their insider claim at the all important, senior levels may become less tenable. This highlights the importance of acknowledging the variety of actors involved in consultancy.

Actors—Multiplicity and Complexity

In our discussion of the consultancy literature, we saw how clients and consultants should be distinguished according to hierarchical levels and roles–insider/outsider with respect to whom? And we have already mentioned some of these relations in the cases such as those consultants who have a relationship management role—'finders'—and senior consultant–junior client relations. When assessing these individuals and their roles comparatively against the numerous bases for insider/outsider relations, a large number of permutations or simultaneous insider–outsider relations emerge. Here, we mention only a few of them. For example, the *Stratco* Partner can be seen as an insider in relation to client organizational knowledge and some personal relationships, but as a relative outsider in terms of technical knowledge of the team and compared to his counterpart at *Elite* in terms of personal relations at senior levels. Likewise, the main consultant at *Prison* can be seen as a relative insider with the main client socially/spatially compared to his peer at *Network* and in terms of management knowledge compared to other client team members, but was very much an outsider in relation to organizational and (prison) sector knowledge. At *Imperial* and in keeping with contrasting formal roles, the *Techno* Project Manager shared a common IT knowledge and working space with many of the client's employees, but was socially more distant from the senior clients than the Client Manager who was often observed 'taking the side' of the clients in meetings (see Chapter 7). Sometimes, these roles are performed by the same person so that, at *Prison* for example, the consultant appeared more of an outsider when playing an expert project management role than when he was encouraging the client to apply his new knowledge, through questioning and mentoring for example (see Chapter 6). By contrast, roles can be performed by different firms such as in the case of *Global*, who appointed a consultant to facilitate a key meeting with *Stratco* because of his close *organizational* knowledge of Global and its senior staff, but relative distance from the specificities and technical knowledge of the project.

The complexity of insider/outsider relations in consultancy arising from multiple boundaries and actors can be compounded by a lack of clarity or agreement over the status of the client/s, particularly as a project progresses. For example, at *Prison*, the main client or, in Schein's terms (1997), the 'contact' client, as we saw in Chapter 3, was working under Prison Service authority to commission and manage the consultants, in part to legitimize the head office role in helping prepare the bid. In this role, he was the 'primary' client in assuming ownership of the test bid even if the 'ultimate' client might be seen to include the prison and even its prisoners. Indeed, as the project developed, the consultant came to see the 'primary' client as the prison Governor who, to an extent, also saw himself in this way, seeing the role of the 'main client' as an 'external' resource, an internal consultant even, there to free up his time. This situation led the consultant to contact the Governor independently, resulting in a 'heated exchange' with the main client and an apology from the consultant. At *Global*, although there was not the same ambiguity or confusion in the 'client system', the Senior *Stratco* Partner similarly sought to bypass the 'primary' client, addressing the *Global* CEO directly, against a prior agreement with the client:

X (the senior Stratco Partner) wasn't supposed to say anything and then he pops up [in a meeting] and starts talking about this [strategic] opportunity and I am looking at him thinking [X] 'shut up'. (Global Project Manager)

Similarly, over time, tensions developed over the extent to which the consultants needed to engage the views of *Global* operational managers versus those of the initial client group, the Strategy Department. The need for 'buy-in' from broader client constituencies led the client team and its knowledge base to become less central or even marginalized. Thus, a strategic analyst joining the *Global* project team would have been very much a (project) knowledge insider at the start of the project, but much less so at the end where operational knowledge began to hold more sway. This can be seen as a common phase in consulting projects, but it also illustrates the importance of adopting a dynamic as well as complex view of insider–outsider relations.

Dynamics and the 'Fragile Negotiation' of an Insider Status

The above instance illustrates how the knowledge domain against which to assess insider/outsider relations may change. But it does little to reveal how this occurs interactively, as part of an often fragile and sometimes conscious, tactical, and political process of negotiation and influence. This applies to personal relationships too, but in relation to knowledge, it can be seen as a form of translation or transformation (Carlile 2004; see also Chapter 6 for a more detailed consideration). For example, a *Stratco* consultant described the delicate process of introducing strategic (i.e. 'outside') ideas from the project team to the operational managers through a series of tactical consultations

... it's a constant interaction and the fine balance is about not jumping too far ahead otherwise immediately you are in the cross wires of 'oh, *I* hadn't heard about that' and you can get very senior [client operational] managers very upset very quickly if that doesn't happen in an appropriate way.

Likewise, at *Prison*, some initial reluctance from the main client to take on project management practices was evident to the consultant. As we have seen in relation to his contrasting consulting roles and use of informality, he adopted various relationship practices to lessen both the personal and cognitive distance between them. For example, he used humour to help create a 'them and us' framing when working late before Christmas, by suggesting distributing the draft project report as a Christmas present 'wrap it up for them. Stick it under the tree! Read it after your Christmas dinner' (see Chapter 7 for a detailed consideration of the use of humour in this instance and more generally).

He would constantly re-orient discussions with the client/s away from operational detail towards planning (i.e. project management) and often did so in a gentle, if persistent, and amusing way—'Right, we seem to have got into the comfort zone of talking about nitty-gritty detail, because planning's too hard! <laughter> So.... ' Such practices seemed to be successful to the extent that, over time, the broader client team were brought further inside the project management discourse. It seemed to lessen or, at least, suspend the cultural (knowledge) outsider status or 'cognitive' distance of the consultant (see also Chapter 6).

This transition is by no means inevitable. We noted, for example, the conflict he caused with the main client at *Prison* and the similar event with the *Stratco* Partner and *Global* CEO. Also, and as we shall see in Chapter 7, humour may obscure or suppress the expression of underlying differences and be used by clients too, to impose outsider labels on others and resist consultants' insider tactics. Here, we see how an 'outsider' might not be just a latent identity that is subject to change, but can be a 'manifest' or experienced identity (Gouldner 1957) or tactic, an 'outsider-trying-to-get-in' (Smith 2008). This dynamic was especially evident at *Imperial* where some client managers, including the CEO, viewed the *Techno* Project Manager (TPM) with scepticism, recognizing some conflicts of interest.

[Some people here] like to think that he's gone native and loves the organization so much. And [the TPM] will play along with that because he knows then that if we think he's going native then we'll be more likely to trust him . . . [but] he has his own boss in the [Techno] division—that's who he reports to—to justify his existence. . . .

This dynamic is illustrated vividly in an exchange over identity badges which, for *Imperial* insiders, were red in colour. The TPM requested a secondee (Susan) onto the project team which would incur extra costs to *Imperial*, but he did so as if he was an *Imperial* employee. This was seen by the *Imperial* Project Manager, Belinda, as a claim to insider status which was rebuffed with humour at the TPM's expense and, at the same time, effectively defined herself and others present as insiders—'*he's after his red badge!*' (see Chapter 7 for a more detailed account).

A contrast can be made here with the situation of the *Stratco* Partner, mentioned earlier, who was proud of having successfully acquired his *Global* identity badge. However, it is important to note that different dynamics and practices are possible. As we have seen, insider tactics are most evident at senior consulting levels where generating new business through close ties and/or dependency is highly regarded and rewarded. It is likely that junior consultants would feel differently, valuing a diversity of client experiences and their outsider identity (also Kitay and Wright 2004; Sturdy and Wright 2008).

Clients and Others as Outsiders—A Politics of Exclusion

Our analysis so far has shown that with an extended view of the bases and actors in dynamic consultancy relations, consultants can in many respects be seen as insiders in relation to their clients. They sometimes share and co-produce various knowledge domains as well as social ties, spaces, and backgrounds, and this status is achieved interactively, over time. This raises the question of who are the outsiders in such contexts, for an insider is a meaningless category except in relation to its other (Weber 1968: 42–3). This is not simply a matter of classification, of identifying fields of 'cognitive' distances or experienced identities. As we noted in Chapter 2, it is also a political issue in terms of exclusion and/or silencing. This has been largely neglected in studies of consultancy to date in favour of seeing power in terms of influence and legitimation such as through the rhetorical, market, 'brand', and tactical power of consultants, clients, and their organizations (Fincham 1999; Gluckler and Armbrüster 2003). Indeed, to a certain extent, all of the case study clients were using consultants as a form of legitimation for decisions, actions, and outcomes. Similarly, we have seen how consultants seek to identify and influence the key power brokers in client firms such as the CEO at *Global* and Governor at *Prison*. However, little attention is given to the concomitant exclusion or silencing of others.

A potentially useful approach to begin exploring those excluded or silenced from consultancy is to draw on Schein's different categories (1997) of clients. This might initially identify 'unwitting' clients, those who are affected, but not aware of the fact. As we shall see, this typically involves those at the lower hierarchical levels, but not exclusively so. Alternatively, it refers to 'indirect' clients who are aware of the effects of the consultancy, but are unknown to the consultant, or 'ultimate' clients such as various stakeholder groups. However, to this list we should add a new category, *'proscribed'* clients—those who are affected and known to the consultant, but consciously excluded. This can be quite explicit. For example, the *Global* project was considered highly confidential with only a small number of the *Global* Strategy Department and operational Heads initially even aware of its existence, let alone its content, and an even smaller number directly involved. The project consultants were not allowed to discuss it with their own colleagues, and for all participants, project documents were available in hard copy only and all electronic files were destroyed.

This situation, when discovered, was not well received by senior operational managers and their representatives on the project team. In keeping with the view of consultants as allies of the primary client, this relationship was seen as more problematic by the *Global* Project Manager than that with the ostensibly external consultants. Rather, the operational members were characterized as 'willing victims' of the portfolio analysis process and the Strategy Department. While this portrays the strategists at *Global* and their consulting partners (agents) as at the hub of power and knowledge, this should not be exaggerated. Indeed, one *Stratco* consultant felt that the CEO was not easily convinced even by those relatively close to him internally.

I've got another hypothesis as well, which—I wouldn't say it's a trust issue, but they [the CEO and Board] want to draw their own conclusions, so they want to see the raw data, Y [CEO] wants to see what's actually behind it, as opposed to being fed a story.

Once again, this highlights the relative or graduated nature of an insider/outsider status with only a small group, perhaps including the *Elite* Partner, at the political core.

More generally, exclusion followed largely hierarchical lines, with relatively junior managers and consultants on the team 'exposed' to 'high-level issues' through the 'filter' of their superordinate. A similar broad pattern was evident in the other cases although without anything like the formal and planned level of secrecy and with some greater levels of participation. At *Prison*, for example, one junior project team client member felt hurt when the consultant had 'come out here in the office and decide[d] things ... [when] we should have been involved' and when the main client made an announcement to the prison management team before doing so to the project team. However, the prison management was otherwise largely excluded or, at least, absent from the project. This was reinforced by physical segregation and the fact that the main client was an external, head office employee. Despite this (and in a similar way to that at *Global*), we have seen how, as the project progressed, explicit attempts were made to gain buy-in with respect to the non-team members. Initially at least, this exposed the (project management) knowledge boundaries between the two groups or, literally, the language with which to achieve voice:

Lesley: You've got to be careful because you can see that vacant look as if to say 'What are you talking about?'

Lisa: You're losing them, yeah.

Lesley: And I think you can become very . . . the terminology becomes very much, you know, into business planning talk, and it's not the talk that they want to hear.

At *Imperial*, both branch staff and, in particular, senior IT management were effectively excluded from the project. The lack of representation of the IT management on the Project Board reflected a broader agenda of the *Imperial* Board of Directors to shift from an in-house to an 'off-the-shelf' IT system. Paradoxically, this shift to an unfamiliar technology resulted in *Imperial* IT managers becoming relative technical as well as political outsiders, at least compared to the consultants.

Thus, we have seen how, politically too, consultants can be comparative insiders. At the same time, other groups and voices are excluded although consultants may be required to speak for them. This exclusion may vary in extent, occurring by design, in terms of what we might call 'proscribed' clients such as the operational managers in the early stages at *Global* and IT management at *Imperial*. Or it may occur by default, such as the local management at *Prison* who were segregated from the consulting space. Such exclusion has clear implications for issues of change management such as reduced trust and restricted knowledge sources (see also Moore 1984; Portes 1998; Sturdy et al. 2006).

Discussion and Conclusion: Under- and Overestimation of Knowledge Flow Potentials

In the above analysis of boundaries in the case study projects, we presented a counter view to that of consultants being outsiders by drawing attention to some of the different ways and moments in which they could be seen as insiders in relation to their clients. In particular, we explored shared knowledge domains, personal relations, social space, and activity in the context of multiple actors and roles which were sometimes quite fragile and subject to negotiation, but also necessarily involved the exclusion or distancing of others, especially client groups—the outsiders. Clearly, we could also have drawn attention to the ways in which the consultants could be seen as outsiders, either in keeping with the dominant view or in relation to other boundary types and dynamics and, even, fellow consultants. Either way would illustrate the framing of consultancy relations as a series of multiple, dynamic, and simultaneous insider–outsider exchanges which was set out from our earlier analysis of the literature on client–consultant relationships and boundaries. Central to this was specifying the what, who, and when of boundaries as a process of structuring.

But what does all this mean for knowledge flow? To begin to address this, we need to return to our discussion in Chapter 1. Here, the knowledge and organizational 'outsider' view of consultants was shown to be based on a fundamental tension in terms of both the 'strength of weak ties' and 'burden of otherness'. This contrasts with the more developed notion, outlined in Chapter 2, of optimum cognitive distance according to different knowledge flow processes and knowledge types and the idea that shared or 'redundant' knowledge and social characteristics can act as knowledge 'bridges'. In addition, knowledge flow was seen as mediated through a multiplicity of dynamic and graduated physical, cultural, and political boundaries and liminal spaces which compare with those identified earlier in the context of consultancy in Chapter 1 (see Table 4.2).

Table 4.2. Frameworks of knowledge flow

	Dominant view of consultancy	Boundaries and knowledge flow	Consulting projects as complex
Key principle	• Strength of weak ties but burden of otherness.	• Optimum cognitive distance and shared knowledge/ social characteristics as bridge.	• Specify boundaries, actors, and dynamics—insider/ outsider continuums.
Boundaries	• Fixed organizational and knowledge boundaries.	• Multiple boundaries and liminality: • Physical • Cultural (cognitive/emotional) • Political (contractual/material).	• Space/activity. • Knowledge domains and personal ties. • Interests and exclusion.

By combining these insights and taking the view or situation of consultants being insiders with respect to their clients, it can be argued at a conceptual level that the 'outsider view' both underestimates and overestimates the micro-structural potential for knowledge flow in consultancy. In particular:

- in relation to cultural (knowledge) boundaries, it *overestimates* the possible novelty of the knowledge that consultants bring to clients (and vice versa) and therefore also the potential for knowledge exploration which is seen as facilitated by high levels of cognitive distance;
- it *underestimates* the possibility of cultural or cognitive closeness which might better enable the flow and development of tacit knowledge as well as knowledge exploitation;
- it *overestimates* the social distance between many clients and consultants by presenting them as being embedded in wholly different social contexts and therefore *underestimates* the possibility of shared 'redundant knowledge', social characteristics, and close personal ties lubricating other knowledge flows between actors—characteristic-based trust.

Similarly, the implicit unitary and organization-centric assumptions of the outsider view, whereby consultants and clients' interests are *organizationally* defined,

- *underestimates* the possibilities for shared interests or alliances between particular client/consultant actors and roles at particular times such as those of project team members when working together or between the 'primary' client and consulting Partner;
- *overestimates* the likelihood that the interests of such actors will be shared with the others within the client and consultant 'systems'— the 'indirect', 'ultimate', or 'proscribed' clients for example.

This absence of shared interests does not mean that knowledge will not flow, but rather that it will be mediated through relations of commitment or compliance, for example, according to dependency relations.

The implications of this analysis are not that potential barriers to knowledge flow are more or less than those implied by the outsider view. Rather, it is that they are contingent, not just on the type of consulting project, but in relation to various and graduated boundaries and different actors and dynamics in particular contexts. Indeed, the outsider view is not only universalistic, but also static and thereby underestimates how relations can change both within and between projects.

We can illustrate some of the above over- and underestimations of knowledge flow potential from our case study projects (see Table 4.3). First, in the *Global/Stratco* case, for example, the overestimation of the novelty of consultant knowledge was evident in the tensions produced over the apparent 'failure' of the consultants to challenge clients sufficiently. But the relative cognitive closeness of team members in the strategy and, in some cases, sector knowledge domains helped in the development and promotion of new portfolio options (knowledge/exploitation). Second, the close extra-project social activities (e.g. attending sporting events) and the development of close personal relations between some of the senior clients and consultants in the *Imperial* case support the view that social distances are overestimated. Likewise, and as we shall see in more detail in the following chapter, one *Techno* consultant in particular shared considerable 'redundant' knowledge and ties around the client's sector with the *Imperial* CEO and Board members. This potential as a bridge seemed to be realized when it came to conflict situations and the development of trust between parties.

Third, the expectation of conflicting (organizational) interests between consultant and client initially seemed to be realized in the *Prison* case when the consultant sought an opportunity for selling on with another client. However, over time, through working jointly and sometimes in close operational proximity, the main client and consultant developed a clear and shared focus on achieving the project objectives. Indeed, in all the cases, those consultants working actively and directly on the project—the 'grinders'—demonstrated shared interests with their fellow team members from the client organization. This helped in their learning of project and consultancy processes (Sturdy et al. 2008). Fourth, the overestimation of shared interests between the core project team members and others in their respective client and consultant systems is illustrated in the *Borough* case where the consultancy firm was, following the failed tripartite partnership arrangement with an IT supplier, keen to withdraw from the engagement with the client. Likewise, the senior client manager and client CEO were quite resistant to the use of consultants in general and to *OpsCo* in particular. Nevertheless, the project progressed and the new approach to staff procurement began to be implemented, with varying levels of compliance among the indirect client groups.

Table 4.3. Examples of boundary processes in case study projects

	Boundaries and knowledge	Consultancy literature	Case study examples
Dynamism	• Boundary interplay as enabling and constraining.	• Project phases and other changes (e.g. from repeat business and liminal transitions).	• Changing importance of knowledge type from strategic to operational (*Global*).
Physical boundary	• Operational proximity; technologies; architecture; (boundary) objects.	• Liminality of joint working and communication.	• Segregation of project team at *Prison*.
Cultural (cognitive/ emotional) boundary	• Multiple knowledge domains and identities; optimum cognitive distance; redundant knowledge; personal characteristics; belonging (NIH) versus outsider attraction.	• Personal/social ties; knowledge domains (e.g. shared/contrasting personal, general management, functional, organizational, and sector knowledge).	• Developing personal ties at *Imperial/Techno*; shared backgrounds and strategic knowledge at *Global/Stratco*.
Political boundary	• Knowledge at stake; structured interests (e.g. contractual/ dependency relations); inclusion/ exclusion.	• Contract (e.g. partnership vs. transaction); political interests (e.g. project objectives, sell on, job loss, and legitimation).	• Partnership and joint 'product development' at *Borough/OpsCo*.
Generic context/actors	• Liminality and projects.	• Organization; individuals and/or roles/hierarchical levels; project team.	• Shifting consulting style at *Prison*; dual knowledge insider (organizational) and outsider (strategy) status of *Global* Partner.

To conclude, our analysis of boundary relations does not simply challenge common sense and other existing views and put forward an approach for researching knowledge relations in consultancy. It also has potential for a basic assessment of likely knowledge flow bridges and barriers. Indeed, and as already noted, consultants often do something similar already in their use of power mapping—who is in/out politically? In this case, however, the focus is also on knowledge flow, even if this is only sometimes an explicit objective of clients and consultants. For example, an assessment of multiple boundaries or distances might help target areas of likely difficulty and prompt the use of commonalities, such as, say, shared sector knowledge, as potential bridges or boundary 'objects' (Carlile 2002; see also Chapter 5) in other knowledge domains. Moreover, the framework might be used dynamically, for mapping changing insider–outsider dynamics as an indication of learning—knowledge outsider becomes knowledge insider. For example, a decline or disappearance of a difference in organizational knowledge between parties should reflect an element of learning (or unlearning) on the part of the consultant/s and/or client/s.

Despite its potential analytical and empirical value, our analysis needs to be developed further. In particular, broadly outlining some of the multifarious bases, actors, and dynamics of boundaries and identifying consultants as insiders and/or outsiders reflects a concern with structural characteristics such as knowledge and interests *ascribed* to the various actors and phases of a relationship. In short, the bases of boundaries constitute 'attribute', more than relational or processual, data (Scott 2000). Likewise, the insider/outsider concept has been treated largely, but not exclusively, as, in Gouldner's (1957) terms, a 'latent' identity rather than one which is necessarily 'manifest', experienced, pursued, and/or resisted as a socio-political tactic within structural contexts (cf. Zabusky and Barley 1997). The very value of a more manifest insider/outsider identity to both clients and consultants, in terms of inclusion/exclusion, social capital, and as a learning bridge for example, renders it subject to negotiation and contestation. We have some insight into this process from studies of consulting rhetoric where consultants seek to present themselves *both* as experts in new knowledge and empathetic to clients' particular contexts—as outsiders *and* insiders (also Sturdy 1997a; Werr et al. 1997). However, we know very little about the *interactive* and dynamic practices of clients and consultants, either generally (cf. Christensen and Klyver 2006) or in the context of the negotiation of insider/outsider identities (see Smith 2008). We now turn to a more direct concern with such issues by exploring selected characteristics of the client–consultant relationship in action. First, we take a closer look at one particular knowledge domain, that of sector knowledge and its ambiguity and negotiation. We then focus more directly on interactive practices in Chapters 6 and 7 through analyses of challenge and the use of humour.

5

Outside expertise and sector knowledge

Introduction

The previous chapter critically explored the idea of management consultants as outsiders and their 'outside expertise' in particular. As we have seen, this expertise is typically associated with mastery of some technique or an area of abstract skill bought in by the client organization as it is not possessed internally. This kind of professional knowledge flow certainly was apparent in some of our cases, such as in the domain of project management at *Prison*. However, we have argued that the outsider view consistently neglects the extent to which such expertise is shared by clients and consultants in project teams and how this can enable knowledge flow and knowledge exploitation. Also, we have seen how it largely fails to consider other knowledge types and domains such as functional, organizational, personal, and, our focus here, sector knowledge. Such neglect is surprising as consultants partly construct their appeal to the client through various kinds of knowledge, and build occupational identities around esoteric skills of divining clients' problems. These identities do not stress transferable or applicable knowledge, but knowledge more as a *context of problems*.

This chapter examines these elements of outside expertise. We ask in particular what is 'outside' the experience and capability of clients—and suggest that one way of specifying this is to see consultants as *sector specialists* and the industrial sector as a relevant knowledge formation. A central part of the appeal to the client, it is suggested, derives from the knowledge accumulated from repeated assignments in the industry where the client organization resides (Werr and Stjernberg 2003). Anecdotally, this can be seen to fit the image of consultants as market-wise figures who

93

pick up comparative information across a range of experiences. The consultant discourse is one that encompasses rival organizations and groups relevant to the client—and, as we shall see, this fits the case study projects and the expertise utilized by many of the consultants. However, in keeping with a more fluid and dynamic notion of insider/outsider boundaries, we also saw how clients and consultants may often share sector knowledge, although our emphasis has been mostly on how consultants developed and co-produced inside, organizationally based knowledge. But the view of clients simply as insiders also needs challenging; clients too need to be considered as more active agents of management knowledge, or as agents of *external* sector expertise. In short, while consultants have been shown to occupy various insider statuses, clients need to be examined in terms of their role in the construction of extra-organizational or outside knowledge.

In focusing on sector knowledge, we find ourselves engaging with what, in organization theory, has become something of a Cinderella concept. Perhaps because of other foci in organization studies (the marketplace, networks, industries), the notion of an external structure of bodies to which managers orient their decision-making has received only sporadic attention except perhaps in terms of the broader notion of institutional fields (Morgan and Sturdy 2000). Nevertheless, its promoters have stressed the importance of the arena in which firms operate as a formation in the minds of managers. The sector represents a set of coherent boundaries, more relevant to managers than vague ideas of markets or environments, and hence relevant too for consultants as a client-dependent group. The industry sector where competitors and peers operate is the source of vital information about technologies in use, and networks of contacts, and intermediaries who bring news of this are crucial figures. For 'outside experts' like consultants, we might well conceive of their expertise having a component of sector-based knowledge. Their expertise claims would be helped by being embedded in experience of solutions and problems in a particular industry grouping—benchmarking-type judgements and decision-making recipes in circulation. Knowledge configured in this way enables consultants to play the role of the disinterested outsider *and* to draw on a language and experiences held in common with the client.

Our four case studies provided significant opportunities for sector-based interaction and the role of consultants as sector intermediaries. In two of them (*Imperial* and *Borough*), consultants used sector experience for framing their understanding of the client problem, while the central narratives of these projects involved sector knowledge being mobilized in project teams. The other two cases were slightly special in demonstrating some of the more subtle and unexpected ways in which forms of knowledge are used. In one (*Global*), direct sector know-how did not seem to be circulated, instead this knowledge (which was certainly present in the consultant team) tended to be diffused into the quality and creativity of solutions. In the fourth case (*Prison*), consultants were not sector experts and we were able to examine problems of knowledge legitimation in the absence of this context of knowledge—though here again we saw a twist to the story and there actually was relevant sector knowledge, but from a source other than the obvious one.

The chapter explores sector knowledge from two distinct angles. First, the process of knowledge construction focuses on how consultants utilize this form of expertise in decision-making and how they solidify it to support claims of legitimacy. Their 'sector knowledge' represents a summation of experiences of past projects; the experience of problems and solutions in a particular sector represents a way of framing clients' problems and claiming special skills. However, while management consultants may be well placed to acquire this outside knowledge, boundaries are not rigid and clients obviously will have knowledge of their markets and industry sectors. As we have seen, the so-called insiders will have outside knowledge and client organizations are also actors in their industry sector. Hence we seek to develop the conventional model of knowledge being acquired by an expert group, that of the consultant, as outsider who brings privileged knowledge in. This leads to the second perspective which focuses on 'the sector' itself, viewing it as a knowledge formation in its own right. Here client–firm dynamics can be seen as not only constrained by pressures from sector rivals, but also being negotiated with external networks, giving rise to the sector as a separate institutional space. Before developing these ideas in conjunction with our empirical material a framework for these aspects of sector knowledge will be briefly developed.

Consultant Knowledge and Sector Knowledge

Sector knowledge as an element of expertise is developed partly within consulting firms as collective knowledge. Consultant firms, particularly larger ones, have been regarded as knowledge systems for generating new management ideas (Clark 2004; Suddaby and Greenwood 2001; Werr and Stjernberg 2003), but a neglected part of this knowledge-fabricating activity involves the development of sector know-how in trainee consultants. As an example of the modern knowledge-intensive firm (Alvesson 2004), the big agencies in particular tend to have structures that combine bureaucratic, functional, and disciplinary aspects—but these complex organizational designs are also divided by industry and sector-based concentrations of activity. As noted in Chapter 1, consultants are often groomed within these structures, and with related groups of clients, before moving on to other kinds of experience. In the context of working on projects, experience accumulated around particular client groups further contributes to tradable knowledge, especially as clients often expect this in their consultant project teams. For a sector speciality to develop, knowledge comes through repeated assignments and extra-project contacts with the main players and their technologies and networks. For consultants, the sum total of interaction with a group of related clients has been shown to equate to this sector-based experience. For example, Fosstenlokken et al. (2003) highlighted the importance for consultants of learning from clients and interaction in joint project teams as a form of knowledge development. As we have seen, this viewpoint reverses simple assumptions about knowledge transfer in client–consultant relationships being only an expert-to-client flow.

Such alternative knowledge sources and formations may represent forms of know-how that are reliant on esoteric skills and sensitivity to client needs, yet provide relatively stable combinations of different kinds of knowledge and abilities—cognitive skills in using specific techniques combined with practical know-how of applying them that builds with experience. Our cases had some clear concentrations of industry and client experience among the consulting members of the projects and, as we are now about to explore, they provide a breadth of examples of different kinds of sector knowledge in circulation. These were examples in which such knowledge was intensively used and limiting cases where it was more diffuse and even apparently absent; the cases also dispel any simple notion of the consultant as a figure in sole possession of privileged outside knowledge; once again, this view of the outside expert (cf. Chapter 4) matched none of them.

In the building society, *Imperial*, we mentioned in Chapter 3 that as well as a project manager, the consulting firm was represented by a specific client relations consultant. This division of labour (which is common practice on big projects) allows for a 'commercial' consultant or account manager to look after contractual aspects and relations back in the consultancy head office, as well as a senior technical consultant who concentrates on project management. In this case, the client relations consultant, Gordon, was deeply networked with other building societies with which the consulting firm did business and was effectively a specialist in sector contacts. But as well as this strong element of sector specialization in the consultant team, client managers too possessed wide-ranging knowledge of other societies' doings. The sector as seen from *Imperial* was a close-knit group of largely regional organizations that was intensely 'present' in discussions about the new IT system.

The local authority, *Borough*, was also a client that was a large organization and the consultant in this case a global consulting firm; and here the two senior consultants were steeped in work with other councils and had deep experience of procurement in the public sector (the junior consultant on the team had little of this experience and had mostly an analytic and fact-finding role). However, statutory requirements and other institutional practices in local government meant that internal managers (the *Borough* procurement group) also had privileged knowledge and access. The client–consultant project team debated what other authorities were doing, particularly in relation to the model of procurement they should adopt, and it would be hard to say which side brought more to the table.

The multinational, *Global*, ranked as an extremely important client and the strategy project was staffed by director (Vice President)-level and senior associate-level consultants with coordinating involvement across many projects with that client, as well as experience of other clients in the sector. There was a strong sense in this case that the client demanded and got this level of experience in the consulting teams put together over the different phases of the project. However, *Global* was the most 'corporate' of our cases and had layers of complexity (the power position of the client came most to the fore and there was also the complicating presence of a rival consulting group and extreme secrecy surrounding detailed content). Here sector knowledge appeared the most ambivalent; this knowledge tended to inform solutions more generally and consultants did not directly trade-off their sector know-how. This may be, in part, a consequence not only of our restricted research access compared to the other cases, but also of the scale of the client organization's business which could be seen to span a number of different 'sectors' and of the strategic level of the project work.

Prison was our limiting case of absent sector knowledge on the consultancy side. The knowledge transfer wanted from the consultants involved

Table 5.1. Levels of sector knowledge

Imperial	Sector very frequently represented in discussions
Borough	Sector recipes and models regularly fed into decision-making
Global	Sector contacts and experiences tend not to be directly discussed
Prison	The consultant had no knowledge of the immediate sector

specialist skills (mainly project management) and they had no prisons experience. This, as we have said, was a case where there appeared at first sight to be no sector knowledge in circulation (though, as we see below, further understanding of the case effectively redefines what 'the sector' really was and re-evaluates the consultants' wider experience).

If we begin the process of comparing the case organizations, some preliminary 'scale' of sector knowledge in circulation in descending order might look like Table 5.1. This needs embedding in the prior discussion in order to account for differences, but sector knowledge did seem to be used more or less intensively (or at least openly) in the cases. In the building society, client and consultant were almost part of an extended family of local societies which seemed to exchange information about each other constantly; at the other end of the scale, in the prison, consultants started with no knowledge of the sector which led to initial apprehensions from staff insiders about their suitability for the work. These considerations are useful as a starting point though there was no sense that crude levels of knowledge in circulation led to simple functional outcomes.

Role of Sector Knowledge

Of the four cases, the building society probably best confirms the importance of seeing knowledge constructed around an industrial sector. At *Imperial*, senior managers spoke of being 'building society people' and knowing managers from other societies on personal and professional terms. As we saw, the 'client relations' consultant was a sort of sector specialist, but senior *Imperial* managers too possessed wider-ranging knowledge. The Managing Director, Paul, for instance, had high-level contacts in the City and the Financial Services Authority and tended to be more knowledgeable about institutional constraints and statutory changes even than the consultants. (For example, many of the issues around the new system were fuelled by new Treasury reporting requirements, and he was able to confirm progress and changes in the institutional constraints.) Between them a discourse was kept up involving the network of channels and institutions like the IT user group and relations between managers. Other societies were akin to a peer group, in the sense of an intense and constraining set of relationships, while the sector comprised an almost normative sphere of action. In the building society community, we were told, 'word gets round' and the community was a 'kind of discipline'. There were factors of affiliation and conformity over and above purely technical or market pressures (i.e. the high-risk nature of the IT implementation) and managers simply did not want to look bad in the eyes of other societies in the event of systems going down and the branch network having to suspend some of its customer facilities. These were relatively collaborative relations among companies that were sometimes supposedly rivals in economic terms.

It's an odd industry. It's odd—building societies—and I never see it as strange but other people do. But some of the best friends I have work for building societies, and it's just second nature to people. If I need an answer to something and we haven't got it here, I'll go to building societies I've got a contact with, and say how are you doing this. And they'll tell me. (Senior client manager)

In the local authority, *Borough*, the sector was invoked more intermittently. The consultants, as we have seen, were investigating the supplier interface with the agencies from which temporary staff were employed. What we might think of as the regular inhabitants of the industrial sector, the group of organizations similar to the client organization (other councils, in this case) were not competitively linked (it was the agencies that were in a competitive private sector). But how other councils tackled problems and the kinds of deals they were obtaining from supplying agencies was important information for internal decisions. A feature of this case, often referred to in consultancy literature, was an issue of clients being suspicious of consultant encroachment on their knowledge (Hislop 2002). Normally this would be internal knowledge that is market-sensitive and pertains to the competitiveness of an organization and thus is valuable to an external agent (like a consultant). But under certain circumstances it could also be knowledge of groups or organizations in the sector. Common statutory links with central government meant that *Borough* managers had knowledge of other local authorities' operations and needs. This meant potential conflict over fractions of sector knowledge and client and consultant differentially valuing their access to the sector. The belief was that the consultants brought in conventional business skills, but because of the way that local government works, they, the client, possessed valuable sector knowledge that the consultant wanted access to.

Under the normal project you've employed them [consultants] because you haven't got that expertise, and therefore because of your knowledge gap you're sort of the weaker partner. And that wasn't quite the case on this one. We sort of started off with equal knowledge and on areas of public procurement we had more knowledge. I'd say it was 50/50 but there were certain elements of that about the structure of procurement within a local authority which was to their business advantage. (Local authority manager)

Implied in the above two cases are differences in the immanence and free circulation of sector knowledge. At least broadly, a distinction could be drawn in terms of the intensity with which sector knowledge figured in decision-making. In the building society we glimpsed an intricate industrial sector. Comparisons were frequently made with other institutions and information from them was frequently sought. In the local authority, networking and contacts with other councils, while considerable, seemed less intensive. Council officers had good collegial contacts with other officers, but parochial and personal relations were not common (contacts tended to be formalized, such as visits to other councils). These differences in internal discourses in project groups seemed at least partly to be caused by the nature of the respective sectors. Special circumstances of the *Imperial* case reflected a group of organizations with strong cultural and historic links, which set the tone of the client–consultant relationship. *Borough* in a sense conformed more to a straightforward transactional relation and provided examples of some typical client–consultant activities (such as a level of suspicion about how knowledge might be used by the consultant group).

In *Global*, 'outside expertise' had a more distinctive role in the work consultants were doing. Developing operating models for areas of the business and identifying 'opportunity areas' and 'lenses' through which to view major investment/divestment decisions meant a positioning of *Global* within sector borders. But second-hand strategy from industry rivals was not what the client wanted. Project managers insisted that 'war stories' about previous clients should form no part of the justification for new strategic ideas, which should stand on their intrinsic merit. (There was little or no exchange of information about this or that sector player as there was about other building societies and councils in the *Imperial* and

Borough cases.) The consultant had to walk a narrow line: there had to be understanding of the sector but the initial stages in the strategy process were about ideas generation. Also, in this case, as noted above, power dependency added layers of complexity and uncertainty for the consultant. The project managers actively maintained a political ascendancy over the consultants; the strategy process was their turf—an established planning and investment round that the consultants had to adjust to— while the consultants were anxious to establish a foothold in this level of work. Adding to the pressure, *Elite*, the strategy consulting firm that *Global* usually employed, had been passed over and the work given to *Stratco*, but, as we saw earlier, *Elite* was still in the background, doing other work for *Global*, and placing *Stratco* on trial.

Against this layered and complex background, the sector knowledge of the *Stratco* consultants was submerged and diffuse though no less important than in other cases. There was a great depth of experience of the industry sector within the consultancy team and the client expected this knowledge to be infused in the opportunity areas identified. Also, what constituted the sector shifted in that the focus was often on business opportunities in retailing rather than the specific product sector of *Global*. The quality of these solutions were evaluated as the extent to which they provided something new and creative and 'challenged' existing assumptions of the portfolio (see also Chapter 6)—the extent to which they were not mere 'extensions of our team'. In this sense, the case provided a rather singular example of sector knowledge. We have been treating this as a reasonably well defined aspect of consultant knowledge, but here it reverts to something closer to the original and arcane image of the consultant as outsider in the sense of supplying something 'different' from the client group's own inputs. The elements of the case—the demanding client, demands of having to come up with high-quality 'creative' solutions, and the comparisons with another strategy consultant— conspired to define the notion of the 'outside expert' as a kind of *deus ex machina* that differentiated what consultants could bring that insiders could not.

One of the things that we think a consultant can give us is external perspective, and in a way during the last six months we had already learned all the external perspectives that Elite could give to us. So these [Stratco] are new persons in the team, they are going to provide external perspectives and they also have a lot of incentives to do a really good job and keep the relationship with us.

(Global Planning Analyst)

In the final case, *Prison*, it appeared at first sight that sector knowledge from the consultancy side played no role. The project was to assist the client in preparing a benchmarking review—the so-called PTB (performance test bid)—a formal request to government for continued investment that stipulated a range of performance criteria. The niche consulting firm hired to do the work had no previous experience in prisons. Hence this case seemed to contrast with the other cases given the lack of any insider experience in the consulting team. Yet the project was successful— the transfer of project management skills initially seen as alien to a prisons culture did take place—and on the surface at least it undermines the thesis that sector knowledge is necessarily an important ingredient in consultant decision-making. However, there were significant contingent factors that made this case in a sense an exception that supported the rule.

There was a strong emphasis on the client wanting specialist skills. This may have been to an extent making a virtue of necessity—in the selection process other consultants who had done this work in other prisons had not impressed—but even so, client managers kept stressing that 'we were very clear about what we wanted'. They were not looking for implementation from the consultant, as we saw in the main account of the case in Chapter 3; what they wanted was skills transfer to the prisons team—specifically skills in project management and financial analysis— and quality assurance. These were the skills or performance standards required in producing bids which at that stage the prison service had little experience of. And though lacking prisons experience, the consultant firm (*Network*) had wider public sector experience, specifically in health, which gave it adequate skill levels for the bid, and explained why the lack of direct sector experience was deemed to be acceptable if not desirable.

A key point in this case, even more so than in *Global*, is that the identity of the sector itself was elusive. Arguably, the environment most relevant to the success of the project was not the obvious and immediate sector (namely prisons). The audience for the PTB was central government (specifically the Home Office) and the performance standards it had to meet were those of Whitehall not the prison service. Hence we ought to understand 'the sector' as partly being that of prisons but also partly (and maybe the major part) the wider public sector. Even so, the rapport that developed between client and consultant took some months to come good and project success probably has to be seen as contingent and uncertain. The consultants' lack of prisons experience initially and for some months did cause a rift; client managers' disregard

Table 5.2. Role of sector knowledge

Case and project	Relationship to the sector
IT systems implementation in *Imperial*	• The sector a powerful and coherent 'peer group' reference • Client relations consultant a conduit for sector knowledge • Links to sector players normative, informal, and personal
Improved procurement model in *Borough*	• Sector actively but intermittently discussed • Links to sector players formalized • Conflict over elements of sector knowledge
Strategy formation in *Global*	• Consultant team experienced with client and industry • Sector knowledge mediated rather than directly discussed • External perspective translated as high-level creative solutions and functional (retail) as much as product specific
Performance improvement in *Prison*	• Consultant had no direct (prison) sector knowledge • Emphasis on specialist not pragmatic skills • Absent sector knowledge was problematic for clients, but moderated by wider (public) sector knowledge

of some consultant 'advice' emanated from what they saw as ignorance of the pressures of running a prison. So although client managers became enthusiasts for these methodologies, this did not wholly detract from the absence of immediate sector knowledge.

Across the four cases, then, sector knowledge played different roles and no single factor determined these (Table 5.2). In certain respects, there was a dividing line between, on the one hand, *Imperial* and *Borough*, and on the other, *Global* and *Prison*. Sector knowledge seemed more of an immediate 'presence' in client–consultant interactions in the first two cases and more 'distant' in the other two. In the building society and local authority, outside knowledge contributed in fairly straightforward rational ways towards solutions, while in the multinational it was used more indirectly and infused with the power relations and some ambiguity, while in the prison the nature of the sector itself was complex. In explaining these differences a number of contextual factors came into play, including the nature of the sector, the task at hand, and what kinds of knowledge were being sought. In the building society the strength of networking seemed to be a function of the sector itself and its intense 'peer group' relations. The local authority was engaged in a search for workable recipes, and it seemed to be this that fuelled the use of sector contacts (albeit not at the same level of intensity as in the building society). In the multinational, the more implicit industry experience expected of the consultants on the team reflected in part the magnitude of an operation that itself involved competitive and market pressures coming from inside the firm (many decisions had major implications for where to invest and divest); to a degree at least, the stress on novelty and creativity in the solutions consultants were generating was measured against internal criteria from the strategy process. In the prison, sector knowledge again showed a different face reflecting the nature of the project and the parts of the sector that were relevant to it. In the other cases, 'sector knowledge' tended to mean the pragmatic experience of actors and groups (how they tackled problems and evolved solutions), but this client was having to 'step up' a level to new standards of performance, and the consultant was being asked to provide the special skills (in financial analysis, project management, etc.) to meet these demands.

In understanding these differences, we now propose to explore two aspects of sector knowledge—first the manner in which it fed into decision-making and sustained solutions. Here, knowledge from the simple sharing of experiences towards actual solutions can be tracked. Second, there is a more complex and political level of understanding insofar as this 'knowledge' is an object under construction. To see sector knowledge solely as something that exists 'outside' is really to give it an idealized material status and to credit consultants with its possession. In fact, these outside references are constructed inside the organization by consultants (and clients) on a continuing basis.

Sector Knowledge and Decision-Making

A basic function of sector knowledge was the contribution of this kind of know-how in achieving decisions. Here we can make further use of Carlile's (2002, 2004) idea of knowledge integration in a context where individuals with quite different kinds of expertise have to come together. However, in our cases, consultant expertise represents more an 'extension' of managerial knowledge. This was certainly the case in *Global* for example (where internal managers would hardly have credited the consultants with any novel skills at all), and to varying degrees in the others. Likewise, in *Imperial*, there were still internal IT people though they did not have command of the computer package being installed. Nonetheless, there clearly were degrees of differentiation in experience and access to outside knowledge, and there were also inherent problems and potential conflicts in client–consultant relations, making knowledge integration or flow problematic.

Carlile pictured successful integration in decision-making occurring on a number of separate levels or boundaries which we loosely compared to our own framework in Chapter 2. Here, his concerns with achieving first a shared basic language between different decision-making groups and, second, the development of shared meanings or viewpoints both relate closely to what we have seen as cultural (cognitive and emotional) boundaries. If we take the first of these, aside from physical or techno-logical limitations,[1] problems of basic communication can often arise. As we have seen, consultants have often been seen as outsiders in the sense of talking a language alien to managers (e.g. Kieser 2002*b*). In this situation, however, the 'language' of firms is partly an insider language, but is also based on a shared industry language and can be accessed via consultants' outside experience. Such a common vocabulary at least allows basic information processing to go ahead (Carlile 2002: 443) and can even serve as a bridge for knowledge flow in functional areas for example, as 'redundant knowledge' (Nonaka 1994).

In three of our cases, knowledge of the sector helped consultant outsiders to acquire a language in common with client managers and understandings generated in project teams were instrumental in the skilful handling of work. Financial services, for example, are essentially information-processing industries, and in the building society case a lan-guage that combined IT functionality with the technicalities of the sav-ings and loans business was the common ground of the client–consultant relationship. Similarly, the procurement models of local government were embedded in the unique nature of local authorities as spending institutions while distinctive concerns were the procurement language of contracts with vendors, the detail of labour markets, and councils' spend and budgets. The same was true of the multinational case where there was a distinct sense of client and consultant inhabiting the same functional world of corporate-level strategy-making. In all these cases, a mass of detailed knowledge was familiar both to managerial insiders and to consultants.

In *Prison*, in contrast, no shared sector language existed except rather generic references to the public sector, and the reality of learning was difficult. As we saw in Chapter 3, the client knew they wanted some skills

---

[1] Carlile does not effectively engage with physical boundaries although they can clearly be linked to his concern with basic communication channels or semantic boundaries (see also Chapter 2).

transfer, but the realities of actually adjusting to the new ways of think-ing implied in this change were painful. There was much early tension over the kind of project-management 'jargon' that the consultants used, effectively symbolizing the rift.

Sometimes it's complete crap, isn't it? In the managerial process you can fall short on those things and just be more straightforward in terms of how you speak. But I think some things, like [the consultant] always talks about process and deliverables, and he says things like 'best in class' and stuff, and 'fit for purpose'. It just has no resonance, I think it has very little resonance. I mean fit for purpose isn't terminology I would ever choose to apply. But even the more neutral stuff that doesn't really jar isn't necessarily immediately understandable, I don't think, in the prison service. (Client manager) (See also Chapter 6)

Integrated decision-making, however, means overcoming cultural bound-aries which separate deeper, more emotion-laden value systems than simply a shared or familiar language. Innovative relationships, according to Carlile (2002), require a process of interaction and common cultures that create wider empathy for each other's positions and priorities. For example, in the prison, after an initial period of hostility, the beginnings of a more stable relationship between client and consultant were marked by stereotypes that were initially sources of conflict (the consultant was deemed to be distant and 'difficult to love'), becoming accepted and laughed about such that the client managers came to accept that the consultant had something to teach them. As noted in Chapter 4, it seemed as if the persistence of the consultant worked in the end, and the client 'learned' and identified with the language of the consultant (see also Chapter 6).

At *Imperial*, we didn't see integrated decision-making signalled by this kind of dramatic change, but there was a clear integrative function per-formed by the client relations consultant, Gordon. The fact that he had known senior managers for some time combined with his shared cultural characteristics of 'age and seniority' enabled him to get close to senior client managers, to cross seamlessly between work and social contexts, and to create wider empathy for each other's positions and priorities—characteristic-based trust. In this case, the work of the Change Board (our main data source) included reviewing the 'issue logs' which for-mally recorded progress and logged outstanding problems and queries (see Chapter 3 for details). However, the client could get intimidated by this list of problems, and Gordon tried to maintain a sense of proportion—in a way, to keep spirits up—often by comparisons with other implementation processes. Client members of the Change Board confirmed how the consultant used sector contacts and experience to bring their perception of the problem in line with his own. Knowledge transferred from other building societies meant the consultant could tell them what happened in this or that society, whether they had had similar problems and how they had learned from them. The strength of the consultant's contacts extended 'even to actually giv[ing] us a name to ring. You know, you actually talk to somebody and say, "Right, we had terrible problems with this functionality. How did you get round it?"' Rather than trying to persuade by force of argument or technical finesse, sector examples and contacts were more concrete and seemed to provide reassurance and common understanding.

Absolutely. I mean the actual go live I think we did have something like 20 issues. It would be 20 things that came up that we needed to look at. And I think we've got them down to two now. But Gordon [the relationship manager] said he almost wanted to bring somebody else's issue log to us, at go live period, just to show how little we had in fact. . . . Obviously he couldn't because of confidentiality, but, yeah, they do bring that, absolutely.

Collaboration in decision-making marks the removal or suspension of political boundaries and is often achieved when actual solutions are identified or created. While we argued in Chapter 2 that the politics is much more than Carlile's notion of 'knowledge at stake' (2002: 445–6), practices within which new knowledge is embedded and invested almost by definition unite political interests. The knowledge being formed in the process is felt as 'their own' and not tainted by past conflicts or hostilities. In our cases too, sector knowledge was a practical resource contributing in some way to the tangible outcomes of a functioning IT system in the building society, a bid document in the prison, acceptable new strategies in the multinational, and new procurement methods in the local authority.

More generally too, consultant knowledge played a key role in these outcomes although this varied between the cases. In *Imperial*, although they were engaged in 'buying in a package', this remained a complex form of technology transfer that inevitably spread new knowledge around. Managers relied on the consultants in the conversion process which constantly threw up problems. Sorting through these, using the consultants' experience, brought managers and employees (as well as consultants) intimate knowledge of the new system and how it integrated with their working methods. In *Prison*, it is obviously impossible to say whether or not the bid would have been successful without the consultant input. Nevertheless, it was evident that expert knowledge of project management techniques and the outlook required in bidding for central government support had rubbed off and passed between client and consultant. In *Global* and *Borough*, there was less differentiation between internal and external skills, and clients placed little emphasis on any learning process they had gone through, though the consultant input was still distinctive and significant beyond simply legitimating existing knowledge.

Firm–Sector Negotiation

The above considerations show how the sector served as a managerial reference point or bridge in client–consultant relations and knowledge flow. However, sector knowledge, like all knowledge, is complex and needs to be considered in a more critical sense. First, there were *uncertainties* in the knowledge itself and in the multiple voices of client–consultant project teams. Second, knowledge *construction* in terms of the interaction between internal and external actors and the networks that cross firm boundaries has to be considered. Here, we see another aspect of the shifting nature of knowledge boundaries—even knowledge apparently obtained from outside sources is invariably 'internal' in that these aspects of client and consultant know-how were constructed internally and brought together in project teams and groups in the client organization. This meant that while sector knowledge as a form of external institutional knowledge was often a touchstone in decision-making, it was not one that automatically led to convergence between firm-level competences and external constraints. Clients and consultants engaged in active and reflective learning from other sector actors, and courses of action represented a process of pooling knowledge in the context of internal needs.

Sector knowledge thus needs to be seen as an object-under-construction. It is subjectively defined insofar as 'the sector' is what internal managers and outside experts says it is, that is, the ever-changing sum of relevant actors, groups, organizations, and contacts which managers and consultants perceive and define. Of course, this has an objective aspect as there will be actors and groups that anyone in a particular industry is constrained to recognize (and others they are not). But possibilities of variation in knowledge and perception mean that people may share or dispute views of what knowledge of the sector means, and what is deemed relevant or irrelevant, so that new knowledge is pragmatically constructed and fought over. In our terms, sectors supplied examples of new understandings that were not only possessed by outside experts and 'brought to' the client, but could be co-produced. The sector was a field of activity where decisions and perceptions were actively shaped. Decision-making was about 'reading' the actions of other players and justification might be derived for diverse courses of action. Information on authoritative ideas was sought, but decision-makers took on board differences that could lead to divergent strategic responses which did not ape market and technology leaders.

Borough provided a number of examples of these more contradictory aspects of decision-making. Here, achieving efficiencies in procurement meant that a single set of bureaucratic rules had to accommodate some very different purchasing decisions and markets of supply. Some uncertainty could be eliminated if they could decide beforehand on a particular principle of 'vendoring', so one of the central decisions, debated back and forth, involved the vendor model they should adopt. This represented a classic management dilemma (like make vs. buy, or centralization vs. decentralization) in that pros and cons, and the 'right' choice, were complex and contingent, and in project meetings, items of information were put together, like pieces of a jigsaw. The basic procurement methodology could be an in-house solution, or go to a favoured main supplier, or several different suppliers. Each had a balance of factors around control and efficiency. A dominant choice did seem to exist in the shape of the favoured single supplier model—the 'master vendor'.

A lot of them are keen on master vendor at the moment, understandably. Sets some extremely tight monetary-rewarded performance measures around some of the analysis and some of the things you want to get done. So the additional premium you're paying is going to be paid for by the better performance that you get. (Consultant)

But council officers were not necessarily aping the strategic actions of other groups when sector knowledge was imported. Their reading of the sector was that there were many models out there, but they leaned towards flexibility and had stories to support different choices: one council rated as a great success was much smaller than the client so their model was less relevant; another that used the master vendor approach had apparently seen no benefit in cutting staff costs, and yet another had obtained benefits but had done this by tightening internal management which was deemed unsustainable. In short, sector knowledge was being used as a discipline and reassurance and to keep options open. Though the 'master vendor' model was as an emerging recipe, the alternative 'neutral vendor' (broker) model needed evaluating too and there were inputs from a wide variety of contacts and experiences from which information was drawn. (As well as other councils that outsourced using neutral vendoring, contacts included a legal firm specializing in procurement contracts and the contracting group that acted as a clearing house for local government procurement.)

Discussions such as these illustrated the ambiguities surrounding knowledge in circulation. The very term 'knowledge' implies certainty and a kind of correctness (truth, in other words). Managed knowledge is almost always seen as knowledge that is 'right'. However, and as noted in Chapter 3, one of the cardinal advantages of conducting observational research (as opposed to interviews where there is a measure of rationalizing and hindsight) is that the sheer uncertainty of much 'knowledge' is brought home with force. In the meetings we observed in *Borough*, there were doubts about the models being developed and what they were examples of, uncertainties about people they had come across and the positions they adopted, whether initiatives under way may have got stalled, and so on. Positions were adopted or reinforced during this pooling of half-known facts and semi-certain events which paved the way for an eventual rationale to be constructed where coherence compensated for lack of objectivity.

In focusing on expertise and knowledge 'outside' the organization boundary in this chapter and the potential bridging role of sector knowledge in particular, it must be recalled that ultimately there remains a potential tension with other knowledge domains such as that of the organization. In other words, sector and other outside knowledge still bears a potential 'burden of otherness' to clients (and consultants). Again there were variations in our cases in this regard. At *Borough* and *Global*, the consultants' knowledge was probably the least different from that of the clients. It is impossible to say whether this contributed to any less enthusiastic client evaluations of the consultants' contribution. But in both *Prison* and *Imperial* it could be said that outside knowledge did have a dominant status; in the prison the consultant's special knowledge of project management was eventually valued highly, as was the technical knowledge of the new package in the building society. However, limits were still discernible. In *Prison*, consultant knowledge (specifically knowledge of project management) was perhaps the most alien to the client and difficult for them to absorb. *Imperial* was a more pointed example because this was where a particularly respected individual (the client relations consultant) was a conduit of sector knowledge. Even here, the consultant did not trade on this knowledge in an unreflective way and admitted that while he shared the knowledge of other societies' experience, each client ultimately demanded his concentration on the resolution of *their* issues and problems. These constraints on the ultimate relevance of outside knowledge meant there remained a boundary between firm and sector and the firm itself was a domain that had to be 'respected' by consultants. In short and in keeping with most accounts of consultancy, clients required some measure of tailoring to their own specific organizational context.

Conclusion

As 'outside experts' consultants possess disciplines and knowledge which are, at least *in part*, 'external' to client insiders, and our case material demonstrated the sector as being the construct around which a significant part of outside knowledge was formulated. In decision-making, sector knowledge helped to provide a context for reaching complex and uncertain decisions and much organizational work went into discussing and developing it between client and consultant. The cases showed instances of sector knowledge circulating continually in decision-making, while its absence created difficulties that had to be surmounted before meaningful progress could be made. Knowledge of the sector was, moreover, actively negotiated across project boundaries. Management consultants were well placed to acquire this knowledge, but the boundaries were not rigid and, in the same way as we argued in the previous chapter that consultants often held significant client-related (e.g. organizational) knowledge, 'insiders' also had 'outside' knowledge. In our cases, multiple knowledge sources, conflict over ownership of knowledge, and uncertainty in decision-making were the order of the day in the sector domain.

In a way, this leads back to what is always the 'sixty four thousand dollar' question with consultants: what exactly is it they offer? This category of expert labour has expanded greatly since the 1980s—yet assumptions about professional levels of expertise have been challenged in critical research. So, is there any distinctive expertise? The category of sector knowledge enabled us to explore this central question in a way that allowed credibility without conferring unrealistic status on an activity like consulting. The sector does not represent a knowledge construct exclusively 'known' by one party, the consultant, but a construct that is developed in interaction, made by the context (Orlikowski 2002). Indeed, some of the knowledge possessed by client managers was distinctive. Senior managers at *Imperial*, for example, were experienced industry insiders who could confirm or dispute sector information and rumour. At *Borough*, there were similar structures of 'inside' knowledge that council officers claimed reflected their special access to institutional sources (see also Hughes et al. 2007).

But this was a complex knowledge field and consultants too could claim distinctive knowledge. In some cases, direct experience of other clients meant they claimed benchmarking-type skills—in *Borough* there was a sector-wide claim to having developed professional models of procurement. *Imperial* provided an instance of a sector specialist in the consultant team who claimed familiarity with other societies on a par at least with managerial insiders. In the *Prison* case, the sector that had crucial relevance (which only the consultant had experience of) was the wider public sector, and this was effectively outside the actual industrial sector that would normally be regarded as the relevant reference point. Perhaps, at the end of the day, a more broadly political role of sector knowledge was most evident. This was intertwined, as we have stressed, with the *uncertain* nature of much of this 'knowledge'. Given that what other sector actors were doing and how this should be interpreted was often uncertain, consultant and client team members needed a level of status and trust gained by claims on this experience. In cases where sector knowledge circulated freely (the building society and local authority), possessing this knowledge—having contacts, knowing the stories of events, analysing events for their relevance to current problems—was a passport to mutual understanding and even decision-making. It was valued by both parties and could serve as a bridge to transcend other boundaries. Those without this contextual knowledge (often the junior consultants with only analytical skills) tended to be denied expression and influence—inclusion.

6

Boundaries in action—challenge

Introduction

In the previous chapter, we saw how the exposure of management consultants to multiple clients across an industry can give them a particular form of 'sector knowledge' which many clients—by their very position *inside* their organization—do not have. A conventional claim from many consultants is that, as *outsiders*, they bring (generalized) sector knowledge to (specific) client problems, interpreting those problems in terms of sector-level principles, and then offering solutions more or less tailored to the client's context and needs. The emphasis here is on knowledge-as-content. An important theme in the literature on organizational development is that while 'content' is important, a repository of sector or other knowledge brought by consultants is often insufficient to instigate change in the client: what is also needed is an appropriate process which facilitates changes in clients' actions and ways of thinking. Furthermore, as we have seen in the previous chapter, sector knowledge itself is not simply developed and held by consultants and clients, but co-constructed within projects and is often quite fluid, negotiated, and ambiguous in form. This suggests that it is important not only to look at the *content* and domain of knowledge brought to (or given by) clients, but also to explore further the *processes* by which knowledge is shared, adapted, and translated to achieve and/or legitimate change or learning.

By placing emphasis on knowledge as a process, we re-orientate our attention to the sorts of interactions, sequences of events, and situational contexts which influence the ways in which clients and consultants *come to articulate what they 'know'*. A conceptual re-orientation towards the process of knowing permits a recognition of the complexities involved in organizational decision-making and action. The literature provides many illustrations of how ideas 'travel' or flow across boundaries between people and within organizations, and how those ideas come to be translated, transformed, and perhaps distorted during that process (e.g. Czarniawska and Sevon 1996; Latour 1987). With the perspective of hindsight, these changes may be seen either as appropriate adaptations to a new context or as distortions that destroy the value of the original idea. Whatever the judgement, the ideas have nevertheless 'travelled' and evolved in the process. Moreover, the boundaries through which ideas travel are themselves subject to construction, variation, and negotiation. As we saw in Chapters 2 and 4, physical, cultural, and political boundaries represent a weak structuring for knowledge flow, one which is socially produced through action.

In the context of client–consultancy projects, consultants frequently have an explicit remit to facilitate organizational change. Such a remit often carries an implicit assumption that some sharing or co-production of knowledge will take place, or at least that the consultants will support a process by which clients can articulate organizational issues and identify ways to change their organization (e.g. see Schein 1987). Indeed, consultants are often positioned as 'agents of change', subject to negotiation or resistance by the parties involved. Questions which then arise are how consultants accomplish their role as 'agents of change', and what clients expect of them. The dynamics of organizational change are likely to involve multiple intervention strategies and actions between different actors in different phases of a project. However, while recognizing this complexity, it is also analytically helpful to look separately at elements in the change process.

A dominant theme in the prescriptive consulting literature is that 'challenge' is an important catalyst for change, and furthermore that clients expect their consultants to adopt some form of role as challenger. These assumptions are prevalent in the traditional 'innovator' discourse on management consultancy where consultants are positioned as outsiders challenging their clients to discard existing positions and to identify with 'new' outside knowledge. In this conventional sense, a challenge intervention can be defined as a summons to the client to take a demanding and risky step (such as adopting new ideas and policies) for a potential reward in the form of personal or organizational success. It is seen as almost inevitable that these challenges will generate resistance from clients whose knowledge (and perhaps their sense of identity) is threatened or 'at stake' (e.g. see Heron 1990; Reason 1988). The consultant is thus positioned as teacher or challenger; the client as the fragile or insufficiently informed recipient who may initially resist, but will eventually learn and change. Two key assumptions here are that challenge *instigates* a process of change; and that consultants are the primary challengers.

In our research, the use of challenge interventions to effect a desired outcome was evident in all four cases to varying degrees (though sometimes with unintended consequences). Furthermore, the interventions changed over time as the nature of the client–consultant relationships shifted, or as different project problems emerged or were solved. In this chapter, we seek to give a flavour of the longitudinal development of challenge interventions to illustrate their impact on relationships, interpretations (e.g. of language), and client readiness for change. In doing so, we show that, in practice, challenges may be made by either party (client or consultant), and that an *experience* of being challenged may result regardless of the other actor's intentions.

The four cases had different contexts which influenced the possibilities for challenge interventions as well as the way they were enacted (and by whom). For example, each case presented a different power/dependency structural context which had a significant impact on the direction of challenge: either from consultant to client or—less conventionally in the *Global* and *Borough* cases—from client to consultant. In the *Global* case, as we saw in Chapter 3, the clients were mostly sophisticated and experienced users of consultancy services and had hired *StratCo* to provide a 'second opinion' surrounding the work of the dominant consultancy competitor, *Insight*. The *StratCo* consultants were acutely aware of the negative power dynamics which that position implied and acted carefully and cautiously with their client. Their apparent reluctance to offer challenging recommendations unless they could be robustly (and almost unequivocally) advocated had the unintended effect of prompting the client to call on the consultant to be 'more challenging' with their opinions. The *Prison* case provided a counter-example in that the principal client was, in his own words, completely inexperienced in the recruitment and management of consultants, and was ready to accept the traditional discourse of the 'consultant as helper'. However, as we show in this chapter, the client–consultancy relationship evolved over the duration of the project in ways which illustrate the effects and limitations of challenge interventions.

Turning now to the remaining cases, an important contextual difference at *Imperial* and *Borough* was the life-cycle stage of the consultant/client relationships. In our initial description of the cases in Chapter 3, we introduced the metaphorical narratives of the 'extended family' of

Techno/Imperial and the 'failed partnership' of *Borough/OpsCo*. In the former case, the enduring quality of the relationship—'through thick and thin'—meant that all parties could be relatively, but by no means completely, secure in 'challenging the other' provided those challenges respected social ('familial') norms (see also Chapter 7). By contrast, the relationship between *Borough* and *OpsCo* had become somewhat formulaic, typified as polite exchanges of advice but without a real desire to convince the 'other side'. Thus, the wider structural contexts created an arena in which challenges were made, accepted, resisted, avoided, or negotiated.

The remainder of this chapter focuses on two of the cases: *Prison/Network* and *Borough/OpsCo*. These cases have been chosen primarily because they offer an opportunity for contrast in the identity of the primary challengers: client or consultant. We present accounts of meetings, interviews, and other interactions and discuss the dynamics of the challenge interventions in relation to the physical, cultural, and political boundaries outlined in Chapter 2. Before presenting the cases, we introduce key themes from the literature on the role of challenge interventions to effect organizational change and individual learning.

The Challenge of Change: Perspectives from the Literature

We argued earlier that in the literature on client–consultancy relationships, a challenge intervention is conventionally seen as a summons to the client to take a demanding and risky step (such as adopting new ideas and policies) for a desirable reward such as personal or organizational success. For analytical purposes, the content and process of challenge can be investigated at each of the three boundary levels introduced in Chapter 2: physical, cultural, and political.

At the physical boundary, consultants and clients must be able to interact physically or virtually if challenges are to be made or received. Given the growing sophistication of ICT mechanisms, a lack of physical co-location is technically no longer an insurmountable barrier and may indeed facilitate communication. However, research suggests that many factors, including physical proximity and/or a shared sense of purpose, mediate the effectiveness of these technologies. Research on geographically dispersed organizational teams, for instance, suggests that a lack of co-located physical space tends to prevent teams from identifying and then managing conflict, with negative consequences for performance

(Hinds and Mortensen 2005: 290; Tagliaventi and Mattarelli 2006). A key problem here is the relative lack of shared group identity of the sort developed in co-located teams where members can see what colleagues are doing, empathize with their problems, share information, engage in spontaneous communication, and experience the 'noise' of the project (Grabher 2002).

At the cultural boundary, the barrier of 'cognitive disequilibrium'—a state experienced by individuals which acts to challenge preconceived assumptions—is fundamental to a constructivist theory of learning and change. On the other hand, contemporary perspectives on learning which emphasize socio-cultural and situated 'ways of knowing' help to explain why an individual may ignore an experience of cognitive disequilibrium, for example to protect the integrity and coherence of beliefs shared by others in one's community (Lave and Wenger 1991). Challenges made at the cultural boundary may focus on questions of interpretation and meaning (e.g. about language and symbolic objects such as 'issue logs', or more fundamentally about values and belief systems). To some extent, one can label this the 'content' dimension of the challenge. It is also important to recognize the 'processual' dimension of challenge interventions, and the constraints which may apply at that level. For example, if a challenge intervention is to be 'heard', it must usually be delivered in a way which fits the behavioural norms and practices of client organizations or projects. This may be impossible to achieve without some degree of shared (and/or 'redundant') knowledge, or 'cognitive closeness' (Nonaka 1994). It is this cultural boundary issue which is the focus of traditional theories about the dynamics of challenge, and which we elaborate in the next section (see also Chapter 7 for the use of humour as a socially acceptable form of challenge).

Finally, at the political boundary, challenges made by one party, even if presented in a culturally appropriate way and apparently understood by another, may still fail to be acted upon if they are rejected for political or existential reasons (Carlile 2004). Or, as set out in Chapter 2, the challenges may be merely complied with (but not fully accepted) in the sense that the required behaviours are adopted even though some resistance continues. This may be the case even if the rational logic of new ideas appears irrefutable.

Having outlined the three boundaries, we return our attention to the cognitive dimension of the cultural boundary, which is the most widely theorized in traditional accounts of challenge particularly in relation to processes of learning and organizational change. Two contrasting themes are prominent: in constructivist accounts of change, we see a focus on challenge as an *internal* experience of the individual which instigates change through a process of 'internal disequilibrium'; in the organizational development and change literature, on the other hand, we see a focus on the *external* and visible events and processes which provoke disequilibrium in others.

Constructivist accounts of individual learning emphasize the mind's continual (re-)evaluation of existing knowledge in the light of new experiences. Piaget (1970) argued that individuals experience 'cognitive disequilibrium' when they encounter events which do not fit—and therefore challenge the validity or utility of—their existing mental schemata. Faced with a strong and uncomfortable internal sense of disequilibrium, individuals typically seek to avoid contradiction and reconstruct their mental schemata through processes of 'accommodation' and 'assimilation' with the effect of 'correcting' their ways of making sense of their world. In other words, the experience of disequilibrium prompts them to learn. In the constructivist perspective then, challenge is an uncomfortable internal experience. This may or may not be provoked by the explicit challenges of others (a possibility which is neglected in this perspective), but is always a function of some form of dissonance between expectations based on experience and perceived reality. There is an implicit but important assumption that disequilibrium will prompt internal reflection and mental reconstruction (Kolb 1984: 43).

The organizational change literature emphasizes the external processes which might provoke disequilibrium in individuals or collectively at an organizational level. For example, Lewin's classic model (1951) prescribes how change agents can encourage organizations to 'unfreeze' existing knowledge and beliefs as a precursor to constructing new knowledge/beliefs and then consolidating or 're-freezing' them. According to the process-consulting model in its pure form, consultants explicitly do *not* bring new knowledge and ideas; instead consultants help their clients to help themselves by engineering challenging interventions which unfreeze the client's existing knowledge and beliefs so that the clients can then think more creatively about their problems at hand (Schein 1988). Authors and practising consultants such as Heron (1990) and Reason (1988) have proposed typologies of intervention styles to suit the client's emotional readiness as well as the task and problem at hand. Heron (1990), for example, distinguishes between interventions that are authoritative (prescriptive, informative, or confronting) or facilitative (cathartic, catalytic, or supportive) (see also Tichy 1975). For example, Cockman et al. (1999: 102) describe a common form of intervention where the clients are perceived by the consultants as 'part of the problem . . . there are discrepancies between what [clients] say they do and what they actually do in practice. Confrontation highlights the mismatch.'

In contrast to the emphasis on process which characterizes the organizational change literature, the importance of content and networks is prevalent in debates about knowledge transfer and social networks. For example, and following Granovetter (1985), 'weak ties' are seen as valuable in bringing external and challenging knowledge into the organization in a way which questions the validity of existing assumptions and ways of thinking. Yet, as Nooteboom et al. (2007) point out, echoing Festinger (1957), the novelty of external knowledge may be too great for the recipient to understand or even recognize without considerable intellectual investment: the 'cognitive distance' may be too great. As we set out in Chapter 2, the effect of this distance is that the knowledge brought by weak ties may not be heard. Similarly, Nooteboom's suggestion that cognitive distance 'yields both a problem and an opportunity' (Nooteboom 2004: 291) is also evident in the field of management consultancy where consultants' status as knowledge outsiders is double-edged: helpful in that new ideas promote knowledge 'exploration' (cf. 'exploitation'); but limiting if the knowledge poses a threat to the integrity of the clients' current understandings (i.e. their mental schemata, Piaget 1970) or if its strangeness leads clients to reject it (Antal and Krebsbach-Gnath 2001; Holmqvist 2003).

Such accounts bring into question the effectiveness of challenge interventions in client–consultant relationships. Furthermore, other accounts question the conventional assumption that the consultant is the principal challenger. For example, we have seen how many highlight the conservative and (purely) legitimatory role of consultants (McKenna 2006), as well as the commercial pressure on consultants to conform to the view of their immediate clients (Sturdy 1997*a*; Sturdy et al. 2004). In these accounts, consultants are presented more as conciliatory and conservative than challenging even if legitimation can still serve to support change initiatives.

The implicit image of the 'fragile client' seeking knowledge is also problematic (Fincham 1999). Indeed, Macdonald (2006) showed how inexperienced users of consultants could be especially demanding of consultants for clear solutions. The image also reinforces the view of the client in a subservient role and as one whose own knowledge base is deficient. In practice, and especially in recent decades, clients who are sophisticated and routine employers of consultants may have come to embrace a collaborative discourse emphasizing the co-production of knowledge and solutions (Christensen and Klyver 2006). In this discourse, each party to the collaboration brings relevant knowledge and experience, and each has a stake in the validity and credibility of that knowledge (Carlile 2004). Here, the likelihood of being defensive against the critique of others and thereby creating or reinforcing barriers at the political boundary is crucially mediated by trust and familiarity in specific relationships or contexts.

Such trust can be exploited or manipulated by either party in a way in which one of them, usually the client, feels as if they have developed an idea themselves and the other, typically the consultant, encourages this view, but sees it as an outcome of their own heavily disguised challenge. In short, either party may deny co-production in favour of their own contribution (Sturdy 1997a). Finally, challenges may be successfully resisted by either party. In a related study of how people deal with dissonant feedback, Chinn and Brewer (1993) catalogued a number of successful strategies for resisting change, such as rejecting all or part of the dissonant challenge, or discrediting the challenger and by implication also the message carried. Similarly, we have seen how consultants and/or the ideas they promote are frequently resisted by various client groups (Sturdy et al. 2006).

In summary, the literature develops a number of themes in relation to challenge, which we have defined as a summons to the client (or to the consultant) to take a demanding and materially or existentially risky step for a potential reward in the form of perceived organizational or personal success or competence. First, the constructivist perspective on learning and change positions the internal experience of 'disequilibrium' as the (potential) engine for change: new experiences which challenge the validity and coherence of one's world view provide an impetus for change— or are resisted if that change is too uncomfortable. Second, from the organizational development literature in particular, there is a recognition that external actors such as consultants may be significant in encouraging individuals or organizations to confront the challenging nature of their experiences. While the constructivist perspective emphasizes the inherent power of experience (or 'content') to effect change, the organization development (OD) literature emphasizes the important mediating role of outsiders. Challenge may come from clients or consultants as each party challenges the knowledge of the other, or (as a defensive move) challenges the other's competence and authority to make a challenge in the first place. Paradoxically (and as we discussed earlier in the context of *Global*) clients may press their consultants to be even more challenging, for a variety of reasons such as political manoeuvring or information-seeking.

Case Studies

Following our review of the literature on challenge, we now turn to an empirical investigation of our cases and ask how the interactions between client and consultant manifested in practice. The cases presented here are *Prison/Network* and *Borough/OpsCo*. These are relevant because they offer comparable *organizational* settings in contrasting *relational* contexts. Both cases involve UK public sector clients: one in the prison service and the other in local government. Furthermore, both clients share an institutional context emphasizing a service ethic and a concern for 'value for money' for the tax-paying public. However, the two clients differed in important respects which had implications for the way they interacted with their consultants. The client individuals differed in age, business experience, and career stage, but more significantly this manifested as different levels of expertise in dealing with consultants: the prison clients were self-proclaimed naïve users of consultants who almost felt guilty with what seemed to them like 'flying first class'; the local government clients, on the other hand, were experienced and to a degree even jaded or sceptical from their repeated involvement with consultancy-supported initiatives and in particular with the consultancy firm employed on their project (see Chapter 3 for a contextual overview).

Prison/Network

The *Prison/Network* case offers insights into the use of management con-sultants by a public sector organization traditionally closed to outsiders. We begin by presenting the client's rationale for the use of consultants as well as their expectations of the relationship. Following this introduction, we outline some of the problems of relationships and knowledge flow as they relate to physical, cultural, and political boundaries.

The main actors in this case were the two associate consultants, Stuart and James (members of *Network*), and the two main clients, Martin and Cara. The main clients had no prior experience of negotiating with man-agement consultants, and expressed their concerns about their naïveté in an early meeting with the researchers. Indeed, Martin commented that it felt 'quite indulgent' to 'have someone come in and quality check on a regular basis', especially given their internalized sense of caution about using public money: 'why are we asking for help with a job that someone has assigned to *us*?'

The clients were using consultants because the UK government Home Office had recommended and budgeted for it in the performance-improvement programme for failing prisons. By 'being there' as a physically present resource, the consultants were expected to be able to transfer their experience to the prison context, overcoming barriers to knowledge flow. At the same time, it was expected that the consultants would provide some legitimation to the process and outcome of the bids for the Home Office.

To some extent, the expectation at *Prison* was that the knowledge transfer process would be unproblematic. The two consultants were hired for different purposes: James for financial management, and Stuart for project · management. The expectation was that these consultants would have the knowledge and skills to advise on and facilitate the financial and project management activities, and would do so during scheduled four to six hour project meetings where client/s and consultant would sit together to discuss and resolve issues. In practice, most of the client activity was with Stuart, who is the focus of our case study.

The clients, Martin and Cara, were seconded to *Prison* from the UK Home Office. Martin, having completed his Masters in Public Administration at a UK university while Cara finished her MBA at another, felt he knew the theory but not fully the practice of project management, and he looked forward to learning from the consultants. As Martin explained— Stuart gave the clients the confidence to insist to the client team that project management was important, and that time should be spent on it. Innovation and legitimation motives were thus combined.

[Cara] and I were sold on the idea of project management—I'd done my project management module at University, and I thought it was quite interesting—I quite liked it, and I thought I could become a convert....

I think what Stuart did was really give me confidence to say—to think we really must do it this way. [Stuart would give advice]...and suddenly we thought 'This is for real, this is how people do it.' And because he's our one and only consultant, we thought—this was what consultants bring.

The main consultant, Stuart, positioned himself (and was positioned by the client) as an outsider with transferable project management skills. Cara and Martin explained:

Cara: Not knowing [the Prison] context was actually an added benefit... sometimes things do need re-questioning.

Martin: I found it more probing having someone in from the outside.... It was more difficult and challenging than Helen [boss to Martin and Cara] who just wants to know that everything is going OK, which is not the same as having someone working alongside you.

As we saw in Chapter 4, Stuart was able to influence Martin and Cara by sitting with them individually or together for significant lengths of time. In all, we observed seven meetings, each of up to six hours' duration. As we shall illustrate later, Stuart's approach was to challenge, gently but persistently, his clients' assumptions and to model the thinking processes of a project manager. This approach was perhaps unexpected by the clients, who thought that a relatively simple process of 'knowledge transfer' was all that was required. Nevertheless, it became apparent that Stuart provided a forum for 'thinking aloud' so that deep-seated assumptions or 'misconceptions' were revealed. This meant that the cognitive distance which separated client and consultant was exposed and then subject to challenge by the consultant. For example Martin explained:

Stuart comes in and checks what you're doing and asks you some probing questions, because although you can probe yourself in that way, you just don't. You just don't get the opportunity to stand back, and even sometimes when we're justifying and explaining to Stuart what we're doing, that in itself is useful, even though it's not necessarily progressing the work, I think it is a real quality check on what you're doing and whether we really truly understand what we're doing and why we're doing it in that way, and whether the plan is manageable.

Echoing psychodynamic views of consultancy (Sturdy 1997a), the *Prison* Governor, Tony, commented that 'Martin would have felt very lonely' without Stuart because there was no one else to turn to in that situation. Another perspective came from Cara at a post-project meeting; she reviewed Stuart's activities and then cited his contributions, particularly in terms of providing quality assurance advice; questioning about programme and project management; and coaching team members who had limited prior experience in project management. Having completed the project, Martin commented that after 'flying first class' and having the comfort of having a consultant to work alongside, he did not relish the thought of going back to 'economy class'. However, this somewhat rosy picture is not a complete characterization of the project—particularly in the early stages. The nature and some of the problems of relationships and knowledge-sharing can be categorized according to our three types of boundary: physical, cultural, and political.

At the physical boundary, the client–consultant relationship had the benefit of a regular and routinized process of interaction: every two weeks or so, Stuart would visit *Prison* for a project management meeting, and would stay with the main clients for most of the day discussing at length any current plans, issues, and problems. These long meetings became increasingly characterized as mentoring-type meetings between Martin and Stuart: typically, they would sit alone together in an outer office, discuss the issues of the day, take coffee breaks together, and work closely with occasional interruptions from other project members. At the same time, of course, these close interactions were punctuated by long periods of separation, marked only by occasional email and telephone contact.

Barriers to knowledge-sharing were evident early in the project when Martin and Cara reacted against the language and terminology used by Stuart. This represented a significant cultural boundary which manifested as the clients' inability to comprehend their consultant. The language was 'alien' and presented a cognitive challenge which was initially rebuffed. In an early research interview, Martin and Cara talked of the barriers they faced as they struggled with the new language and ways of thinking which Stuart introduced.

Martin: It's a kind of alien learning and thinking style, isn't it?...and I think also [the managerialist language] isn't really in place in the Prison Service. And sometimes it's complete rubbish anyway, isn't it?...Stuart talks always about 'process' and 'deliverables',...and he says things like 'best in class' and stuff—

Cara: And 'fit for purpose'.

Martin: It just has no resonance...Stuart will say 'best practice' and 'best value' rather than 'best in class', but they mean the same thing.

In this last quotation we see an attempt at *translation* of the language, which Martin and Cara were able to do later in the project following their periodic exposure to Stuart. However, as the next quotation shows, the barriers were not solely to do with language: sometimes the project management language was seen to reflect values of a prosaic type of 'order' which was foreign to the prison service culture.

Cara: Some people genuinely have an inherent kind of resistance to [the project management way of thinking] because it clashes so much with the values that they hold, for example about being spontaneous.

These concerns were also expressed by junior members of the client team. The following quotation from one team member shows the extent to which some members felt able eventually to cross these language barriers.

Lesley: At the first meeting, terms were used that I'd never heard! Things like the Gantt chart. I mean, I've heard of a pie chart! [Laughter] a lot of techno-speak. And I don't mean that rudely—it's the way [of speaking and thinking]. I mean I must say, I think [some of us] are now into that. We throw these terms around.

In the early phase of the project, the client also experienced the effect of socio-cultural boundaries. Stuart was aged in his forties and had an engineering/project management background. To Martin and Cara, he seemed to belong to a different era of 'industry' and 'manufacturing', and he initially came across as rather pedantic and old-fashioned. His appearance and approach were noticeably different from that of Martin and Cara, who were younger and with public sector backgrounds. These clients were sensitized to prison service buzzwords and ways of thinking as well as the newer 'cosmopolitan' ideas introduced in their Masters education.

Also at stake (and creating another barrier) was Martin's (and to a lesser extent Cara's) sense of identity. Martin was seen—and identified himself as—a high-flying civil servant. He had just turned 30, had recently completed his Master of Public Administration (MPA), and felt that he had now acquired the theory—albeit not the practice—of management. His sense of identity was on the one hand flattered by the attention provided by the consultancy support, yet at the same time challenged by the implication that he needed teaching or at least mentoring about a topic he 'should know'.

The knowledge and skills which Stuart brought to the project were alien and therefore challenged the utility and validity of Martin's MPA studies and his extant understanding of project management. This meant that Martin's identity as competent—or at the very least his 'knowledge at stake' (Carlile 2004)—initially stood in the way of open engagement and knowledge-sharing between client and consultant.

These boundaries were overcome to some degree over the course of the project. However, as we shall see later, Martin was anxious to preserve his growing sense of managerial identity; for example, he bridled when that identity was challenged by Stuart in the presence of the prison Governor, speaking of 'raised blood pressure' if Stuart had gone further and copied the Governor on emails. Nevertheless, a growing level of comfortable humour and banter was displayed in the observed meetings (see also Chapter 7) which appeared to reflect a sense of mutual respect and collegiality: Martin even invited himself to a post-project meeting between Stuart and the authors so that Martin could 'catch up' with him.

The consultant's challenges were persistent, sometimes humorous, and often delivered in an avuncular manner. For example, in an early project meeting, Martin and Cara, with Stuart, discussed the projected content of the bid document which was to be the written outcome from the project. They discussed the likely expectations from the eventual recipient—the Home Office Prisons Service—which would evaluate the bid based on the report as well as a later Evaluation Day visit to the prison.

Martin: This is a bid to say 'will you [Home Office Prisons Service] let us [Prison] do this'. . . . We're not necessarily going to say when it's going to be done, or by whom, or the dependencies . . . or how. These senior managers won't be in a position to ask these questions [at the Evaluation Day visit].

Stuart: Don't underestimate them. If they're worth their salt, they'll ask a few probing questions, and then make their judgement. *But if that's how it'll be, I think they've missed a trick. . . . OK. You've replied; I'm comfortable.*

[Martin then discussed the [Prison Z] bid document]

Martin: It's waffle, and without a delivery plan—although they have gone further by prioritizing the improvements. . . .

Stuart: *I'll ask the question another way around, because I'm surprised.* You're not expecting the Evaluation team to go to [one of the bid team] and say—'good idea; how are you intending to deliver it?' You'd not expect it to be a problem if she said 'I don't know' or if she just ad-libbed? You'd not think that was a problem?

Cara: We'd [give] ownership back to senior management. . . . [The discussion then moves to another topic] [emphasis added]

A second example is taken from a meeting two months later, and which immediately preceded the Evaluation Day. This example shows Stuart in a more confident exchange with Cara and Martin as Stuart cajoles his clients into thinking about the best way to plan for this important day. The following exchange follows a long discussion, mainly between Martin and Cara, about how prison staff might behave on Evaluation Day, and how the staff might feel uncomfortable about promoting themselves to the Home Office Bid Committee.

Stuart: OK. So where are we? Are we saying . . .

Martin: Oh god! [Laughter]

Stuart: Just an observation, we're not being terribly focused this morning [Martin: No. Cara: No.—said in acknowledgement]. And I'm conscious I'm being a bit of a bully; But what does that all mean? Practical action. You're starting with a big action plan, you need to delegate responsibility. Now, are you saying, are you sticking with your focus group option? [i.e. Stuart brings the discussion back to the planning for the Evaluation Day]

... [After a long digression]

Stuart: And again Martin, sorry again, I know you're going to want to stab darts at my photograph, but who? who is going to make it happen?

Stuart, during research interviews with the authors, acknowledged his conscious use of humour (especially self-deprecating humour) as a way of easing his relationship with clients (see also Chapter 7). Our observations suggest that by downplaying his own role and apparently deferring to Martin on occasions, Stuart was able to encourage Martin's self-questioning and reflection without overtly challenging Martin's identity and authority. Stuart enhanced them by treating Martin as an emergent project manager. Over time, these interactions had the apparent effect of reducing the clients' resistance to the alien language; indeed the clients were observed to adopt some of the project management language and practice as their own.

We also see Martin and Cara re-positioning their identity as 'translators' of Stuart's engineering-infused project management language, rather than being mere recipients of his knowledge. As translators for others, their role was enhanced yet they also preserved the integrity and authority of their existing prison service knowledge.

Cara: What we end up doing is bridging some of that gap, to some degree, trying to interpret and put some of the learning that we've gained from Stuart back into Prison Service language. And I think that's worked reasonably well.

...

Martin: Cara and I are almost acting as consultants to Tony [the Governor].

Indeed, as the project unfolded, there was a growing sense that Stuart was being shepherded away from the rest of the client team even though, as discussed later, other team members valued Stuart's interactions. After an initial workshop with all team members, Cara and Martin had seemed reticent to continue to expose their team to the challenge of this rather 'different' project management culture, as personified by Stuart.

Cara: When you see him sometimes interact with some of the members of the project team—I could be wrong, but I just think he would end up being frustrating [to them]. I think we're a little bit conscious that we don't want to do people's heads in when they're managing quite a lot of work anyway.

The client–consultant relationship was not solely one of compliance and control, however. There was also evidence of resistance as the client rebuffed some of the admonitions of the consultant. Martin or Cara used various strategies such as ignoring Stuart, signalling 'no-go' areas, or re-negotiating the task. At other times Stuart seemed to choose to desist from his cajoling rhetoric.

For example, during an early research interview, Martin commented on Stuart's 'rigidity'. He relayed a story about Stuart not liking the term 'slack' in the plan and suggesting that the term should be changed to 'contingency'. Martin explained to the authors that he had not changed the wording, and that Stuart continued to make the same corrective comments. This story was told in a somewhat mischievous way, like that of a schoolchild knowingly shunning the advice of a headmaster.

Another example shows how Martin signalled a 'no-go' area of discussion, after a long day discussing the print layouts for the final bid document. Martin was initially reluctant to show Stuart the layouts, but Stuart expressed interest and asked several questions such as '. . . and what about the cover and executive summary?' Martin answered the questions but also signalled areas that he wanted Stuart to leave well alone. For example, in answer to Stuart's question about the quality of the photographs, Martin replied rather crisply: 'the photos will probably be black and white; it's not a key issue; we've already agonised about that'.

An example of task re-negotiation occurred in a meeting where Martin and Stuart had been reviewing the Gantt chart.

Stuart: At the risk of being a pain, should I insist you update it now to make sure you do it right?

Martin: I can do it. I don't particularly want to do it now. [Said with feeling]

[Stuart and Martin then agreed that Martin would update it and send it to Stuart]

Stuart reflected later in the project on the way in which he tried to encourage as well as challenge Martin. In doing so he recalled how he held back from pushing his client too far.

Stuart: I think at the end of the day I always left feeling there was more to do but I just sensed that I'd pushed him as far as I wanted to, without really annoying him. . . . I want the guy to feel I'm trying to be constructive and I just felt to load on any more, or to offer any more criticism—albeit constructive—possibly could have undermined the delivery altogether, so I didn't do it.

When Stuart overstepped the mark (as perceived by the client) it was in relation not to challenges of knowledge, but to challenges to the client's identity and status. As we noted in Chapter 4 in our discussion of the possible ambiguity of the client identity, one instance of significant conflict arose between Martin and Stuart. This was provoked by Stuart's self-initiated meeting with Tony (the prison Governor) which Martin later found out was to discuss the possibility of follow-on work. Martin explained that he was extremely annoyed, and that he had said so to Stuart in a subsequent telephone conversation.

Martin: Stuart just kept saying sorry; he didn't even try to explain his actions.

Cara: He seemed very concerned about not spoiling the relationship [with us].

Thus the consultant's challenges were not wholly successful. The client demonstrated various strategies, either to ignore the challenges, re-negotiate their meaning, or reject them. These responses resonate with those observed by Chinn and Brewer (1993) in their research on how individuals responded to dissonant feedback. They noted that, in order to pre-serve a coherent and integrated domain of knowledge, individuals would not necessarily accommodate the new knowledge implicit in the feed-back; instead, they displayed other responses, such as evaluating the feedback to be irrelevant, rejecting its validity, or making superficial rather than fundamental changes to their beliefs.

While Martin's relationship with Stuart was the primary focus of client–consultant interactions in this project, other relationships are relevant in illustrating aspects of challenge. An interesting dynamic was evident in the relationship between Stuart and Lesley, a long-standing Wing Officer at the prison who had been co-opted onto the bid team. Lesley spoke of the insights brought by Stuart, of his role (from her perspective as an insider who was more 'inside' the prison than Martin and Cara), and of missing Stuart's coaching as he began working more closely with 'manage-ment'. Lesley had two individual meetings with Stuart, for example, when he helped her to plan her strand of work. She explained, 'he brings a fresh mind; he's [an outsider] and so he can ask questions such as "why did you choose that route?"' Lesley commented at the post-project meeting that she 'missed [him] towards the end, even for reassurance and keeping me on board and focused because it felt I was like a pin-ball machine without understanding everything'.

The Governor, Tony, also spoke of Stuart's role as *agent provocateur*.

Tony: Stuart has been challenging. He was pushing us to think about wider issues. I wouldn't necessarily say that all of us agreed on everything he was saying, but it's certainly thought-provoking and gives you that time to actually step outside your current role, within a busy establishment and all the rest of it, to think about things differently.

The *Prison/Network* case began with a public sector organization accepting the discourse of consultant as 'expert helper', with clients acknowledging their naïveté in dealing with management consultants, but nevertheless expecting to learn from them. The difficulties of 'alien language', and the inexperience of project management practices were overcome to a large extent by the principal consultant's use of a gently persistent challenging manner softened with self-deprecating humour. These challenges were not always passively accepted, and were sometimes resisted. Furthermore, as the consultant acknowledged during interviews, he 'held back' and pushed the main client, Martin, 'only so far to avoid annoying him'. By doing so, the cultural and political boundaries did not become barriers. Thus, the consultant brought legitimation (it was 'OK' to spend time on project management) as well as challenges which facilitated learning and change in the clients but only up to a point.

Borough/OpsCo

The historical background to this case study, which we introduced in Chapter 3, is particularly relevant to its interpretation because it framed (and perhaps soured) the nature of the working relationship between *Borough*, a public sector client running one of the London Borough Councils, and *OpsCo*, an IT/performance improvement consultancy. The main points of contact between these organizations were Colin, the account manager at *OpsCo*, and Damon, the procurement manager at *Borough*. These two individuals had developed a relationship of mutual respect over several years as they worked together to try to make effective the 'strategic partnership' between *Borough*, *SystemsCo* (the main partner providing IT and systems support), and *OpsCo*. By the time of our case study, and for reasons outlined in Chapter 3, the strategic partnership was suffering serious problems. The planned Tier three e-procurement project was shelved, and *OpsCo* was instead commissioned to do two smaller procurement reviews with the aim of identifying potential cost-efficiencies: the first of which related to spending on agency staff.

Colin and Damon were equally disappointed about the shelving of the larger e-procurement project which they had been planning for twelve months. Although employed by different organizations, Colin and Damon shared common understandings and political orientations about the e-procurement project; in some ways they were 'on the same side' of the boundary (see also Chapter 5). As we shall see, these understandings influenced their interpretation of the scope and effectiveness of the agency-staff project.

While Colin and Damon enjoyed a relatively close working relationship, the context surrounding the agency-staff project was potentially unfavourable. The original client sponsor of the e-procurement programme had been replaced by a new Finance Director, Dennis, who was a self-professed sceptic of consultants (including, specifically, *OpsCo*). The new *Borough* CEO brought a scepticism about the underlying motivation of consultants, believing that they eschewed out-of-scope work if it could instead be sold as a 'new' project. This meant, according to Dennis, that the project was tinged with 'an element of that emotional stuff as well as the perhaps harder value-for-money issues'.

A key feature of this case (as with the *Global/StratCo* case) was that the clients, rather than the consultants, were the more vocal in their urge for challenge. By way of illustration, this chapter focuses on two types of occasions where the challenges were manifest: in the clients' desire for speed-over-accuracy of data collection; and in the clients' desire for more specific (even 'directive') interventions from the consultants. Both represented challenge in the sense of preferred actions in a particular context rather than the more conventional sense of presenting new knowledge. In this way, it can also be seen in contractual or political terms. Indeed, as we shall see in the following chapter, such disputes and tensions were evident in the other cases.

The agency-staff project involved a review of the way the *Borough* Directorates were recruiting temporary (i.e. agency) staff, particularly in view of a perception of costly inefficiencies such as the rolling renewal of some temporary staff rather than the recruitment of new permanent staff. Another reason for choosing agency staff for the focus of the first project review was that this was a politically weaker or less sensitive group in comparison with other staff groups employed in *Borough*. The review involved several project meetings and one workshop event—all of which we observed as part of our research. Some of the meetings were relatively short, and at times perfunctory—especially towards the end of the project. As an indicator of the status of the project meetings, Dennis admitted that he only had exposure, in total, to a few hours with the consultants, and that he did not plan those meetings in advance with his *Borough* colleagues. The lack of routine and/or long-duration physical proximity meant that, unlike at the *Prison* case, the clients and consultants had insufficient opportunity to talk *at length* about the issues of the project, and to communicate in a way which could potentially smooth interactions at the cultural or political boundaries.

We argued earlier that 'challenge' is not necessarily confrontational (Heron 1990); indeed consultants may try to avoid it and instead to cajole (as we saw in relation to *Prison/Network*) or deflect conflict (as we shall see later). While the behaviours towards the consultants of some *Borough* clients such as the Finance Director can be described as challenging, the clients deferred to the consultants on logistical decisions about how to organize the mid-project workshop. The workshop was to be an important event in which operational managers from the four Directorates in *Borough* were brought together to hear the consultants' review of agency-staff spending.

Terry (client): How many managers are you trying to get along?

Andrew (consultant): I think sixteen, four per directorate. . . .

Terry (client): How many half days then are you doing, or two hours?

Derek (consultant): A couple of hours I would have thought, realistically. . . .

Terry (client): Is that something you're running on your own with the managers?

Derek (consultant): No, it's everybody.

Dennis (client): From the communication side it's probably key that you two are there [meaning the client managers, Terry and Damon].

Terry (client): Yeah, I'd like to hear the views on the ground . . . but I'll change my identity before I come in [Laughter]. . . .

Derek (consultant): My personal view is that this is going to be primarily a communications session if you like. I think it needs to be fronted by Borough because I think if we front it then it'll risk being seen as being something external. . . .

Dennis (client): Do you think you might facilitate some of the discussion?

Colin (consultant): I mean the way these are always run is that we do all the work [Laughter] and then you're at the sharp end! [Laughter]

Already we see some positioning occurring as the clients ask how the consultants will run (and facilitate) the session, and the consultants give advice but also imply that the clients need to lead the discussions. This positioning around the political boundary became particularly important in this case, as the consultants tried to maintain a position as advisers only, while some clients challenged them to *propose* solutions and act as a catalyst for change.

The first illustration of challenge surrounds the question of data accuracy. As part of the review, *OpsCo* collected data on agency spending and on the procedures adopted by each Directorate for agency recruitment. In some cases, the agency-recruitment procedures were ad hoc and did not strictly comply with *Borough*'s standard policies. In the project meetings between client and consultant, it was evident that all parties had a shared knowledge of agency-staff issues. In the following two extracts— from the same meeting six weeks before the project's completion—the clients (especially Dennis) challenged the consultants to complete the data collection phase more quickly; the consultants eventually deferred to this request.

Dennis (client): I had it in my mind that the workshop might be in two weeks' time.

Derek (consultant): Well we could certainly do it by then, but I'd be reluctant to [confirm] because we don't have the questionnaire returns back yet and then we've got the analysis to do and then we've got the baseline, the benchmarking, to do.

Damon (client): In terms of the actual structure, as opposed to the detail of what we spend on it, presumably within the next ten days we'll be in a position to have some drafting around approaches we might take [in relation to agency procurement]?

Derek (consultant): Oh yes.

Dennis (client who has been silent for some time): The longer that we keep on deferring [the greater the problem].... Let's get on and start doing it. I'm nervous that you can lose a couple of months by waiting for firm figures when actually we can be more decisive earlier and actually take action and deliver efficiencies—

Derek (consultant) [interrupting]: My only concern about jumping ahead is that we risk jumping in and making uninformed decisions and there's a cost of that. So we just need to balance that somewhere along the line. We do need these numbers to support the case, otherwise it's going to be a pack of cards which might collapse. *But you're right*, I mean the bits are there. I think probably sitting in this room now we've probably got some idea of what the shape might look like, but we do need to make sure that we've got the quantitative information to support it as well. *But yes, you're right, we can certainly start working on what the shape of the options*. [emphasis added]

LATER IN THE SAME MEETING

Dennis (client): I recognize all the caution that you rightly exercise, but I'd much rather we get it 85–90% in the right direction and we do something.

Colin (consultant): If you get 85–90% [accuracy], that's a win. The issue for me is that the boroughs in particular are so complex, so devolved and so independent that actually getting even 40% or 50% compliance [and therefore accuracy of data] is a battle. So it's not—*I completely agree* that if you've got to 'Pareto' (80%), that's

133

enough. Absolutely. But it's got to be done mindful of the fact that there's a still a lot of work to get to that. *But we'll advise a way as we go through.* [emphasis added]

The next illustration of challenge concerns the client expectation that the consultants would lead the project in proposing solutions for generating efficiencies in agency-staff spending. When planning for the workshop, Dennis was explicit with his remark that 'a major problem we have at *Borough* is that we have no enforcement mechanism. The more explicit and directive you can be the better.' Here, the client wanted the consultants to become change agents and to be involved in planning for implementation. The problem faced by the client managers was that their operational managers were accustomed to a degree of freedom around their day-to-day operations. Talking of a nearby local council—a sector peer—which operated strict recruitment policies, Terry said:

The CEO's approach was to tell all managers, give me a business case by Friday or [agency staff are] stopped—they're not working here. But you couldn't do that here; there would be a revolt!

Later in the project, the same client reiterated the point:

Terry: The solution [to the perceived agency overspending] is fairly obvious; it's just how well you implement it, really. It's just a matter of how you actually get people to buy in and comply basically. But *that's a bit of a Borough issue from my point of view.* [emphasis added]

However, we see the seeds of conflict when we hear the alternative viewpoint of the junior consultant talking early in the project with the authors about his expectations for the workshop. *OpsCo* intended to present the outputs from its data analysis phase at the workshop to illustrate the apparent inefficiencies in the agency-spending processes across the four Directorates. These outputs resembled what *OpsCo* called 'templated data', such as comparisons of actual versus budget spending across several years. Andrew, the junior consultant, hoped that *Borough's* operational managers and the client managers would 'drive' the workshop, and would give feedback and ideas on the basis of the templated data which *OpsCo* had presented. He added:

Andrew: We might have work in just facilitating the whole process...but it needs to be internal and we can't drive that....I think that's going to be another problem for these guys to truly to take ownership and actually to see the seriousness of this whole process and actually take ownership of it.

In a similar—though less direct—manner, the *OpsCo* account manager tried to position expectations about the workshop in a client–consultant project meeting.

Colin: We've got to think quite carefully about where we're going to leave people at the end of next Tuesday.... Are we just going to say we're going to do something about it, or are we actually saying 'we've highlighted a major issue here.'... We've just got to think about that.

The consultant used the term 'we', but it became clear during research interviews with the authors that he intended to prompt the client managers to take the lead in working to gain commitment from the operational managers regarding new procurement procedures. Rather than directly challenge his client to 'take ownership' (as the junior consultant had suggested during interviews with the authors) the language used by the account manager was relatively ambiguous. The response from the senior client manager, Dennis, suggests that he did not interpret the comments as a call-to-action to take ownership. Instead, he reiterated (using the same ambiguous 'we') that 'we are looking [to you, *OpsCo*] for realistic and workable recommendations'. The challenge from the clients was either misunderstood, or implicitly not accepted by the consultants.

At the workshop, the consultants' data were duly presented and acknowledged to be a good enough representation of agency-staff procurement processes. Most of the operational managers claimed already to be following standard procedures, which 'may have been slightly exaggerated' according to one of the consultants in a later interview. Interestingly, that claim was not challenged by the *Borough* senior management even though they believed that agency procurement was largely determined by localized, pragmatic processes. Another unexpected response—this time from the operational managers—was that they did not 'revolt' when the client managers suggested that agency contracts might be cancelled after a duration of twelve months—the so-called cliff-edge approach. In a post-workshop project meeting, an *OpsCo* consultant said he was encouraged by the fact that

Derek: Even when you got to the point of talking about the cliff-edge type approach, they didn't immediately say 'well you can't do that'. It was 'well that's fine; we'll use it as a warning and we'll take some actions now' which I thought was actually really good.

The *Borough* HR manager, however, was more sanguine about the workshop's outcome, no doubt due to his long-standing experience with these managers—knowing how change was sometimes avoided by prevarication after giving implied consent:

Terry: There are still opportunities and challenges around.... They'll say 'ah, well you can't really enforce this'. You know, people are resisting.... I think we sort of felt like we ran out of time but we actually didn't address some of the harder issues.

The resultant report to *Borough*'s Executive Committee was perceived as weak by the client: it listed options, but contained no advice about the 'pros and cons of the different optional arrangements'. The consultants continued in their resistance to take up the mantle of prescribing a path of implementation. The *OpsCo* account manager was willing, however, to produce recommendations but only *in collaboration* with *Borough*; in other words if the client took ownership:

Colin: My sense is that the five of us [main clients and consultants at the table], if *we just get together for a couple of hours and work it through*, yeah? And I think that's that. Because there's some really interesting data—really powerful in terms of where we are—but to really drive home the benefit we need to think two things: one is what are the best quick hits?... and secondly what's the smartest way of setting things up. [emphasis added]

The *OpsCo* account manager's apparent reticence was confirmed in a post-project meeting when he explained to the authors that he had 'learned to avoid playing the client' (i.e. as an insider) when trying to encourage buy-in because 'he'd had his fingers burned in the past' when attempting to do so (see also Chapter 7 for an illustration of this in the *Imperial* case).

The pressure from the client Financial Director strengthened as he himself was challenged by *Borough*'s CEO to produce efficiency savings. He was 'again looking to be very directive about timescales'. Yet at the same time, he acknowledged that he was

Dennis: Mindful of the fact that with the best will in the world, projects can slip, and there's very good reasons why they slip, and a lot of those reasons being around not necessarily OpsCo's work, but actually the organization's [Borough's] capacity to give you the information and... you know playing Ping-Pong.

While recognizing that this game of ping-pong was hindering progress, he was

Dennis:.... disappointed that they [OpsCo] were perhaps not as proactive as they could have been around some of the objectives... not bullish around the recommendations.

A rather different perspective on the project was provided by Damon, the client procurement manager who had worked for eighteen months to try to launch the more ambitious e-procurement project with *OpsCo*.

I think OpsCo provided everything they were asked to provide, but then people were making unreasonable demands at the end. They were almost asking them to rework stuff to the *n*th degree.

What seemed to be occurring here was a positioning of roles, as client and consultant each implied that 'the other' should be leading the drive for change, and pushing forward recommendations to the point where they were not just suggested, but also accepted and implemented. The challenge here was positioned largely at the political boundary. There were few cognitive boundaries because both client and consultant had knowledge and experience in the procurement area. Nevertheless, as we saw in the previous chapter, *OpsCo* did lack depth in some aspects of sector knowledge such as about some of the statutory and regulatory compliance processes of local government, and this acted as a barrier to some extent. The procurement client management and the HR manager both acknowledged this but also accepted its inevitability: the consultants were, after all, external to the *Borough* organization and could not 'know' what an insider knows. As the *Borough* HR manager explained:

Terry: Consultants don't always quite pick up the vibes as to what the local cultural issues are. Often the solutions are very good but it's often the little subtleties about how we operate as opposed to other boroughs [that make a difference].

Discussion

The two cases were presented in narrative form with the aim of reflecting the projects' development *over time*, and in particular, to show the relative success of challenge interventions in shifting the behaviour or understandings of clients (or consultants). The contexts and objectives for the two projects were different in important respects, but there were also similarities. Furthermore, both projects could be said to have been successful in that they were formally completed and 'signed off'. Yet the tenor of the relationships were significantly different: at *Borough/OpsCo*, the relationship had become perfunctory with no real sense of collaborative achievement; on the other hand, at *Prison/Network*, the relationship between the primary points of contact—Stuart and Martin—had developed from sceptical beginnings (from the client) to a point where consultant and client demonstrated a degree of respect for and engagement with each other.

Critical challenge interventions at *Borough/OpsCo* were routinely deflected by each party: for example, the clients did not acknowledge the consultants' implicit suggestions to 'take ownership' of the management workshop; and the consultants deflected the clients' requests to specify and prioritize options for implementation. The resultant stalemate was quietly condoned; the only explicit signal of dissatisfaction from *Borough* was that *OpsCo* was not recruited to do more spending reviews. As has been argued elsewhere (Alvesson 2004; Clark 1995), project failure and any blame for it is notoriously difficult to 'prove', and often clients' only sanction is to decline to re-hire the consultants, as in the *Borough/OpsCo* case. A rather different story could be seen in the *Prison/Network* project. Here, the challenge interventions of the primary consultant were initially resisted by Martin and Cara, but came to be listened to and accepted as valid and useful (though they were not always translated into action).

To shed some light on the different unfolding relationships and behaviours in these projects, we can consider the dynamics in terms of physical, cultural, and political boundaries. First, the *possibility* for challenge seems to have been directly influenced not only by the physical availability of project meetings, but more importantly by the frequency and duration of those meetings. At *Prison/Network*, Martin and Stuart experienced what one might call a 'prolonged exposure' to each other: sitting for up to six hours at a time in an outer office, and sharing the same artefacts and resources (e.g. Gantt charts and whiteboards). They had informal coffee breaks together, and were seen by others, such as Lesley, as a working unit. On the other hand, at *Borough/OpsCo*, there were few opportunities for clients and consultants to meet informally—or at least, none were offered or requested. Physical proximity thus appears to be important (but not sufficient) because it allows interactions to happen. Unless the physical boundaries are overcome, challenge interventions cannot 'take place' except through the medium of communications technologies such as email, telephone calls, or video conferencing—methods which have important deficiencies (as well as opportunities).

The processes of breaking down such barriers are also important in allowing consultants and clients to work on boundaries at the cultural level. In our account of the *Prison/Network* project, we showed how Stuart consciously deployed a strategy of persistently but gently questioning Martin's decision-making processes. Initially, Martin and Cara rejected these attempts, pointing at the incongruity of language and implied values of phrases such as 'fit for purpose', and downplaying the value of Stuart's manufacturing background. Over time, and with prolonged periodic operational proximity, Stuart was able to present himself as a sensible, pragmatic, and ultimately credible project manager who warranted attention from his younger clients. In short and in Nooteboom's terms, he was able to overcome what was initially experienced as a high cognitive distance. At the same time, however, it is unclear as to what the consequences would have been if Stuart had been on site for longer periods. This would have tested the relationship more intensely and potentially exposed the consultant's knowledge to greater scrutiny (cf. Menon and Pfeffer 2003).

At *Borough/OpsCo*, both clients and consultants had comparable knowledge and experience in the field of procurement, which meant that there were few cultural boundaries (i.e. low cognitive distance) in this respect. However, some, but not all, of the client managers were sometimes critical of the consultants' apparently limited understanding of the internal processes of the local government sector and, as we saw in Chapter 5, *Borough* in particular. This was seen as reducing their ability to recommend implementation policies. In other words, they were seen as organizational knowledge outsiders. Indeed, we saw how Damon seemed to criticize his boss, the Finance Director, Dennis, for expecting too much of external consultants—for example, by asking for 'accurate' data on operational spending while also wanting speedier data collection methods; and an implementation strategy over-and-above the original brief. The consultants and clients each recognized the importance of collating sufficient data with which to propose a case for change, and both recognized that the point of difficulty would come when trying to enforce changes. The challenges from each side to the other to initiate the changes were rebuffed, and so the project ended by completing only a basic interpretation of the project objectives: a simple review of agency-staff spending at *Borough*.

The lack of further progress in the *Borough/OpsCo* project can also be explained at the political level. Neither party in the project was willing to accept responsibility for 'taking ownership' of implementation; yet neither party was willing to state explicitly that 'the other side' *should be* responsible. Challenges tended to be implicit as though there was a vague hope that responsibility would be voluntarily accepted by others. An underlying issue seemed to be that it was 'identities' more than knowledge which were 'at stake'. We have already seen how, during a post-project interview, the *OpsCo* account manager said he resisted 'playing the client' because 'he'd had his fingers burned in the past' when attempting to persuade middle managers to change their behaviours. The client Finance Director, on the other hand, continued to push back on the consultants. A similar type of impasse is discussed in the literature on issue-selling: senior executives are reluctant to accept middle managers' calls to place a new issue on the executive agenda if that issue is high-risk and unlikely to lead to successful closure (Dutton and Ashford 1993). Another political aspect was that neither party to the project had clear support from its own senior management: Colin was under pressure to recoup some fees, given that *OpsCo* lost considerable time working on the abortive e-procurement proposal; and Dennis was under pressure from the *Borough* CEO to deliver significant efficiencies as part of the government's Gershon efficiency initiative.

Conclusion

The two cases illustrate the outcomes and limitations of challenge interventions as well as the analytical utility of the boundaries framework. We have shown how cultural barriers at *Prison/Network* were overcome through periodic physical proximity and through Stuart's use of a coaching style of challenge softened with humour. Time and physical proximity also appeared to be key enablers in this case, as well as Martin's growing confidence in Stuart's sensitivity to the prison context. Martin and Cara came to understand, enact to some degree, and translate (for others) the practice of project management. Political boundaries were negotiated through the early acceptance of the consultants as 'given by the Home Office to help as experts' and by the resolution of the unsolicited approach of Stuart to the prison governor. The *Prison/Network* case contrasts with *Borough/OpsCo* where the political boundaries were expressed as a resistance to taking responsibility or ownership for the problems of implementation, even though each party recognized this to be the key project issue.

In the spectrum of consultant (or client) interventions, 'challenge' goes beyond a mere request or an authoritative demand that action must be taken. We argued earlier that a challenge intervention is conventionally seen as a summons from the consultant to the client to take a demanding and risky step (such as adopting new policies) for a desirable reward such as personal or organizational success. In contrast to the trials-of-strength which are the hallmark of war stories, challenges in the client–consultancy context—as we have seen in these cases—are often more tentative because of the fear from all parties of a devastating rupture in the relationship. Calls for change are often subtly issued, and if not accepted, may be ignored or quietly resisted in order to maintain the semblance of good relations: the challenge to adopt the 'alien' project management discourse was eventually accepted by Martin and Cara— although Stuart was careful not to push too far. However, the challenge to design a project implementation strategy was largely ignored by *OpsCo* in the *Borough* case. An important difference in these cases was the perceived desirability of potential rewards matched against the risks of taking up the challenge: Martin and Cara saw the rewards of bid success and career enhancement as worth the risk of taking up Stuart's challenge; in contrast, *OpsCo* saw that the time and resources required to design a project implementation strategy were unlikely to lead to more consultancy business given *Borough's* drive for cost-reduction. The perceived gap between risk and reward resulted in acceptance or rejection of others' challenges to act, and these perceptions were shaped and changed by actions at the boundary level: physical, socio-cultural, and political.

7

The micro management of boundaries through humour and laughter

Introduction

We have already seen how there may often be tensions in the client–consultant relationship. Various structural conflicts such as that between problem resolution for the client and 'sell on' for the consultant can be linked to a range of issues which place actors' identities and material (e.g. career) interests at risk. As we saw in the previous chapter, both parties may challenge each other and; in the process, their respective knowledge bases or sense of competence and commitment are brought into sharp relief. Challenge can be an uncomfortable process and, unless well managed, put the client–consultant relationship at risk. Although the four case studies upon which our research is built represent different forms and contexts of consulting, some of the tensions displayed in each were similar and characteristic of joint project work more generally (Tempest and Starkey 2004). For example, strains in the relationship were evident with respect to timescales (e.g., project and task over-runs); potential and actual increases in costs in relation to the budget and what might be considered reasonable additional items; the demarcation of roles and responsibilities; the commitment of resources; and the range of parties involved in the delivery of the project. Such concerns are often exacerbated where the task at hand is relatively ambiguous, which is common, if not ubiquitous, in consultancy (Alvesson 1993; Clark 1995). This creates problems in relation to the definition of issues and division of tasks which are further exacerbated by the fact that clients and consultants are, to an extent, locked in contractually and socially (i.e. in terms of norms derived from exiting relationships) in order to achieve the overall objective of the assignment. At this stage in the relationship, they cannot easily escape one another. This is a common problem for 'temporary organizations' such as project teams where 'all the participants must interrelate with the other participants as they jointly struggle to arrive at viable solutions' (Goodman 1981: 3).

If the issues identified above had been left unaddressed, working relationships could have become more strained which in turn would have impacted on the success or otherwise of the project. Indeed, some of these issues became so serious that there were moments when we, as researchers, wondered if there would be another project meeting, especially at *Imperial*, where the role of the consultant was most crucial for the client organization's ability to function. Here, one of the research team attended a meeting when the intensity of the clients' anger over the inability of the ATM network to link into the new IT system and associated cost issues nearly resulted in the cancellation of the contract. More generally, even though there were sometimes powerful eruptions in the relationship between the clients and consultants, these were temporary in that moments of discord were, for the most part, smoothed over, suppressed, or managed in order not to ostracize particular members of the project team so as to become permanently situated as outsiders. The exception here perhaps, as we saw in the previous chapter, was the case of James, the accounting consultant at *Prison*. Indeed, all the projects we observed were delivered to the main clients' satisfaction, albeit with varying degrees of enthusiasm.

Having been present at episodes of near collapse in which bubbling tensions appeared to have the potential to escalate out of control, we asked ourselves how these moments were overcome or diffused. In particular, how did clients and consultants manage to establish a continuing rapport or working relationship such that differences of opinion or priorities could be safely expressed without permanent divisions emerging? The issue here is not that the differences were eradicated, but rather that they were mitigated or hidden in some way. Their impact was limited as they were located within a space which allowed differences to be expressed, but in such a way that the relationship was not critically questioned and destabilized. As noted in earlier chapters with regard to the consultant Stuart, in the *Prison* case, one critical way in which tensions and the mini crises that emerged from them were dealt with appeared to be through the use of humorous remarks that led to laughter. In other words, at key moments, problems and difficulties were 'laughed off' and seemingly treated as not that serious.

Even if, as we shall see, humour and shared laughter by no means always reflect harmonious relations, perhaps by their very contrast to rational and other cultural norms (e.g. politeness), they can shed an important light on not only the nature of client–consultant relations, but also their negotiation in action. Furthermore, following Lavin and Maynard (2001: 454), if we initially define 'rapport' as the extent to which those present respond to humorous messages by engaging in shared laughter, a detailed analysis of humorous episodes can reveal some of the ways in which the various parties are included and excluded or uninvolved in relation to particular humorous comments and so reveal something of the other shifting cultural and political boundaries between them (see Lamont and Molnar 2002). Through the lens of humorous acts and laughter, we shall explore some of the ways in which boundaries are constructed *in the moment*, how they temporarily unite and divide people, and how this is experienced.

Such unifications and divisions result from numerous micro moments in interactions which build upon one another to establish agreed-upon (and other) definitions of a situation. Thus, an examination of moments where clients and consultants laugh together, or some laugh and others do not, points to the extent of their like-mindedness and whether those present display themselves as an 'in-group' that share a common perspective in relation to the matters at hand. The degree to which clients and consultants engage in displays of reciprocal laughter can therefore indicate whether, *at that time and in a particular respect*, they constitute themselves as insiders or outsiders and how this shifts over time. In this way, humorous messages and the laughter they evoke can momentarily delineate group boundaries and determine who is in and who is out at that point in time (Glenn 1995; Meyer 2000) in a way which does not always follow organizational roles (i.e. client vs. consultant). This underpins our broader view that the nature of the client–consultant relationship is not wholly determined by relatively stable organizational, contractual, and other social structures at the outset but is also constituted and reconstituted on a moment-by-moment basis, thereby reproducing and transforming those structures.

This chapter is organized in the following way. Initially, we link some themes in the consulting literature to that on humour to inform our broad discussion of boundaries in the client–consultant relationship. We then discuss three types or objects of laughter in the client–consultant relationship and show through examples from our data how some forms of laughter are more unifying than others. We end by arguing that in

managing these humorous episodes, clients and consultants are sometimes able to maintain rapport and test the strength of the boundaries
and relationships within the project team. Thus, through the micro
management of humour and laughter, clients and consultants were able
actively to manage cultural and political boundaries in a way that stabilized and solidified the relationship at particular moments and, in the
process, established a key foundation block for the relationship as a
whole.

Consulting, Ambiguity, and Liminality

Before we discuss our analysis of humorous remarks and the laughter they
induced, we wish to highlight a few connections between the focus on
humour and the broader consulting literature. In Chapter 1, we critiqued
the dominant 'outsider' view of consultants which is particularly evident
in studies of consultancy and knowledge flow. Rather, we pointed to alternative roles, such as legitimation, and a multiplicity of actors and bases
for relationships. Furthermore, we highlighted various aspects and trends
in consultancy, such as consultant knowledge of clients derived from
repeat business and increased client sophistication, which have come
to blur the traditional insider–outsider distinction and certainly render
such a generalized assumption implausible. This was then developed
empirically in Chapter 4 where the multiplicity of boundary relations
was the focus, one of which, sector knowledge, was explored in depth in
Chapter 5. As with the previous chapter, the following analysis focuses
more on the dynamics and experience of boundary relations than on
their structural multiplicity. However, we are particularly concerned with
exploring this at a micro level in conditions of ambiguity and liminality,
two key features claimed of consultancy and professional services more
generally.

In a seminal paper, Alvesson (1993) highlighted that the work of
many knowledge-intensive firms, such as management consultancies, is
inherently ambiguous. He argued that few 'knowledge-workers operate
according to a handbook of scientific methodology . . . [this] makes the
impact of the "knowledge-factor" or esoteric expertise much less clear-cut
in practice' (p. 1002). Not only are the results of consulting knowledge
and work ambiguous, but also it is ambiguous what role knowledge plays
(see also Clark and Fincham 2002; Clark and Salaman 1996, 1998). As we
have seen, this does not imply that knowledge is not an integral, if varied,

feature of consultancy, as with any other interactive relationship. Rather, the dominant conceptions of consultancy outlined in earlier chapters as either innovation (i.e. discrete new knowledge transferred) or legitimation are inadequate. Likewise, we have seen how the client–consultant relationship is structured along organizational and contractual (i.e. service) lines, but only partially. The complexity, multiplicity, dynamism, and indeterminacy of relations renders them too ambiguous. Building on this point, we focus in this chapter on the haziness between insider and outsider statuses.

As we noted in Chapter 2, Merton critiques an overly restricted view of insiders and outsiders when he states that 'individuals have not a single status but a status set; a complement of various interrelated statuses which interact to affect both their behavior and perspectives' (1972: 22). Thus, we do not possess a range of mutually exclusive statuses and switch from one to another one and so on. At any one time a person can be a collection of statuses—simultaneously insiders and outsiders. In this respect, our relationship to any group is highly ambiguous since we are both a member and a non-member at the same time. Our status as an insider or outsider is thus potentially unclear and so is subject to negotiation and confirmation.

In Chapter 1, we discussed Czarniawska and Mazza's (2003) view that (organizational) insider–outsider distinctions are particularly ambiguous in consulting projects because they occur within a blurred space in which statuses and boundary differences are suspended (see also Clegg et al. 2004). Drawing on the work of the anthropologist Victor Turner, Czarniawska and Mazza define consultancy as 'liminal' and argue that it is 'more than a personal state; to use a traditional vocabulary, it is an objective condition, a working arrangement, which we shall call a *consultant condition*' (2003: 273). A key problem with Czarniawska and Mazza's argument (2003) is that it assumes liminality is a constant condition which applies throughout a consulting assignment; there is little variability in its intensity (cf. Sturdy et al. 2006). As Turner (1984), and before him Van Gennep (1909), argues, these liminal or transitional spaces are short-lived. They are special temporary spaces that enable people to 'think about how they think, about the terms in which they conduct their thinking, or about how they feel in daily life' (Turner 1984: 22). In this respect liminal spaces provide an opportunity in which the normal conventions and strictures that guide social activity are momentarily suspended. Importantly, for our purposes, they are a moment of commentary in which people reveal otherwise hidden realities about ongoing social action. Put another way, they are apertures or interruptions in the rational and serious discourse of consultancy which expose 'seen but unnoticed' aspects of boundary management work within project teams (Garfinkel 1967).

The link between this work on liminality and the present focus is that Turner (1984: 27), following Bateson (1955), identified humour as an important liminal space in that it is a form of communication set apart from the talk which precedes and succeeds it. The implicit message of such a frame is that 'this is not real' and 'this is fantasy'. What is occurring is fun rather than serious. Mulkay (1988: 26) distinguishes between the 'play' frame and the 'serious' frame in the following way:

Whereas ambiguity, inconsistency, contradiction and interpretive diversity are often treated as problems during serious discourse, and attempts are made to remove them or to reduce their impact, they are necessarily features of the humorous mode. In contrast to the unitary character of serious discourse, humour depends on the discursive display of opposing interpretative possibilities.

The critical point here is that the serious frame should reflect a relatively clear and one-dimensional picture of social reality whereas humour is like a prism, reflecting and refracting light in many directions (Boland and Hoffman 1983; Fox 1990). The picture is therefore distorted and uncertain. Where you stand in relation to the prism determines the nature of the picture that emerges. From this perspective, humour permits a greater acceptance of multiple interpretations of a situation. The various tensions and differences between clients and consultants are thus revealed since it is a liminal space which allows participants to simultaneously hold and display alternative 'frames of reference' (Boland and Hoffman 1983). Clients may find the status of their knowledge being questioned and consultants may be criticized for being late for a deadline or over-budget. However, because people invest humorous remarks with multiple sources of humour in order to maximize the chances of laughter, recipients can consider a number of possible reasons for laughing and select the one that has most meaning for them at that time (Greatbatch and Clark 2003). Consequently, in humorous situations when people laugh 'they move across several frames of reference, always entertaining several possible frames simultaneously, never reducing to just one that can be relied on for a literal analysis of the situation . . . [and] without explicitly defining what those frames of reference are' (Boland and Hoffman 1983: 192, 196). More than one understanding of a humorous situation is therefore possible. These are partially revealed in the extent to which people laugh together, decline to laugh, or laugh half-heartedly in response to humorous messages.

Humour, therefore, is a particular liminal space (i.e. a play frame) which celebrates or allows ambiguity and supports the simultaneous display of different points of view. Given that people may show a range of responses to an invitation to laugh, an apparently unifying act when examined in greater detail may in actuality both unite and divide a group at the same time. The power of humour to be both a unifier and a divider has been noted by Meyer (2000: 328) who writes that humour 'can be a kind, human, friendly, pleasant means of communication...or it can be wry cynical, cutting, and even mean....Thus does the duality paradox of humour allow rhetorical unification or division—or both at the same time.' In this respect humour cuts both ways. Thus, the extent to which clients and consultants laugh (or do not laugh) together can be seen as indicative of different degrees of intimacy and cohesion and/or distance and division between those present (i.e. whether they consider themselves as insiders or outsiders at that moment in time).

With respect to differences, Lavin and Maynard (2001: 456) note that '*non*-reciprocal laughter can create relational distance, negate the formation of an alliance between parties and undermine rapport'. Displays of non-laughter or minimal laughing may therefore be seen as indications that there is no or little agreement between the parties. In this respect, the differing types of laughter displays and their absences in the meetings between clients and consultants can indicate varying levels of rapport and like-mindedness among those present as well as the shifting alignments and affiliations between clients and consultants. In what follows we draw selectively upon our case studies, especially that of *Imperial*, to demonstrate how these shifting alignments relate to different forms of humour and laughter in the client–consultant relationship.

Laughter and Client–Consultant Boundaries

Although disparaging jokes about consultants are a key element of the popular business discourse (see Sturdy 2009; Sturdy et al. 2007), consultancy project meetings may seem a strange place to study humour. It is a context where rational norms operate and where one might expect relationships to be relatively distant and reputations to be at stake. Indeed, humour was not especially evident in one of the four case studies, namely *Global*. Given our more restricted and formal access to meetings in this case, our interpretation is necessarily tentative in this regard. Nevertheless, in those interactions observed, as well as through interviews, relationships appeared to be highly rational, emotionless, and professional. The parties operated at and around very senior, strategic levels of a large multinational client and a 'serious' strategic consulting firm, jointly engaged in a highly confidential project with potentially very significant consequences under analysis and discussion. Furthermore, the consulting firm was on trial in a project which could lead it to a more long-term place at the 'top table' of this client. This was not fun, nor could it be seen as such. This certainly appeared to be a context in which making a humorous comment and laughing were not considered appropriate, at least, not on the front-stage (Phills 1996).

The rational, cultural norms of business, consultancy, and meetings were also largely evident in the other cases. However, here they were contrasted with occasional and sometimes even habitual laughter, suggesting an element of rapport between clients and consultants. Indeed, the extent of their 'playfulness' was identified by a number of those involved in *Prison* and *Imperial* at least, as a barometer of the level of closeness or familiarity in specific client–consultant relationships. However, laughter can also reflect tensions in relationships and contexts or, rather, their release as 'nervous laughter'. Indeed, in highly formal contexts, it is common to observe laughter at their margins such as at the start and end of meetings. Indeed, it is most visible at these times because of the contrast it presents.

In examining the incidences of laughter across the case studies we found that three types of joke were especially common. People laughed in response to remarks about (*a*) absent third parties, (*b*) consultants, and, much more rarely, (*c*) clients. Each of these types of humorous remarks entails disparagement of an individual or group. They are therefore inherently critical and can be seen as 'put downs' since people laugh 'because they feel some sort of triumph over them or feel superior in some way to them' (Meyer 2000: 314). Indeed, this type of humour 'relies on making fun of a perceived weakness of the target (whether a person, thing or institution) for its success' (Lennox-Terrion and Ashforth 2002: 58). In what follows we describe examples of each of these types of humorous remarks and the type of laughter they initiate. In the process we show how the response was organized and whether it was collective or more differentiated. In other words, the analysis indicates whether certain kinds of humour appeared more unifying or excluding than other kinds and therefore shows how humorous comments can both reveal and actively shift the boundaries in the client–consultant relationship.

Laughter at Third Parties

The most frequently observed form of humour was jokes made in relation to third parties. These individuals or groups were not directly involved in the project and so were not present. They thus can be seen as an attempt to create a sense of group identity and cohesion and in the process maintain a clear separation between themselves and some external party or, at least, to have that effect. In this respect they are an affirmation of, or attempt to construct, the insider status of the project team and the outsider status of a named third party—a 'common enemy'. In the case of the building society project, these jokes were frequently aimed at the other building societies and consultants, and the regulator, the FSA. As we saw in Chapter 5, in other contexts, building societies were seen as insiders within a 'sector community'. In terms of the *Prison* case, the targets included prisoners, prison officers, and the inspection team. For *Borough*, the targets included employment agencies (the focus of the assignment), other consultancies, and local authorities. In terms of Schein's characterization (1997) of the different types of client, targets tended to be 'unwitting' (i.e. not aware that the assignment may impact on them) or 'ultimate' clients (i.e. not directly involved but nevertheless must be considered in the assignment) clients.

In one example of this type of humorous remark, which we noted in Chapter 4, a consultant in the *Prison* project joked with a client about distributing a draft report to other client managers late in December:

EXTRACT 1—'MERRY CHRISTMAS'

Consultant: Wrap it [the report] up for them. (Tell them to) stick it under the tree! Read it after your Christmas dinner.

[*Much joint laughter*]

Client: I have to go with you there mate.

Consultant: ... I know I said it in jest but a big part of me is saying you do give it to them and say Merry Christmas! But ... no, no ... OK.

This brief extract demonstrates the key principles related to these types of jokes. Critically, the person making the joke, in this case a consultant, identifies something which not only differentiates them but also the recipients, in this instance other members of the project team, from the butt of the joke. In this case, the sentiment underpinning the joke is a feeling that the two members of the project team have devoted a considerable amount of time to the project and that this has been in excess of what might have been expected. Delivering the report as a Christmas present can be seen to acknowledge (*a*) that their own work and time commitments have been hidden and so would come as a surprise to others in the prison (as an unwrapped present) and/or, (*b*) it would force those others to make similar sacrifices (i.e. working during time typically identified for other activities, such as a break from work for a public holiday). The client acknowledges they are mutually implicated in the consultant's remarks by laughing and also confirms their agreement with the initial comments when they say after the laughter 'I have to go with you there mate'. The joke therefore momentarily affirms that the consultant and client are like-minded about this issue and so are constituted as an 'in-group'. By confirming their difference from the target of the humorous remarks, the joke and joint laughter celebrate and affirm their insider status and both signify and mark out a cultural boundary between them and others, some of whom are also in the project team.

The next extract similarly is an example of a third-party joke which creates a momentary 'in-group' in that everyone laughs. However, in this case the target is less clear. It occurred at the very outset of our observation of the meetings between *Imperial* and *Techno* Consulting. The lead researcher on this case study entered the room without having previously been introduced to anyone present except for Paul who was the Managing Director. In the following extract, Paul begins by introducing the researcher and then asking him to explain his research project. Once he has done this he offers to answer any questions in relation to the research. This could represent an opportunity for the other participants to discuss his status in the meetings or ask for clarification with respect to his purpose in relation to the project before the meeting. Before any other person present takes up this offer, and without a pause, Paul makes a joke. It concerns one of his colleagues—Joyce—being played by Gwyneth Paltrow in a film based on the research the researcher has just described. Everyone laughs and as the laughter dies away Paul announces the formal start of the meeting and so terminates the laughter and any further opportunity to discuss the researcher's presence by moving the focus to more serious issues, in this case the minutes of the last meeting.

EXTRACT 2—'GWYNETH PALTROW'

Paul: Welcome everyone. (.) I want to introduce you to [researcher]. He works at [university business school] and is going to be observing our meetings. [Researcher] Would you like to tell us something about your project?

Researcher: Thank you for letting me sit in on your meetings. I am conducting research into the transfer of knowledge between consultants and their clients with colleagues at two other universities [. . .] and [. . .]. We are sponsored by the ESRC, the main funder of social science research in the UK. It is not intended to be evaluative in any way. I look forward to learning more about your project over the coming months and am happy to answer any questions you may have.

Paul: Great. Joyce when the research is finished and the film of the book is made [*turns and looks at person to whom remarks addressed*] you will be played by Gwyneth Paltrow. [*Said in laughing voice*]

[*Turns to look at group as a whole and displays an expansive smile*]

Participants: [*Much joint laughter*]

Paul: Right (.) let's follow the agenda. [*Said in a laughing voice*] Minutes of the last meeting. Any comments, updates?

Paul does not rely solely on the content of his remarks to establish the relevance of laughter and the 'play frame'. He gives the audience early warning of his humorous intent by smiling and using a laughing voice (i.e. laughter particles are mixed into his speech). In addition to these cues, the speaker signals the humorous nature of his remarks by using at least two incongruous images. The first concerns his colleague—Joyce. While she has blonde hair, she bears little physical similarity to Gwyneth Paltrow. Joyce is also at least twenty years older than Gwyneth Paltrow. Outside of the humorous frame, such a comment may be interpreted as an insult and hurtful. However, within the play frame, clearly indicated by Paul, this comment is more likely to be understood as an 'affectionate poking fun' (Lennox-Terrion and Ashforth 2002). The fact that Joyce joins in and laughs audibly possibly indexes that she understands this and can take a joke. She does not indicate that she feels isolated and the target of the rest of the group. The laughter is collective. Everyone laughs together on cue. Second, he contrasts academic research with that of a mass medium known for its populist inclinations. The elongation of the phrase 'when the research is finished and the film of the book is made' underscores both the lengthy time frame in which academic research is produced and the priorities attached to different outputs. In this case, the research is conducted, then a book written, and eventually a film made. The very absurdity of this comment—it is highly unlikely that a piece of academic research (i.e. this volume) would ever be made into a film starring Gwyneth Paltrow—underpins the commonly held notion that academic research has limited popular appeal, and so represents the antithesis of a film with a well-known actress.

Paul could have framed this situation seriously by stating that he fully supported the researchers' presence or through a discussion that led to some degree of consensus. As we pointed out earlier in the chapter, the use of the humorous frame offers a multi-dimensional view of reality whereas the 'serious' frame tends to assume or require a unitary understanding of reality. Thus, in this episode the recipients are asked to resolve at least two incongruities. We also argued earlier that offering several images concurrently increases the likelihood of generating a collective affiliative response in that people are given more than one reason to laugh and less reason to decline. However, it also increases the ambiguity and interpretive diversity that underpins the subsequent response. Although this is a put-down joke, it is not clear who is the butt. Is it the researcher or Joyce? Consequently, participants are free to constitute one or the other, or both, as the target. The fact that everyone laughs, including both the possible targets of the comments, indicates that no one feels they are being positioned as an outsider at this moment or that they choose not to risk this by taking offence. This humorous remark therefore enables those present to demonstrate that they are an in-group and to test and display the cultural/emotional boundaries of the group. The researcher is shown to be able to 'take a joke' and is also made aware of the other members' scepticism of the value of academic research and therefore the fact that he does not represent an immediate threat.

This incident demonstrates the power and usefulness of a 'play frame'. A group can momentarily constitute itself as an in-group without having to share a common perspective on the issue at hand. It is not clear whether people laugh because they appreciate some aspect of the joke, find some of the actions or activities related to its telling funny, or wish to support, or not openly oppose, the speaker (Clayman 1992; Greatbatch and Clark 2003). This implies that what might appear to be a unifying act undertaken to affirm the participants as insiders actually hides important differences. For example, it is possible that the consultants especially may have not been entirely happy with the way the researcher was introduced. But given Paul's hierarchical and contractual positions, as MD and client, they chose not to object or place the issue in a serious frame. In order to ascertain why people laughed at some of the humorous episodes in the Change Board meetings we observed, we were sometimes able to discuss this issue as part of our informal conversations with participants as we left the meetings and attended lunch (see also Lennox-Terrion and Ashforth 2002: 66–7).

One such episode, also at *Imperial* Building Society, is detailed in Extract 3. This follows an extended discussion of issues surrounding the interface between the new IT system and the Society's network of automatic telling machines (ATMs). Ensuring that the new system interfaced with the ATMs was a major undertaking that could potentially shut down the ATM network for a significant period. Given the importance of ATMs to the Society's customers, this was something *Imperial* wished to avoid. They had therefore requested an evaluation of the nature and difficulty of the task from *Techno*. A specialist consultant—George—had been brought in to assess the situation and write a report with recommendations. The humorous remarks can be seen as similar to the episodes referred to in the previous chapter in relation to clients struggling to familiarize themselves with new terminology. In this respect the joke relates to the cultural/knowledge boundary between this particular client and set of consultants.

In the extract, the Managing Director—Paul—evokes laughter after describing his reaction to receiving and reading George's report. This person is not part of the implementation team and never attends the meetings. Paul responds to the consultant Project Manager—Julian's—question with a contrast between a report that he did not understand and a report that he did. This is delivered without a smile, laugh, and/or the use of other recognizably 'comedic' non-verbal techniques. Indeed, the initial sharpness of his remarks could be understood as a direct and overt criticism of a particular *Techno* consultant and by association the consultancy. Paul resolves or transforms this uncertainty by remaining silent and smiling thus indicating that laughter is an appropriate response. When he does so, the participants immediately start to laugh in unison. As the laughter subsides Paul ceases smiling and adopts a serious stance as he continues the discussion about the ATMs.

EXTRACT 3—'ENGLISH VERSION'

Julian: You got Georges's report?

Paul: George sent me something that I didn't have a clue about. Now I've got the English version.

[*Expansive smile*]

Participants: [*Much joint laughter*]

Paul: Right uhm Do we take a machine out of Post Office Row and install some kind of temporary arrangement? It would mean maintaining a limited level of service even if it was limited for a period.

During this brief sequence, Paul's remarks move from being potentially construed as a 'serious' direct and open criticism of George to being understood as non-serious or, at least, as less serious. By smiling, he indicates his humorous intent and that he does not regard this issue as fundamental and to be treated as being of critical importance. He further diffuses the notion that he is openly criticizing the individual and/or consultancy by clearly indicating in his subsequent remarks that he intends them not to be taken seriously or, at least, not completely so. Despite the apparent collective response to Paul's remarks, interviews immediately after the meeting revealed that the participants had very different takes on the incident as the following data demonstrate:

1. Criticism of *Techno*: 'I felt Paul was criticizing *Techno* and the way they can sometimes make things overly technical and complex.' (*Imperial* employee)

2. Criticism of George: 'I agree with Paul. I saw that report and the guy just didn't produce a clear report.' (*Imperial* employee)

3. Criticisms of communication: 'We are all learning fast. Paul was commenting on our frustration at having to make decisions with incomplete information.' 'It was about *Techno*'s communication with us.' (Both *Imperial* employees)

4. Paul's preference for information: 'Paul's not technically minded, I can just imagine his reaction to that report. He likes things in plain English. That's what should have been done.' (*Techno* consultant)

5. Incongruity: 'They think of us as techies and often joke that we speak another language.' (*Techno* consultant)

6. Uncertain response: 'I don't really remember the remark.' (*Imperial* employee)

Several points emanate from these responses. First, for those people who remember laughing at the joke, there is first-order agreement over the nature of the topic that is being invoked in the humorous remark. In this respect, there is an underlying commonality that the humorous episode involves a joke about communication. However, the participants chose different ways of interpreting this common sentiment. They do not necessarily share a common view as to who and what is being criticized. As the responses indicate, at a second-order level there are five possible sources of humour. The first two—criticism of *Techno* and George—relate to the nature of Paul's remarks prior to his indicating that he intended them to be taken as non-serious. 'Criticism of communication' similarly could also indicate criticism of *Techno* and the consultancy process in general (Sturdy et al. 2007). The fourth category suggests that one of the participants was laughing because of their knowledge of the Managing Director's preference for plain language. In this respect, they understand the joke to be self-deprecatory in that the target is the teller rather than the consultancy and its employees as indicated by the previous three responses. Finally, someone laughed because of an apparent continuation of a theme in the banter between *Imperial* and *Techno*. This joke was indicative of a broader stream of humour—the contrast between people with technical and non-technical skills. So, despite locating his potentially critical remarks within a play frame and obtaining an apparently collective response, those present at the meeting do not share a unified view of the source of the laughter. They appear to have laughed for a variety of reasons.

This raises the question of whether, despite shared laughter, we can treat clients and consultants as a homogeneous group at this point in time. Partly, their different recollections as to why they laughed relate to their particular structural position in the organizational client–consultant system. A second important feature of these comments therefore relates to the identity of those making them. In the main, those subscribing to a critical understanding of the source of humour come from the client (*Imperial*). Interestingly, the two representatives of *Techno* identify different second-order sources of humour. Gordon, the Client Manager who was based at *Techno*'s head office and visited *Imperial* primarily for the regular Change Board meetings, is critical of the report's lack of clarity for the client (point 4). He indicates that the report was too technical and should have been written in a clearer style and format to enable the contact client's understanding. He is therefore critical of the actions of one of his colleagues. On the other hand his colleague the Project Manager (Julian), who was based at *Imperial* for the duration of the assignment, viewed this incident as part of an ongoing theme in the teasing between client and consultant (point 5). While he laughed, and admits to laughing, he nevertheless did not view that action as affirming the unity of the group. Rather he laughed because it confirmed the clients' view of their separate identity and special skills. This suggests that the consultants may have responded to the operation of a general pressure or business meeting norm to be polite and conform in order not to disrupt a sense of mutual solidarity and rationality (Norrick 1993, 1994; Raskin 1985). We will pursue this point further later in the chapter.

The general conclusion from this section is that jokes about third parties involve displays of group cohesion and therefore also distancing from others—boundary construction. They include a range of incentives to laugh which increase the likelihood of collective laughter, even if people are responding to different features of the humour. Thus, while the reasons for the laughter vary, clients and consultants display consensus and unity at these points. These displays suggest that at these moments they constitute themselves as an in-group. Our more detailed analysis of the reasons as to why people laughed suggests, however, that third-party jokes are not simply acts of unification which establish boundaries between one group and another but are also sometimes founded on variations of interpretation, based partly on pre-structured positions. However, since these differences are hidden by a collective response they may still contribute to creating a sense of cohesion and intimacy which confirm the clients and consultants as a group of insiders.

Criticisms of the Consultants

Many readers will be aware of a whole host of jokes about consultants. These are without exception critical in tone. One of the oldest jokes, that has been doing the rounds since the 1960s, is that 'a management consultant is someone who will borrow your watch to tell you the time (when you didn't ask to know) and then sell it to someone else (who didn't know that they wanted to buy one)'. Critical consulting jokes have become a central part of popular business discourse. It seems that although their services have become indispensable, people love to hate them at the same time. These many jokes draw on a number of common criticisms of consultants which portray them 'as expensive (charging exorbitant fees) and ineffective (their advice rarely works), as destroying organizations, as repackaging old ideas and developing empty buzzwords, as undermining the long-term quality and confidence of management, as running amok if not tightly controlled. ... Consultancy is presented as a zero-sum game; if consultants are making money someone else must be losing it—inevitably the clients' (Fincham and Clark 2002: 8; see also Sturdy et al. 2007). Overall, consultants are therefore viewed as diminishing rather than further enhancing the wealth and performance of client organizations.

They have thus joined a succession of occupational groups, including the clergy, bankers, and lawyers, that at different points in time have been portrayed as conmen, prostitutes, and parasites in popular jokes. Indeed, a recent study of the law in the USA analysed hundreds of lawyer jokes in terms of broader representations of the law in the mass media, political discourse, and public opinion surveys. It identified an underlying *ambivalence* associated with belief in the law and increasing reliance on lawyers (Galanter 2006). Consultants are a further group whose supposed insidious power and apparent lack of accountability create deep feelings of resentment and distrust that are articulated through the many jokes that are told about them (Engwall and Eriksson 2005; Sturdy 2009).

However, the issue here is not so much whether or not consultants actually have the characteristics and qualities identified in these jokes, or to what degree—there are plenty of popular accounts on this issue (e.g., Craig 2005; O'Shea and Madigan 1997; Pinault 2001)—but whether such criticisms become expressed in the client–consultant relationship. As we have seen, 'put-downs' with respect to third parties can be both integrative and divisive. Furthermore, their location in the liminal space of the play frame ensures that they are viewed as relatively safe or inoffensive (i.e. indirect) ways of expressing criticism. Third-party jokes also generally involve comments about individuals and groups who are not present. Similarly, consultants are not necessarily present when the jokes in the popular discourse are repeated. The issue for us in this section of the chapter is how consultants respond to clients making humorous remarks in meetings which criticize them.

In the previous section, although we noted differences between clients and consultants in relation to why they recollected they were laughing at third-party jokes, the verbal response at the time was nevertheless collective. Everyone laughed together. However, with jokes about consultants, the response is much more uneven. Clients and consultants do not always engage in reciprocal laughter, with the consequence that some members are positioned as insiders and others as outsiders. Some jokes dealt explicitly with such boundaries. For example, in *Borough* in an early meeting, the *OpsCo* client account manager introduced one of his consulting colleagues with the quip 'He *is* one of us . . . you can see the difference can't you?' Similarly, the next extract from the building society case shows starkly how organizational and role boundaries are evident in such humorous remarks. At each meeting the Project Manager from *Techno* presented a technical issues log that detailed every software problem since the last meeting. Typically between twenty and thirty issues were listed. These were in turn designated low, medium, or high priority. In addition, a risk log for the whole project was presented which identified key resourcing issues that may impact on the project as a whole (e.g., staffing, training, staff morale, and other IT projects). The discussion in the extract below occurred in the meeting where the Society had to decide whether to 'go live' with the new mortgage system in the next three weeks.

The Society's General Manager (Duncan) initially expresses concerns at the number of software problems in the technical issues log. The *Techno* Project Manager then responds that there are no 'high priority' issues and so no 'show stoppers'. However, he recognizes that the volume of issues is itself a problem and so asks if a member of the *Techno* project team can be seconded—at an extra cost to *Imperial*—for a further period to help with the issues surrounding the production of accurate monthly and quarterly financial statements. The Special Projects Manager (Belinda) at *Imperial* immediately intervenes and accuses him of wanting his red badge. As noted in Chapter 4, this refers to the security badge worn by everyone in the head office building. *Imperial* staff wear badges with red neck bands, visitors such as *Techno* staff have either green or yellow bands. Ostensibly the humour is initially signalled by Belinda's use of a playful rhythmical tone of voice as she waves her own security badge at Julian (the Project Manager from *Techno*). As the laughter dies away, Belinda uses a laughing voice to make a further comment that she intends to be taken as jocular and additional laughter ensues. The Managing Director, and chair of the meeting, then moves the discussion onto a more serious footing.

EXTRACT 4—'RED BADGE'

Duncan: These seem a large number of problems to fix before the next conversion. We only have one more meeting after that. Can you be confident that we can go live?

Julian: Sure. But if you look at the incident report most of the problems are cleared up on average in less than a day. Many of the active issues are not high priority and so [i.e. not] show stoppers. But it would be helpful if we could have more of Susan's time. I know she's pressed on other jobs but her input would help in fixing Summit to produce the new format MFSs and QFSs.

Belinda: He's after his red ba-hh-dge. [*Waves her security badge*]

Paul, Duncan, Belinda: [*Joint laughter*]

Julian: [*Wry smile*]

Gordon: [*Delayed and muted laughter*]

Belinda: She's our Susan now not your Susan. [*Said in a laughing voice*]

Paul, Duncan, Belinda: [*Joint laughter*]

Julian: [*Smile*]

Gordon: [*Delayed and muted laughter*]

Paul: If we have Susan for a few days can you be confident that you can fix the problem before next week? This is getting close. We then only have one more conversion before we decide to go live.

Julian: Doing it this way is the favoured option, the fastest option and the cheapest option. It's an irritant but not a show stopper.

When asked subsequent to the meeting why they laughed during this episode, the *Imperial* staff gave similar reasons. These related to an understanding of the jocular remarks as referring to the consultant as 'going native' (see also Chapter 4). Typical explanations included: 'it was about them [*Techno*] going native'; 'they've become part of the furniture ... they bring our [company] mugs to the meetings'; 'Susan's become part of the team. She wants to stay because she likes it here'; 'she's just recognizing that the longer they stay with us the more they want to be us'. However, the *Techno* staff interpreted the remarks differently. The Project Manager regarded them as an attack on the extent of his commitment to the client: 'look they want me to be committed and I am, but to the project and them as a client, not as a future employer'. In this respect the *Imperial* staff indicate that *Techno*, in the form of Susan, has already 'converted' to them or wishes to do so. Julian realizes this is an important issue for *Imperial* and recognizes that they want to see him and his team as one of them. But as he indicates, his primary commitment is a structural one, to the project rather than *Imperial* as an organization. In contrast, Gordon the *Techno* Client Manager views these remarks primarily as a resourcing issue rather than one of attitudinal commitment. As he stated in a subsequent interview, 'They're just having a go at our commitment. But leaving Susan in *Imperial* for a couple more weeks has implications elsewhere ... I did feel that we need to talk about this a bit more, but probably outside of the meeting.'

These differences of opinion are also shown by the varying response to the humorous remarks. Although our contemporaneous notes do not capture all the nuances of this incident, they nevertheless show that the consultants' responses were different from that of their clients and one another. Gordon did not laugh at the same time as the client members, but only once the client group had started. His delayed response may indicate that he laughed out of politeness rather than agreement with the foregoing remarks. He does not show fulsome agreement with, or immediate acknowledgement of, the play frame. Likewise, Julian does not laugh, he smiles. His wry or weary smile possibly indicates that he has seen this before; it is part of a recurrent theme. As he remarked afterwards, for him this comment was a further element in a general ploy on the part of the client to get him to 'go native'. It was nothing new. They wanted him to become one of them which he felt inappropriate. His smile is therefore a way of minimally recognizing the humour in the remarks but not offering his complete support for the underlying message. He shows his appreciation but does not join in. However, although he positions himself as an organizational outsider at this moment, certainly more so than his colleague Gordon, he does so in such a way that it is not noticed. Laughing involves a number of facial gestures that look similar to smiling (i.e. accentuation of the eyes and opening of the mouth to show one's teeth) (Pollio et al. 1972). To those present, a smile can therefore look physically similar to a laugh. Given that nobody remarked on or seemed to notice the fact that Julian did not laugh, they may have felt that he was acknowledging the play frame.

In terms of the client–consultant relationship, we can see in this episode a consultant managing Merton's (1972) competing 'status sets'. Julian is a person who worked on site for nearly two years and was regarded by many in the client organization as an insider. When he attended his final lunch at the Building Society, before moving to another IT consultancy, the kitchen staff expressed surprise that he was not a member of staff. Similarly, the receptionists, responsible for handing out the security tags, occasionally had to think twice as to which colour to give him. There was therefore some confusion outside the project team as to his precise status. From Julian's point of view, he was very much an employee of *Techno* and therefore resisted the overtures to enrol him completely into the client organization. Much like the 'implementer' type of consultant discussed in Chapter 1, he appeared to be *organizationally* close, but not in terms of personal ties or organizational identification (also Kitay and Wright 2003)—he did not wish to go native. However, he had to do this in a way that did not offend the sensibilities of his client. His smiling during this episode reflects how he managed this boundary through a form of passive resistance. Drawing on Lavin and Maynard's analysis of laughter declination, part of the consultant's 'tacit knowledge includes conversational competence' (2001: 465). More specifically, they know how to decline to laugh and position themselves as outsiders in such a way that they are able to sustain their rapport with a client. Thus, on occasion they are able to move between being positioned as insiders and outsiders without the switch between the two states being immediately apparent to those present (see also Smith 2008). To all intents they look like and remain insiders.

What we see here can be contrasted with our earlier discussion of third-party jokes. Here, the liminal play frame resulted in collective laughter masking competing understandings. The fact that everyone laughs indicates that there was a general acknowledgement of the onset of the play frame even if it was interpreted differently. However, in the example just discussed the establishment of the play frame is more problematic. The two consultants do not unequivocally confirm its establishment by delaying and displaying more muted responses which can be read as acknowledging the humour, but not in a fulsome manner. In this way, they are able to position themselves ambiguously by being simultaneously outsiders and insiders. They acknowledge the humour, but in a way that also demonstrates their detachment from the client's assessment of them. This is an example of the management of cultural boundaries by the consultants par excellence.

We found that consultants frequently used another technique—the use of self-deprecatory humorous remarks—to repair situations where the client's criticisms or concerns positioned them as outsiders and to further manage cultural boundaries. Such humour involves someone making a joke about themselves through some form of implied self-criticism. For example in the *Borough* project, one consultant frequently used self-deprecatory humour when challenged by the client. In one case the client seeks clarification as to the year on which a budget projection is based. After clarifying the precise year, the consultant then says in an incredulous voice 'Where did you get that? Did I give you that year?' Laughter then ensues. In this way they turned a situation in which they were initially criticized to one where people demonstrated enjoyment of their self-critical remarks (although said in a self-mocking tone of voice).

Clearly, to client employees working in the project team a key potential threat is an existential one, the challenge to their identity as experts or as competent (Sturdy 1997*a*). This is a source of considerable tension, resulting in the common criticism of consultants as arrogant or insensitive. It is also one which some consultants seek to diffuse through humour, including irony and self-deprecation. One of the consultants we observed, Stuart at *Prison*, was quite conscious of this and used it in his direct interactions with the senior clients as the following two extracts demonstrate.

EXTRACT 5—'LAST PAGES'

Consultant: [*Looking through client's workings in a report*] OK.

Client: Enough? [*Said quickly to the consultant while showing him his workings*] Thank God he didn't look at the last pages. [*Said ironically as if this was own train of thought*]

[*Laughter, followed by the consultant grabbing the papers as though pretending to inspect the last pages*]

And later in the meeting:

Consultant: . . . We (all) seem to have got into the comfort zone of talking about nitty-gritty detail, because planning's too hard! [*laughter*] So . . .

Such practices can be seen as maintaining rapport or, at least, as diffusing tensions in several ways. Partly, and as we saw in the previous chapter and noted in Chapter 4, they can soften the challenge implied in a 'teacher–learner' relationship. This gives rise to particular tensions in a context where the client might consider himself or herself as a fellow expert and/or a sovereign consumer, not a pupil, and therefore feels disempowered or threatened. The consultant's actions may reveal them to be inadequate or failing in some respect. To soften such a threat the consultant counters by revealing one of their own weaknesses—'I'm conscious I'm being a bit of a bully' (Stuart). Thus, this is partly an episode of mutual revelation in which the client's anxieties are balanced by the consultant's. But the humour can also be seen as a way for the client and consultant to admit this in a non-threatening way by positioning it in the play frame, and having this confirmed through the shared laughter. Thus, the self-deprecatory humour here plays down status differences. It helps confirm a common bond and reinforce rapport between the client and consultant and construct a cultural boundary between themselves and others. This occurs in another example where a client member criticizes themselves for 'thinking off the top of their head'. Again the consultant in this instance provides reassurance by making an inclusive self-deprecatory joke when they reply 'We all are, so don't worry about it. It's more thrilling that way isn't it?'

The next example (Extract 6) is similar in that it shows how consultants can turn a situation where they are being criticized, and are the butt of a joke about their apparent lack of communication with one another, to one where they realign those present to laugh collectively and demonstrate their like-mindedness. In other words, they transform a moment in which they are distanced and positioned as organizational outsiders to one where they are repositioned as group/project insiders by obtaining a collective affiliative response to a humorous remark. Glenn (1995) has previously noted this movement when he writes that laughing at someone 'makes the other into an object, distancing and disaffiliating laughter and victim. But such distancing is labile and subject to change . . . those being laughed at may attempt to transform the sequential environment into one in which affiliation becomes relevant' (p. 55). We have similarly shown how people can turn a situation in which a humorous comment positions them as group outsiders to one where they are still laughed at but on their own terms. In the process, they turn a fragmentary situation where boundaries between group members are delineated to a more unified one that generates a display of like-mindedness based on their actions.

EXTRACT 6—'VERSION 9.1'

Des: The workaround is working at the moment. It should be. Is that the case Julian?

Julian: Mmmm.

Des: Right, so it would be better if it was included in the next upgrade. We don't want it to be a workaround for ever.

Julian: There's a difference of opinion. You know what I'm going to say Duncan you might have to wait.

Gordon: I am told that it's all in and 9.1 is loaded and tested.

Des: Is? It? [*with emphasis*]

[*Holds his hands out like a set of scales and moves them up and down looking at each of his colleagues with an incredulous expression on his face.*]

[*Blows a long raspberry*] Clients: [*Much joint laughter*]

Consultants: [*Weak smiles*]

Gordon: I will check but I am pretty sure it's in.

Des: That would be helpful.

Julian: Well if it is in we will have saved you some money and I can take a holiday. [*Said in a laughing voice*]

Participants: [*Joint laughter*]

In this extract, there is an exchange about whether a temporary patch to the IT system is to be incorporated into the next version of the software that will be uploaded onto *Imperial*'s system shortly. The client, represented by the Society Secretary, Des, would like it included. However, the consultant Project Manager (Julian) says that 'there's a difference of opinion'. What he means by this is that *Imperial* will have to pay for the inclusion of any additional elements to future versions of the software. From his point of view, they cannot assume that it will be included free in the next version since what is being requested is not part of what was agreed to be supplied. However, before he can complete his sentence his colleague, the Client Manager from head office (Gordon), interrupts him to express a different view. He indicates that he believes that this upgrade has already been incorporated into the next version of the software and furthermore that this has been loaded and tested. In this respect it will be provided free as part of the next version of the software. Des, who is chairing the meeting, exclaims his surprise. Initially, this comes off as a sharp rebuke and could be understood as a direct criticism of the consultants, Gordon and Julian. After a pause he turns to his colleagues sitting either side of him and puts out his hands and mimics a set of scales going up and down. This gesture indicates that he does not know who to believe. At the same time his face shows an incredulous expression and he 'blows a raspberry'. In response to this his colleagues laugh.

Gordon and Julian clearly see this as a criticism of them since they do not participate in the laughter. As we have seen in previous examples, they resist the definition of the situation by both smiling weakly. Gordon is initially silent and then overlaps the laughter by engaging in serious talk. Also by making this talk 'on task' he seeks to redefine this situation as a non-laughing one in which further serious discussion is more appropriate. His actions therefore indicate that he does not see laughter as a relevant response. Although Julian remains silent, he and Gordon exchange eye contact and while Gordon is talking Julian nods his head in agreement. Julian remains silent as Gordon speaks to present a common position and rectify the fact that they have just contradicted one another in front of the client team. Julian then makes a self-deprecatory joke about saving the client some time and money with the consequence he can go on holiday. Everyone laughs in response to this remark.

In summary, this episode represents an example of the client construing the consultants as outsiders, as suppliers, by making them the butt of their humorous remarks. The consultants indicate their understanding of this by not laughing and engaging in serious talk thereby seeking to reduce the humorous tone and move it into a more serious one. One reason for this may be that their professional competence has been questioned. Des is questioning whether they are familiar with their own product? Thus, Gordon's response to the laughter may be interpreted as engaging in 'professional talk' to reassert their expertise in the eyes of the client—not everything can be laughed off. After Duncan has accepted Gordon's offer, Julian then makes a self-directed humorous remark that evokes a collective response and re-establishes an affiliative atmosphere and confirms the group's like-mindedness. In this way, he turns a situation in which he and his colleague are initially positioned as outsiders, and negatively so, to one in which their insider status is re-confirmed or, at least, increased. Put another way, he manages to convert a moment of division into one of relative consensus and harmony and in the process navigate the cultural and political boundaries that may divide client and consultant. This suggests how the boundaries and divisions evident in some of the previous episodes of laughter are occasionally more pre-carious, graduated, and fluid as one definition of a situation turns into another. Thus insiders can become short-lived outsiders and the reverse is also true. In the process, cultural and political boundaries are being reconfigured.

Criticisms of Clients

The final category of jokes is those where client personnel are the butt. In keeping with the structure of supplier and client and the hierarchical discourse of the client or consumer as sovereign or higher in status, such jokes were not very common. We have very few examples in the case studies where the consultants made a humorous comment about their client. The long-term viability of the consultants' business depended on their ability to maintain strong client relationships. Indeed, repeat business and word of mouth recommendation (i.e. an indirect measure of client satisfaction with a consultant based on direct experience) are often used as an indicator of the quality of the consultancies' services (Armbrüster 2006). None of the consultants therefore wanted to engage in any activity that appeared or came off as an overt criticism of their immediate clients, at least not in public (see Phills 1996). Thus, in one of the very few examples of a consultant openly criticizing a member of the client organization (see Extract 7), the impact of their remarks is ameliorated in a number of ways. First, Gordon's comment follows a criticism of this person already made by a member of the client team (Duncan) and further reinforced by another one (Joyce). Their jocular remarks therefore confirm an assessment already made by members of the client team. Second, their comments are positioned within a humorous frame and so are projected as not serious. It is a friendly jibe that builds on one made earlier by Duncan. In addition, the person who is the butt of the joke is a third party and their identity is never revealed. In this way they avoid not only offending a named person within the client organization but also offending anyone who is a member of the immediate client group.

EXTRACT 7—'SACK THEM'

Paul: I understand there is one user jumping from stage thirty to eighty.

Duncan: Inadvertently [*Said in an ironic tone of voice*]

Participants: [*Much joint laughter*]

Joyce: This is a training issue. People have got to understand that this is the way it is going to be.

Gordon: You may need to sack 'em if they don't. [*Laughs as he says this*]

Participants: [*Much joint laughter*]

Extract 5 ('last pages') discussed earlier in the chapter also contains an implied criticism, albeit rather muted, of the client by the consultant. In this case the potential impact of the remarks is softened by the consultant making this an inclusive remark so that they are also implicated in the criticism before engaging in self-deprecation. Similarly in the *Borough* case, potentially critical comments of the client were heavily mitigated. For example, when discussing the difficulty of obtaining information from managers within the council one of the consultants says to a key member of the client team: 'Yeah, I'd like to hear the views on the ground...but I'll change my identity before I come in.' This humorous but critical comment follows from the client previously admitting that communication is problematic. It therefore follows the structure of the extract above in that they confirm an opinion already expressed by the client.

In summary, jokes by consultants at the expense of their clients were exceptional. When they did occur they were heavily toned down in order to lessen the impact of the implied criticism. On each occasion the client members accepted the invitation to laugh and so confirmed their understanding that the remarks were not to be taken seriously and they were part of an in-group with the consultants. This was therefore a humorous comment that was shared and so united the parties.

In contrast, clients, like many family members or insiders, made numerous jocular remarks about their own colleagues (see Extract 7). For example, in the *Prison* case, one of the key clients makes a joke in relation to his concern that colleagues will not willingly meet the inspection team when he says:

I may be taking us on a detour but it's some of my misgivings about the day are that staff won't come forward and won't say 'Here I am, I'm the Reception Senior Officer. This area that I'm in charge of, doesn't it look clean? Aren't my staff well presented? This is the process that we run. It's different from this other prison. In fact, it's better and prisoners will tell you it's better.' They won't. They will be reticent and if they can they'll be on the bleedin' phone out the back. [*laughter*]

In another example in the *Prison* project, when discussing the composition of groups for the inspection visit one of the consultants said 'I think you need somebody chatty in that group', to which a client replied 'Yeah, that's where Julie [a prison officer] would be good'. Much laughter ensued and other humorous comments were made about Julie ('We would have to put her on a no smoking' and 'She'd have to have patches all over her').

These types of jokes are essentially another form of third-party humour in that their butts are individuals and groups who were external to the project team, or the core team at least, and were very rarely named. In those instances where people were named, consultant laughter often was more hesitant and delayed indicating that they were waiting to be led by their client. They did not want to find themselves laughing before the client had confirmed the relevance of that response. Even though they may have begun with a staggered rather than immediate onset, these were episodes of shared laughter and so were public displays of consensus and like-mindedness (Glenn 1989; Greatbatch and Clark 2003, 2005).

Discussion and Conclusion

In focusing on humorous remarks and the different forms of laughter they can evoke, this chapter has been concerned with exposing a particular element of the micro-dynamics of boundary relationships. As we argued earlier, in the majority of the projects, humour was a noticeable feature of the meetings between the clients and consultants in that it provided a contrast to their predominantly serious tone. Moments of laughter therefore stood out from the surrounding talk. As liminal spaces within the structured liminality of an inter-organizational project, they reveal important elements in the social dynamics between the different parties. Our analysis shows that jokes about third parties provided a number of reasons for people to laugh and so generated a unified response. Since the targets of these remarks were typically external to the different project teams those present did not feel threatened. Although the reasons as to why people may have laughed varied, nevertheless their collective laughter was an open display of like-mindedness. Such moments may therefore be seen as an expression of the project team as an in-group and the confirmation of a common cultural–emotional boundary. Similarly, on the very few occasions when consultants made jokes about clients, these jokes were constructed in such a way that they did not challenge the client and so evoked a collective response. Indeed, these jokes frequently confirmed a client member's prior assessment of a person or situation and so were not the threat that they might initially appear to be. Once again the shared response confirmed those present as members of an in-group with a common cultural boundary in that they shared an apparently unified perspective in relation to the situation being described. In contrast, when clients made negative jokes about consultants they frequently positioned the latter as organizational and political outsiders. It was during these episodes that the relationship was most challenged and at risk. Consultants employed a number of techniques either to locate themselves ambiguously in relation to the remarks or to reposition themselves as insiders. In this respect the consultants actively sought to smooth over some of the tensions that gave rise to the critical remarks in order to ensure the maintenance of cultural and political boundaries, cohesion, and an affinity or collective purpose among the members.

The maintenance of rapport was facilitated by the fact that the great majority of humorous episodes were inclusive in nature and where shifts between the insider–outsider statuses occurred, they were momentary. Although, differences within the project teams existed, even in relation to the source of the humorous remarks, these were hidden by displaying a collective response and the fact that the few moments of dissensus were actively managed so that rapport was maintained. As a consequence, those present were able to treat the remarks that provoked the different forms of put-down humour as non-serious. They never threatened to disrupt irrevocably the relationship between the various parties. The implied criticism within the humorous remarks was therefore limited or acknowledged, but at a level where the relationship was not unduly endangered.

Overall, in three of the projects where we observed humour, it enabled the clients and consultants to maintain a sense of social cohesion or, at least, suspend or defer substantive and explicit conflict. Indeed, as we remarked earlier, the presence of laughter was viewed by many of those involved in the projects as an indicator of the level of affinity and closeness between the parties. The fact that clients and consultants could laugh together and at one another created a sense of togetherness and a friendly footing that helped establish a foundation for resolving more serious and structural issues. In essence each humorous episode was a test in relation to cultural and political boundaries. Underpinning jokes were the unspoken questions—'To what extent do we understand one another? To what extent are our interests shared here?' Individual responses were both a sign of participants' understanding of the meanings they attached to these questions and also an indication of the boundaries of shared cultural meanings, even if displayed in a convoluted, hesitant, and qualified manner.

As each humorous episode was negotiated in the ways we have outlined, it enabled the clients and consultants to explore and test in a non-threatening way the shifting boundaries within which their relationship was located. This occurred in part because each laughter episode, whether involving a collective response or not, demonstrated that they jointly understood the interactional rule structure, or grammar, surrounding laughter and its management, and that this in turn showed a willingness to maintain harmony and a sense of group cohesion and like-mindedness. At the level of display, the relationship was generally reaffirmed rather than challenged. Each humorous episode built on the previous one to establish a base of friendliness and common understanding that could be drawn upon when more was at stake; when understandings and objectives themselves needed to be challenged and changed. In other words, more challenging and serious issues could be tackled on a different and potentially friendlier basis than if the relationship between the parties was devoid of humour. The humour thus facilitated the clients and consultants we observed to test the limits and nature of boundaries in a safe manner. In this way they were able to make assessments of where they could work together productively and where they could not; where the boundary of unity and division was. The collaborative achievement of laughter therefore facilitated collaboration more generally. So, for example, it enabled the different parties to determine the parameters for challenge by helping establish the limits of what each party determined as acceptable.

In conclusion, the micro management of humour and laughter enabled clients and consultants to manage cultural boundaries in a way that stabilized and solidified the relationship at particular moments and in the process established a key foundation block for the relationship as a whole. More generally, by focusing on the dynamics and micro level of interaction, we have sought to show how boundaries in consulting projects are only partially pre-structured, in terms of formal organizational affiliation, contractual expectations, and hierarchical and functional roles for example. In keeping with the analysis in previous chapters, insider–outsider relations are also fluid, multiple, and subject to more or less conscious moment-by-moment negotiation.

171

8

Conclusion—beyond consultancy and projects

Introduction

Our primary aim in writing this book was to begin to address an empirical research neglect of management consultancy in action, and to explore the largely taken-for-granted and persistent assumption that, when it comes to knowledge transfer, management consultancy can best be understood as a process where *expert outsiders* bring *new* knowledge to *organizational insiders*. Our focus was on consultancy project work, client–consultant relationships, and the conditions and processes of knowledge flow in these contexts. In exploring these phenomena, we first referred to various studies of consulting relationships which pointed to different dimensions of their multiplicity, complexity, and dynamism, but still largely subscribed to the traditional view of knowledge transfer. In order to develop this towards a better understanding of knowledge flow, we drew on wider studies of boundaries—or structuring *processes*—and inter-organizational learning. This enabled us to construct a broad framework for analysing boundary and knowledge dynamics in the context of consulting projects. Here, we revealed the possibility of the negotiation and co-construction of relations through action as well as the notion of multiple, simultaneous, and shifting insider–outsider positions or continua. In other words, we raised the importance of the need to specify insider–outsider relations with respect to *what, whom, and when* (Table 1.2). These social and symbolic boundaries were shown to have significant implications for understanding the flow of knowledge and its potential—boundaries as barriers and bridges. Indeed, both knowledge and its boundary conditions were understood as being processual, negotiated, and often ambiguous. In the context of client–consultant relations at least, knowledge was shown to be more commonly shared and/or co-produced than transferred like an object from expert consultant to client learner.

These issues were explored in detail through four empirical chapters which each had their own empirical and analytical focus around boundaries and knowledge, but together served to demonstrate a picture of consultancy quite removed from the image of consultants as bringers of new knowledge from the outside, as management innovators or as mere legitimators of existing knowledge. Rather, consultancy, or consulting project work, can be seen as somewhat more mundane in nature, where the 'shock of the new' is more likely to be felt by those outside of the project context, if it is at all. Indeed, while consultancy in general clearly plays an important ideological and legitimatory role in management and organizations, Thrift's (2005) characterization of consultants as the 'commissars of capitalism' is misleading at this level of analysis in terms of its implicit assumptions of consultants' relative and one-dimensional expertise, authority, and primary concern with promulgation and/or compliance, at least in relation to their immediate management clients.

Perhaps, then, both clients and consultants can be seen as commissars. They are both managerial agents located within various other historical and structural relations simultaneously, which shift in significance through social interaction and negotiation. Here, formal contractual (e.g. supplier–customer) and organizational (e.g. employment) relations, roles, and identities are crucial, but may be subsumed, suspended, or translated by those associated with project working and other physical, cultural, and political boundaries. This recognition of the multiplicity of structures and relations is, perhaps, a conventional one, but it is important. Viewing organizational practice close up is almost bound to reveal its complexity and dynamism and its embeddedness in wider social relations. This was illustrated in our account of humour, for example, where familiar social dynamics and norms associated with put-down jokes and laughter were coloured by and informed client–consultant and project relationships with all their tensions, tactics, and alliances.

Our various challenges to the dominant image of consultants as expert, innovative outsiders are only partly derived from the complexity and dynamism revealed by our level of analysis and in-depth and longitudinal methods. The historical and specific contexts of our research are also important. For example and as we argued in Chapter 1, both formal management knowledge and project-based working are more widely diffused among UK managers now. The traditional image of consultant-expert and client-learner are also likely to be least evident in the specific context of project teams, where client experts may work alongside consultants with similar or less expertise, especially when considering a range of knowledge domains (e.g. sector knowledge) above and beyond the substantive focus of the project. This was evident in our case study projects, but clearly, other projects will differ and some may even more closely conform to the traditional image of consultancy. Our point is that the expert outsider position of consultants in relation to their clients *cannot be assumed* and, in contemporary project contexts especially, may even be unlikely. Furthermore, client–consultant relations cannot be reduced to one domain of expertise, a limited conception of formal organizational or project roles, or to a static characterization for an adequate understanding. Here, our focus on boundaries also revealed a different perspective on consultancy practice in terms of its political dynamics. This involved a move away from the literature's primary concern with patterns of influence and dependency towards an additional recognition of inclusion and exclusion, whether in a formal and physical sense of absence/presence or more interactively and purposefully through shifting patterns of boundary—us and them—construction and associated cooperation and conflict.

Consultancy and Beyond

In addition to the above core arguments about knowledge flow and politics in consulting projects, we have shed light on other dimensions of consultancy. Indeed, although the in-depth nature of our study precluded the selection of a full range of project types and conditions, the case studies were quite varied in character. This, combined with our longitudinal approach, allowed us to demonstrate some of the variations both between and within projects (e.g. Chapters 4 and 5). Yet we also revealed some common patterns and dynamics, not least that of shifting insider–outsider positions and the under- and overestimation of knowledge flow derived from the outsider view of consultancy. Such claims were made possible by our analytical framing of various boundary bases, actors, and dynamics as well as our exploration of practices such as humour and challenge. Thus, for example, the frequently sharp distinction made in some of the literature between the small firm and sole consulting practitioner, such as Stuart, and the multinational consulting firm, such as *StratCo*, is not wholly sustainable. Likewise, by focusing upon the commonly and partially shared domain of sector knowledge, we were able to explore a neglected form of consultant and management expertise (Chapter 5).

This was revealed as being negotiated and exchanged in action in different forms, levels, and contexts and as assuming a form which did not fit either of the polar views of consulting knowledge as either concrete and external or wholly ambiguous and contested. Rather, this negotiated and emotionally important knowledge of the organizational 'outside' was co-produced within the liminal space of the consulting project and sometimes served as a bridge for the flow of other forms of knowledge.

The following two chapters focused less on knowledge, its flow, and boundary relations in consultancy and more on the interactive practices which sustain and transform them. First, we examined what is seen by many as a core feature of consultancy in imparting new knowledge to clients—challenge. This notion was developed considerably, by drawing on learning theories, our boundary framework, and forms of challenge in action. Challenges were revealed as not necessarily confrontational, consultant-led, successful, one-off interventions, nor necessarily focused upon imparting new knowledge. Rather, they assumed different, often tentative, forms, and unfolded over time with different responses and outcomes. They also sometimes reflected a broader, more contractual, politics of consulting projects where the issue was not one of knowledge being 'at stake' so much as a conflict of objectives and interests.

The second interactive practice or process to be explored was less conventional, especially in the contexts of consultancy and project meetings. Here, through our analysis of the micro-processes of humorous episodes, we saw how cultural and political boundaries of in-groups and out-groups could emerge and change *in the moment*. They ebbed and flowed as tensions were raised, diffused, hidden, or deferred through the often purposeful and skilful management of humour and laughter. Both were viewed by many as a barometer of the level of closeness and rapport between the different parties, but the 'weather' could change at any moment and in unpredictable ways. This presents a very different view of client–consultant relations from that in the consulting literature where any closeness is seen to develop gradually over time and as relatively robust. By contrast, in addition to presenting alliances which were only partly informed by broader structural positions at the outset, we saw how they could be much more fragile, short-lived, negotiated, or managed. In other words, relations such as continuing rapport between clients and consultants are an active achievement.

Now, although our primary concern has been on management consultancy, the same empirical study could have been carried out with a completely different focus and primary reference point in the literature such as project working or professional or business services for example. After all, management consultancy is simply a facet of management and organizations with particular characteristics. Indeed, even with our delimited focus within consultancy, we have drawn on a wide range of literature from different topics and fields.[1] In an effort to retain this focus, we have not sought to make substantive claims in these other areas, nor is there scope to do so here. However, it is worth pointing to some of these themes and connections and our position in relation to them. First, we have explored boundaries as structuring processes, not objects, and sought to show how they can be used to make sense of consultancy projects and their dynamics, both by us and by the research participants. Here, we have adopted both traditional and (late) modern concerns in terms of developing Merton's notion of multiple and simultaneous insider–outsider positions and identities as well as pointing to physical, cultural, and political patterns of inclusion and exclusion. Boundaries have also been shown to be relative and fluid phenomena, but not completely so. For example, actors may be insiders or outsiders compared to others and their positions are both partially pre-structured as well as subject to negotiation and more or less conscious tactics, such as in the use of humour to mark out insiders or to designate a statement as being within the safety and liminality of the play frame.

These dynamics have helped us to explore knowledge flows which also form the focus of a second stream of relevant studies, that of inter-organizational and project-based learning and management knowledge and innovation. We have already pointed to a number of connections to these broad fields, which have formed an important part of our analysis overall, especially in relation to the role of organizational outsiders for example. Nevertheless, the importance attached to context and dynamics in our analysis suggests that universalist, checklist-type prescriptions for facilitating learning are highly problematic (see also Chapter 3). At best, they might provide some insight into the *potential* for learning, much as we sought to do through our application of the notion of cognitive (cultural) distance combined with physical and political boundary relations. In addition, our account of shifting insider–outsider roles resonates with recent work on insider–outsider hybridity (Birkinshaw et al. 2008; Smith 2008). The notion of adopting multiple and shifting roles may also help reconcile conceptually the tension in the dominant and dualistic view of

---

[1] By contrast, one area of literature of potential relevance to our study, that of meetings, has not yet been explored (Jarzabkowski and Seidl 2008; Schwartzman 1986). This is the planned focus of future research by one of the authors.

consultancy outlined at the start of this book, between the 'strength of weak ties' and 'burden of otherness'. It also reinforces our critique of the dominant empirical assumption that consultancy is primarily concerned with bringing new knowledge or management innovation to clients. This role may be more evident in contexts beyond consultancy projects such as among peer managers and firms or other change agents or consultancy contexts, but this would require further research, an area to which we now briefly turn.

Beyond Projects

Our in-depth focus on consulting projects and knowledge flow has helped to shed new light on both consultancy and broader organizational phenomena. But such an empirical focus as well as our analytical choices also reveals areas of neglect, many of which remain under-examined in consultancy research. We therefore conclude by exploring some of these limitations by way of a recognition of them in our own work and a call for further research from others. In particular, we identify some empirical sites and conceptual themes which have potential to yield further insight into the various worlds of management consultancy.

First, and as we have already noted, our challenge to the dominant image of management consultancy and knowledge might have been less evident in other consulting contexts. For example, our attention was focused on formal projects and, for the most part, in and around formal meetings. A more didactic form of consulting practice could be expected in formal sales pitches and informal selling activity both before and during projects. Here, we should also include the largely hidden promotion, sharing, and construction of ideas or perspectives between, typically very senior, consultants and executives, and policymakers which occur above and/or beyond any consideration of specific projects, at a national or sector level for example (Mohe 2008). At the same time, further insight into the role of consultancy in the development of new management practices could be achieved by extending research back into early product development (Anand et al. 2007; Heusinkveld and Benders 2005) as well as forwards, well beyond the immediate post-project phase that we examined. In addition, we have already pointed to some emerging forms of consultancy where client–consultant knowledge relations may differ. For example the *Borough* case began as a formal partnership with *OpsCo* and an IT company, but other novel arrangements exist such as the triadic relationship between client purchasing departments, clients, and consultants (Werr and Pemer 2007); internal and external consultants (Wright and Sturdy 2008); and projects with multiple client and consulting organizations. In all of these cases, a question remains over the extent to which formal organizational and functional roles persist or dominate in interactions with other parties. While we sought to highlight the diversity of roles in our projects and their enactment and translation in meetings, the participants' organizational control mechanisms and their impact on project practices and knowledge flow were not considered in detail. There is some work in this area, but largely in terms of consulting knowledge management practices—the extent to which consultants are effectively encouraged to acquire, share, and develop client knowledge. This leaves a considerable empirical gap to be filled, perhaps through the method of shadowing consultants and clients as they move between and reflect upon their organizational and project spaces and roles.

If our focus on projects led to areas of empirical neglect, our conceptual focus on boundaries and insider–outsider relations opened up a wide and diverse field of analysis spanning physical, cultural, and political relations. However, each of these interrelated qualities could have been developed further. First, physical boundaries and spatial issues more generally only became a focus as the research work developed and thus receive relatively little attention, beyond concerns with joint working or operational proximity for example. Second, the three boundary forms could have been extended in scope, towards an institutional or national level of analysis in terms of sector or field norms for example (Marchington and Vincent 2004; Robertson et al. 2003) although some consideration of this was given in our account of sector knowledge. Third, and more importantly, our consideration of processes of inclusion and exclusion remained largely at the level of the project actors such as proscribed clients and, even, of micro-interactions. Insufficient attention was given to the possibility of how these might relate to broader structural patterns and dynamics. Such neglect is partly a consequence of our methodological and empirical focus on what was visible (to us) in our observations, but this need not preclude some sensitivity to what or who was absent from the start and the extent to which such absence can be seen as an outcome of active exclusion.

Concerns with broader patterns of exclusion have been touched upon by others in related fields such as that of learning where new knowledge is closed to 'out-groups' such as other organizations and, more generally, those with differing social characteristics (Ebers and Grandori 1997;

Portes 1998). Likewise, some, albeit limited, attention has been given to the exclusion of women, ethnic minorities, and working classes in professional services (Hanlon 2004), including consultancy (Kumra and Vinnicombe 2008; Marsh 2008). To this we might add various categories and groups such as client employees, unions, citizens, customers, and less conventional groups such as those without formal management education, although this was not always evident in our own projects. Moreover, in certain contexts, individuals (and organizations) actively choose not to engage in consultancy. But the questions of precisely who is excluded and absent from, and included in, consultancy and with what effects have yet to be properly addressed. This is especially important given the influence and relative unaccountability of consultancy in public domains. In addition, there is a need to follow the trail of consultancy interventions further to those diverse groups who experience the outcomes of consultancy work most directly, as 'ultimate', but often forgotten 'clients' or insiders in terms of *consultancy effects*.

References

Abrahamson, E. (1996). 'Management fashion'. *Academy of Management Review*, 21, 1, 254–85.

Alvesson, M. (1993). 'Organizations as rhetoric: knowledge intensive firms and the struggle with ambiguity'. *Journal of Management Studies*, 30, 6, 997–1019.

——(2004). *Knowledge Work and Knowledge-Intensive Firms*. Oxford: Oxford University Press.

——and Karreman, D. (2007). 'Unraveling HRM: identity, ceremony, and control in a management consulting firm'. *Organization Science*, 18, 4, 711–26.

——and Robertson, M. (2006). 'The best and the brightest: the construction, significance and effects of elite identities in consulting firms'. *Organization*, 13, 2, 195–224.

Anand, V., Glick, W. H., and Manz, C. C. (2002). 'Thriving on the knowledge of outsiders: tapping organizational social capital'. *Academy of Management Executive*, 16, 1, 87–101.

Anand, N., Gardner, H. K., and Morris, T. (2007). 'Knowledge-based innovation: emergence and embedding of new practice areas in management consulting firms'. *Academy of Management Journal*, 50, 2, 406–28.

Antal, A. B. and Krebsbach-Gnath, C. (2001). 'Consultants as agents of organisational learning', in M. Dierkes, A. Berthoin, J. Child, and I. Nonaka (eds.), *Handbook of Organizational Learning and Knowledge*. Oxford: Oxford University Press.

Argote, L., McEvily, B., and Reagans, R. (2003). 'Managing knowledge in organizations: an integrative framework and review of emerging themes'. *Management Science*, 49, 4, 571–82.

Argyris, C. (1970). *Intervention Theory and Method*. Reading, MA: Addison-Wesley.

——and Schön, D. (1996). *Organizational Learning II: Theory, Method and Practice*. Boston, MA: Addison-Wesley.

Armbrüster, T. (2006). *The Economics and Sociology of Management Consulting*. Cambridge: Cambridge University Press.

——and Kipping, M. (2002). 'Types of knowledge and the client–consultant interaction', in K. Sahlin-Andersson and L. Engwall (eds.), *The Expansion of Management Knowledge—Carriers, Flows and Sources*. Stanford, CA: Stanford University Press.

Arnaud, G. (1998). 'The obscure object of demand in consultancy—a psychoanalytic perspective'. *Journal of Managerial Psychology*, 13, 7, 469–84.

Barley, S. R. and Kunda, G. (2004). *Gurus, Hired Guns and Warm Bodies*. Princeton, NJ: Princeton University Press.

Bateson, G. (1955). 'A theory of play and fantasy'. *Psychiatric Research Reports*, 2, 39–51.

Becker, H. S. (1963). *Outsiders: Studies in the Sociology of Deviance*. New York: Free Press.

Berger, P. L. (1963). *Invitation to Sociology*. Harmondsworth: Penguin.

Berglund, J. and Werr, A. (2000). 'The invincible character of management consulting rhetoric: how one blends incommensurates while keeping them apart'. *Organization*, 7, 4, 633–54.

Bessant, J. and Rush, H. (1995). 'Building bridges for innovation: the role of consultants in technology transfer'. *Research Policy*, 24, 97–114.

Bhagat, R. S., Kedia, B. L., Harveston, P. D., and Triandis, H. C. (2002). 'Cultural variations in the cross-border transfer of organizational knowledge—an integrative framework'. *Academy of Management Review*, 27, 2, 204–21.

Birkinshaw, J., Hamel, G., and Mol, M. J. (2008). 'Management innovation'. *Academy of Management Review*, forthcoming.

Blackler, F. (1995). 'Knowledge, knowledge work and organizations—an overview and interpretation'. *Organization Studies*, 16, 6, 1021–46.

Bloomfield, B. and Best, A. (1992). 'Management consultants: systems development, power and the translation of problems'. *Sociological Review*, 40, 533–60.

——and Danieli, A. (1995). 'The role of management consultants in the development of information technology: the indissoluble nature of socio-political and technical skills'. *Journal of Management Studies*, 32, 1, 23–46.

Bogenrieder, I. and Nooteboom, B. (2004). 'Learning groups: what types are there? A theoretical analysis and an empirical study in a consultancy firm'. *Organization Studies*, 25, 2, 287–313.

Boland, R. J. and Hoffman, R. (1983). 'Humour in a machine shop: an interpretation of symbolic action', in P. Frost, V. F. Mitchell, and W. R. Nord (eds.), *Organizational Reality: Reports From the Firing Line*. Glenview, IL: Scott, Foresman, pp. 371–6.

Born, G. (2004). *Uncertain Vision—Birt, Dyke and the Reinvention of the BBC*. London: Secker and Warburg.

Bowker, G. and Star, S. L. (1999). *Sorting Things Out: Classification and Its Consequences*. Cambridge, MA: MIT Press.

Boyatzis, R. E. (1998). *Transforming Qualitative Data: Thematic Analysis and Code Development*. Thousand Oaks, CA: Sage.

Brockhaus, W. L. (1977). 'Prospects for malpractice suits in the business consulting profession'. *Journal of Business*, 50, 1, 70–5. Cited in Gluckler and Armbrüster, op. cit.

Brown, G., Lawrence, T. B., and Robinson, S. L. (2005). 'Territoriality in organizations'. *Academy of Management Review*, 30, 3, 577–94.

Buchanan, D. and Badham, R. (1999). 'Politics and organizational change: the lived experience'. *Human Relations*, 52, 5, 609–29.

Buono, A. F. (ed.) (2001). *Current Trends in Management Consulting, Research in Management Consulting*, Vol. 1. Greenwich, CN: Information Age Publishing.

——(2002). *Developing Knowledge and Value in Management Consulting, Research in Management Consulting*, Vol. 2. Greenwich, CN: Information Age Publishing.

Burt, R. S. (1992). *Structural Holes*. Cambridge, MA: Harvard University Press.

Camus, A. (1946). *The Outsider*. London: Hamish Hamilton.

Carlile, P. R. (2002). 'A pragmatic view of knowledge and boundaries: boundary objects in new product development'. *Organization Science*, 13, 4, 442–55.

——(2004). 'Transferring, translating and transforming: an integrative framework for managing knowledge across boundaries'. *Organization Science*, 15, 5, 555–68.

Chanlat, J.-F. (1996). 'From cultural imperialism to independence', in S. R. Clegg and G. Palmer (eds.), *The Politics of Management Knowledge*. London: Sage.

Child, J. and Rodrigues, S. (1996). 'The role of social identity in the international transfer of knowledge through joint ventures', in S. R. Clegg and G. Palmer (eds.), *The Politics of Management Knowledge*. London: Sage.

Chinn, C. A. and Brewer, W. F. (1993). 'The role of anomalous data in knowledge acquisition: a theoretical framework and implications for science instruction'. *Review of Educational Research*, 63, 1, 1–49.

Christensen, P. R. and Klyver, K. (2006). 'Management consultancy in small firms: how does interaction work?' *Journal of Small Business and Enterprise Development*, 13, 3, 299–313.

Clark, T. (1995). *Managing Consultants—Consultancy as the Management of Impressions*. Buckingham: Open University Press.

——(2004). 'The fashion of management fashion: a surge too far?' *Organization*, 11, 2, 297–307.

—— and Fincham, R. (2002). *Critical Consulting: New Perspectives on the Management Advice Industry*. Oxford: Blackwell.

—— and Salaman, G. (1996). 'Management gurus as organisational witchdoctors'. *Organization*, 3, 1, 85–107.

————(1998). 'Creating the right impression—towards a dramaturgy of management consultancy'. *The Service Industries Journal*, 18, 1, 18–38.

Clayman, S. E. (1992). 'Caveat orator: audience disaffiliation in the 1988 presidential debates'. *Quarterly Journal of Speech*, 78, 33–60.

Clegg, S. R., Kornberger, M., and Rhodes, C. (2004). 'Noise, parasites and translation: theory and practice in management consulting'. *Management Learning*, 35, 1, 31–44.

Cockman, P., Evans, B., and Reynolds, P. (1999). *Consulting for Real People*. London: McGraw Hill.

Contu, A., Grey, C., and Ortenblad, A. (2003). 'Against learning'. *Human Relations*, 56, 8, 931–52.

Craig, D. (2005). *Rip Off! The Scandalous Inside Story of the Management Consulting. Money Machine*. London: The Original Book Company.

——(2006). *Plundering the Public Sector*. London: Constable.

Czarniawska, B. and Joerges, B. (1996). 'Travels of ideas', in B. Czarniawska and G. Sevon (eds.), *Translating Organizational Change*. Berlin: de Gruyter.

——and Mazza, C. (2003). 'Consulting as liminal space'. *Human Relations*, 56, 3, 267–90.

——and Sevon, G. (eds.) (1996). *Translating Organizational Change*. Berlin: de Gruyter.

Czerniawska, F. (2002). *The Intelligent Client*. London: Hodder & Stoughton.

——and May, P. (2004). *Management Consulting in Practice*. London: Kogan Page/MCA.

De Jong, J. A. and van Eekelen, I. M. (1999). 'Management consultants—what do they do?' *The Leadership and Organization Development Journal*, 20, 4, 181–8.

Deelmann, T. and Mohe, M. (eds.) (2006). *Selection and Evaluation of Consultants, Management Consulting Research*, Vol. 1. Munich: Rainer Hampp Verlag.

Delaney, S. (2000). Email contribution to the *Two days of coding* thread, on the QUAL-SOFTWARE listserv, 14 February 2000. (See http://www.jiscmail.ac.uk for archives).

Duffy, F. (1997). *The New Office*. London: Conran Octopus.

Dutton, J. and Ashford, S. (1993). 'Selling issues to top management'. *Academy of Management Review*, 18, 3, 397–428.

Dutton, J. E., Ashford, S. J., O'Neill, R. M., and Lawrence, K. A. (2001). 'Moves that matter: issue selling and organizational change'. *Academy of Management Journal*, 44, 4, 716–36.

Easterby-Smith, M., Lyles, M. A., and Tsang, E. W. K. (2008). 'Inter-organizational knowledge transfer: current themes and future prospects'. *Journal of Management Studies*, 45, 4, 677–90.

Ebers, M. and Grandori, A. (1997). 'The forms, costs and development dynamics of inter-organizational networking', in M. Ebers (ed.), *The Formation of Inter-Organizational Networks*. New York: Oxford University Press.

Edenius, M. and Yakhlef, A. (2007). 'Space, vision and organisational learning: the interplay of incorporating and inscribing practices'. *Management Learning*, 38, 2, 193–210.

Engwall, L. and Eriksson, C. B. (2005). 'Doing deals despite distrust', in S. Furusten and A. Werr (eds.), *Dealing with Confidence—The Construction of Need and Trust in Management Advisory Services*. Copenhagen: Copenhagen Business School Press.

Engwall, L. and Kipping, M. (2002). 'Introduction', in M. Kipping and L. Engwall (eds.), *Management Consulting: The Emergence and Dynamics of a Knowledge Industry*. Oxford: Oxford University Press.

Festinger, L. (1957). *A Theory of Cognitive Dissonance*. Stanford, CA: Stanford University Press.

File, K. M., Cermark, D. S. P., and Prince, R. A. (1994). 'Word of mouth effects in professional services buyer behaviour'. *Service Industries Journal*, 14, 3, 301–14.

Fincham, R. (1999). 'The consultant–client relationship—critical perspectives on the management of organisational change'. *Journal of Management Studies*, 36, 3, 335–51.

——(2002). 'Charisma v technique—differentiating the expertise of management gurus and management consultants', in T. Clark and R. Fincham (eds.), *Critical Consulting*. Oxford: Blackwell.

—— and Clark, T. (2002). 'Introduction: the emergence of critical perspectives on consulting', in T. Clark and R. Fincham (eds.), *Critical Consulting: New Perspectives on the Management Advice Industry*. Oxford: Blackwell, pp. 1–18.

Ford, R. and Randolph, W. (1992). 'Cross-functional structures: a review and integration of matrix organization and project management'. *Journal of Management*, 18, 2, 267–94.

Fosstenlokken, S. M., Lowendahl, B. R., and Revang, O. (2003). 'Knowledge development through client interaction—a comparative study'. *Organizational Studies*, 24, 6, 859–80.

Fox, S. (1990). 'The Ethnography of humour and the problem of social reality'. *Sociology*, 24, 3, 431–46.

——(2000). 'Communities of practice, Foucault and actor–network theory'. *Journal of Management Studies*, 37, 6, 853–67.

Froud, J., Haslan, C., Johal, S., and Williams, K. (2000). 'Shareholder value and financialisation: consultancy promises, management moves'. *Economy and Society*, 29, 80–110.

Fullerton, J. and West, M. (1996). 'Consultant and client—working together?' *Journal of Managerial Psychology*, 11, 6, 40–9.

Furusten, S. (1999). *Popular Management Books: How They Are Made and What They Mean for Organizations*. London: Routledge.

—— and Werr, A. (eds.) (2005). *Dealing with Confidence—the Construction of Need and Trust in Management Advisory Services*. Copenhagen: Copenhagen Business School Press.

Galanter, M. (2006). *Lowering the Bar: Lawyer Jokes and Legal Culture*. Wisconsin: The University of Wisconsin Press.

Gammelsaeter, H. (2002). 'Managers and consultants as embedded actors—evidence from Norway', in M. Kipping and L. Engwall (eds.), *Management Consulting—Emergence and Dynamics of a Knowledge Industry*. Oxford: Oxford University Press.

Gann, D. and Salter, A. (2000). 'Innovation in project-based, service-enhanced firms: the construction of complex products and systems'. *Research Policy*, 29, 955–72.

Garfinkel, H. (1967). *Studies in Ethnomethodology*. Englewood Cliffs, NJ: Prentice Hall.

Garsten, C. (1999). 'Betwixt and between—temporary employees as liminal subjects in flexible organizations'. *Organization Studies*, 20, 4, 601–17.

——(2003). 'Colleague, competitor or client: social boundaries in flexible work arrangements', in N. Paulsen and T. Hernes (eds.), *Managing Boundaries in Organizations—Multiple Perspectives*. Houndmills: Palgrave/Macmillan.

Giddens, A. (1984). *The Constitution of Society: Outline of the Theory of Structuration*. Cambridge: Polity Press.

——and Abrahamson, E. (1991). 'Champions of change and strategic shifts: the role of internal and external change advocates'. *Journal of Management Studies*, 28, 2, 173–90.

Glenn, P. J. (1989). 'Initiating shared laughter in multi-party conversations'. *Western Journal of Speech Communication*, 53, 127–49.

——(1995). 'Laughing at and laughing with: negotiation of participant alignments through conversational laughter', in P. ten Have and G. Psathas (eds.), *Situated Order: Studies in the Social Organization of Talk and Embodied Activities*. Washington, DC: University Press of America, pp. 43–56.

Gluckler, J. and Armbrüster, T. (2003). 'Bridging uncertainty in management consulting—the mechanisms of trust and networked reputation'. *Organization Studies*, 24, 2, 269–97.

Goodman, R. A. (1981). *Temporary Systems: Professional Development, Manpower Utilization, Task Effectiveness and Innovation*. New York: Praeger.

Gouldner, A. W. (1957). 'Cosmopolitans and locals: towards an analysis of latent social roles I'. *Administrative Science Quarterly*, 2, 3, 281–306.

Grabher, G. (2002). 'Cool projects, boring institutions: temporary collaboration in social context'. *Regional Studies*, 36, 3, 205–14.

Granovetter, M. (1973). 'The strength of weak ties'. *American Journal of Sociology*, 78 (May), 1360–80.

——(1985). 'Economic action and social structure: the problem of embeddedness'. *American Journal of Sociology*, 91, 3, 481–510.

Greatbatch, D. and Clark, T. (2003). 'Displaying group cohesiveness: humour and laughter in the public lectures of management gurus'. *Human Relations*, 56, 12, 1515–44.

————(2005). *Management Speak: Why We Listen to What Management Gurus Tell Us*. London: Routledge.

Grey, C. and Sturdy, A. J. (2007). 'Friendship and organizational analysis: towards a research agenda'. *Journal of Management Inquiry*, 16, 2, 157–72.

Haas, M. R. (2006). 'Acquiring and applying knowledge in transnational teams—the roles of cosmopolitans and locals'. *Organization Science*, 17, 3, 367–84.

Hacking, I. (1999). *The Social Construction of What?* Cambridge, MA: Harvard University Press.

Hagan, T. and Smail, D. (1997). 'Power-mapping: background and basic methodology'. *Journal of Community & Applied Social Psychology*, 7, 257–67.

Hagedoorn, J. and Duysters, G. (2002). 'Learning in dynamic inter-firm networks: the efficacy of multiple contacts'. *Organization Studies*, 23, 4, 525–48.

Hancock, P. and Tyler, M. (eds.) (2009). *The Management of Everyday Life.* Basingstoke: Palgrave/Macmillan, forthcoming.

Handley, K., Sturdy, A. J., Clark, T., and Fincham, R. (2006). 'What type of relationship do clients really want with their consultancies?' *People Management*, 18 May, p. 52.

——————(2007). 'Researching situated learning: participation, identity and practices in client–consultant relationship'. *Management Learning*, 38, 2, 173–91.

Hanlon, G. (2004). 'Institutional forms and organisational structures—homology, trust and reputational capital in professional service firms'. *Organization*, 11, 2, 187–210.

Hansen, M. T. (1999). 'The search-transfer problem: the role of weak ties in sharing knowledge across organization subunits'. *Administrative Science Quarterly*, 44, 1, 82–111.

—— Nohria, N., and Tierney, T. (1999). 'What is your strategy for managing knowledge?' *Harvard Business Review*, March, 106–16.

Hargadon, A. B. (1998). 'Firms as knowledge brokers—lessons in pursuing continuous innovation'. *California Management Review*, 40, 3, 209–27.

Heracleous, L. (2004). 'Boundaries in the study of organization'. *Human Relations*, 57, 1, 95–103.

Hernes, T. (2004). 'Studying composite boundaries—a framework for analysis'. *Human Relations*, 57, 1, 9–29.

—— and Paulsen, N. (2003). 'Introduction—boundaries and organization', in N. Paulsen and T. Hernes (eds.), *Managing Boundaries in Organizations—Multiple Perspectives.* Houndmills: Palgrave/Macmillan.

Heron, J. (1990). *Helping the Client.* London: Sage.

Heusinkveld, S. and Benders, J. (2005). 'Contested commodification: consultancies and their struggle with new concept development'. *Human Relations*, 58, 2, 283–310.

Hinds, P. and Mortensen, M. (2005). 'Understanding conflict in geographically distributed teams: the moderating effects of shared identity, shared context and spontaneous communication'. *Organization Science*, 16, 3, 290–307.

Hislop, D. (2002). 'The client role in consultancy relations during the appropriation of technological innovations'. *Research Policy*, 31, 657–71.

Hobday, M. (2000). 'The project-based organization: an ideal form for managing complex products and systems?' *Research Policy*, 29, 871–93.

Hochschild, A. R. (1997). *The Time Bind: When Work Becomes Home and Home Becomes Work*. New York: Metropolitan Books.

Holmqvist, M. (2003). 'A dynamic model of intra- and interorganizational learning'. *Organization Studies*, 24, 1, 95–123.

Huczynski, A. A. (1993). *Management Gurus—What They Are and How to Become One*. London: Routledge.

Hughes, M., Dalziel, R., Baker, K., and Fox, P. (2007). 'Local government attitudes to external consultancy support'. *Public Money and Management*, 27, 4, 241–3.

Human Relations (2004). Special issue on 'Boundaries or Integration', 57, 1.

Inkpen, A. C. and Tsang, E. W. K. (2005). 'Social capital, networks and knowledge transfer'. *Academy of Management Review*, 30, 1, 146–65.

Jackall, R. (1986). *Moral Mazes—The World of Corporate Managers*. New York: Oxford University Press.

Jarzabkowski, P. and Seidl, D. (2008). 'The role of meetings in the social practice of strategy'. *Organization Studies*, 29, 11, 1391–1426.

Jones, A. (2003). *Management Consultancy and Banking in an Era of Globalization*. Houndmills: Palgrave/Macmillan.

Karantinou, K. M. and Hogg, M. K. (2001). 'Exploring relationship management in professional services—a study of management consultancy'. *Journal of Marketing Management*, 17, 263–86.

Karreman, D. and Rylander, A. (2008). 'Managing meaning through branding—the case of a consulting firm'. *Organization Studies*, 29, 1, 103–25.

Katz, R. and Allen, T. J. (1982). 'Investigating the not invented here (NIH) syndrome: a look at the performance, tenure, and communication patterns of 50 R&D project groups'. *R&D Management*, 121, 7–19. Cited in Menon and Pfeffer, op. cit.

Keegan, A. and Turner, J. R. (2002). 'The management of innovation in project-based firms'. *Long Range Planning*, 35, 4, 367–88.

Kennedy Information (2004). *The Global Consulting Marketplace 2004–2006: Key Data, Trends and Forecast*. Peterborough, NH: Kennedy Information Inc.

Kieser, A. (1997). 'Rhetoric and myth in management fashion'. *Organization*, 4, 1, 49–74.

——(2002*a*). 'Managers as marionettes? Using fashion theories to explain the success of consultancies', in M. Kipping and L. Engwall (eds.), *Management Consulting—Emergence and Dynamics of a Knowledge Industry*. Oxford: Oxford University Press.

——(2002*b*). 'On communication barriers between management science, consultancies and business organizations', in T. Clark and R. Fincham (eds.), *Critical Consulting*. Oxford: Blackwell.

Kinnie, N. et al. (2006). *Managing People and Knowledge in Professional Service Firms*. Research Report. London: CIPD.

Kipping, M. (2002). 'Trapped in their wave: the evolution of management consultancies', in T. Clark and R. Fincham (eds.), *Critical Consulting: New Perspectives on the Management Advice Industry*. Oxford: Blackwell.

Kipping, M. and Armbrüster, T. (2002). 'The burden of otherness—limits of consultancy interventions in historical case studies', in M. Kipping and L. Engwall (eds.), *Management Consulting—Emergence and Dynamics of a Knowledge Industry*. Oxford: Oxford University Press.

——and Engwall, L. (eds.) (2002). *Management Consulting—Emergence and Dynamics of a Knowledge Industry*. Oxford: Oxford University Press.

Kitay, J. and Wright, C. (2003). 'Expertise and organizational boundaries: varying roles of Australian management consultants'. *Asia Pacific Business Review*, 9, 3, 21–40.

——— (2004). 'Take the money and run? Organisational boundaries and consultants' roles'. *Service Industries Journal*, 24, 3, 1–19.

Kolb, D. A. (1984). *Experiential Learning*. Englewood Cliffs, NJ: Prentice Hall.

Kostova, T. and Roth, K. (2002). 'Adoption of an organizational practice by subsidiaries of MNCs: institutional and relational effects'. *Academy of Management Journal*, 45, 1, 215–33.

Kumra, S. and Vinnicombe, S. (2008). 'A study of the promotion to partner process in a professional services firm: how women are disadvantaged'. *British Journal of Management*, 19, 1, 65–74.

Kvale, S. (1996). *Interviews: An Introduction to Qualitative Research Interviewing*. Thousand Oaks, CA: Sage.

Lacey, M. Y. (1995). 'Internal consulting: perspectives on the process of planned change'. *Journal of Organizational Change Management*, 8, 3, 75–84.

Laclau, E. and Mouffe, C. (1985). *Hegemony and Socialist Strategy*. London: Verso.

Lahti, R. K. and Beyerlein, M. M. (2000). 'Knowledge transfer and management consulting: a look at the firm'. *Business Horizons*, January, 65–74.

Lamont, M. and Molnar, V. (2002). 'The study of boundaries in the social sciences'. *Annual Review of Sociology*, 28, 167–95.

Latour, B. (1986). 'The powers of association', in J. Law (ed.), *Power, Action and Belief*. London: RKP.

—— (1987). *Science in Action: How to Follow Scientists and Engineers Through Society*. Milton Keynes: Open University Press.

Lave, J. and Wenger, E. (1991). *Situated Learning: Legitimate Peripheral Participation*. Cambridge: Cambridge University Press.

Lavin, D. and Maynard, D. (2001). 'Standardization vs. rapport: respondent laughter and interviewer reaction during telephone surveys'. *American Sociological Review*, 66, 453–79.

Lefebvre, H. (1991). *The Production of Space*. Oxford: Blackwell.

Lennox-Terrion, J. and Ashforth, B. E. (2002). 'From "I" to "We": the role of putdown humour and identity in the development of a temporary group'. *Human Relations*, 55, 1, 55–88.

Lewin, K. (1951). *Field Theory in Social Science; selected theoretical papers*. New York: Harper & Row.

Lillrank, P. (1995). 'The transfer of management innovations from Japan'. *Organisation Studies*, 16, 6, 971–89.

Lippitt, G. and Lippitt, R. (1986). *The Consulting Process in Action*. San Diego: University Associates Inc.

Long Range Planning (2004). Special issue on 'Boundaries and Knowledge', December.

Macdonald, S. (2004). 'The cost of control: speculation on the impact of management consultants on creativity in the BBC'. *Prometheus*, 22, 1, 43–70.

——(2006). 'Babes and sucklings: management consultants and novice clients'. *European Management Journal*, 24, 6, 411–21.

Maister, D. (1993). *Managing the Professional Service Firm*. London: Simon & Schuster.

March, J. (1991). 'Exploration and exploitation in organizational learning'. *Organization Science*, 2, 1, 71–87.

Marchington, M. and Vincent, S. (2004). 'Analysing the influence of institutional, organisational and inter-personal forces in shaping inter-organisational relations'. *Journal of Management Studies*, 41, 6, 1029–56.

Markham, C. (1997). *Practical Management Consultancy*. London: Accountancy Books.

Marsh, S. (2008). *The Feminine in Management Consulting—Power, Emotion and Values in Consulting Interactions*. Basingstoke: Palgrave.

Marshall, H. (2000). 'Avoiding wrecked heads with magic and machinery', in *Sociological Sites/Sights: Referred Proceedings of the Australian Sociological Association Conference*, Flinders University, Adelaide, South Australia.

Marshall, N. (2003). 'Identity and difference in complex projects—why boundaries still matter in the "boundaryless" organization', in N. Paulsen and T. Hernes (eds.), *Managing Boundaries in Organizations—Multiple Perspectives*. Houndmills: Palgrave/Macmillan.

Management Consultancies Association (2006 and 2007). *The UK Consulting Industry, 2005/6 and 2006/7*. London: MCA.

McGivern, C. (1983). 'Some facets of the relationship between consultants and clients in organizations'. *Journal of Management Studies*, 20, 3, 367–86.

McKenna, C. (2006). *The World's Newest Profession*. Cambridge: Cambridge University Press.

Menon, T. and Pfeffer, J. (2003). 'Valuing internal vs. external knowledge: explaining the preference for outsiders'. *Management Science*, 49, 4, 497–513.

Meriläinen, S., Tienari, J., Thomas, R., and Davies, A. (2004). 'Management consultant talk: a cross-cultural comparison of normalizing discourse and resistance'. *Organization*, 11, 4, 539–64.

Merton, R. K. (1968). *Social Theory and Social Structure*, rev. edn. New York: Free Press.

——(1972). 'Insiders and outsiders: a chapter in the sociology of knowledge'. *The American Journal of Sociology*, 78, 1, 9–47.

Meyer, J. W. (1996). 'Otherhood: the promulgation and transmission of ideas in the modern organizational environment', in B. Czarniawska and G. Sevon (eds.), *Translating Organizational Change*. Berlin: de Gruyter.

Meyer, J. C. (2000). 'Humour as a double-edged sword: four functions of humour in communication'. *Communication Theory*, 10, 3, 310–31.

Meyer, M. W. and Lu, X. (2004). 'Managing indefinite boundaries: the strategy and structure of a Chinese business firm'. *Management Organization Review*, 1, 1, 57–86. Cited in Santos and Eisenhardt, op. cit.

Mickhail, G. and Ostrovsky, A. (2007). 'MetaCapitalism: the dialectics of impoverishment'. *Critical Perspectives on Accounting*, 18, 8, 671–705.

Miles, M. B. and Huberman, A. M. (1994). *Qualitative Data Analysis*. Thousand Oaks, CA: Sage Publications.

Mills, P. K. and Morris, M. (1986). 'Clients as partial employees of service organizations: role development in client participation'. *Academy of Management Review*, 11, 4, 726–35.

Mintzberg, H. (1973). *The Nature of Managerial Work*. London: Harper & Row.

Miozzo, M. and Grimshaw, D. (eds.) (2006). *Knowledge Intensive Business Services and Changing Organizational Forms*. Cheltenham: Edward Elgar.

Mohe, M. (2008). 'Bridging the cultural gap in management consulting research'. *International Journal of Cross Cultural Management*, 8, 1, 41–57.

Moore, G. L. (1984). *The Politics of Management Consulting*. New York: Praeger.

Morgan, G. and Sturdy, A. J. (2000). *Beyond Organisational Change—Discourse, Structure and Power in UK Financial Service*. Basingstoke: Macmillan.

——Quack, Z., and Sturdy, A. J. (2006). 'The globalization of management consultancy firms: constraints and limitations', in M. Miozzo and D. Grimshaw (eds.), *Knowledge Intensive Business Services and Changing Organizational Forms*. Cheltenham: Edward Elgar.

Morris, T. (2001). 'Asserting property rights: knowledge codification in the professional service firm'. *Human Relations*, 54, 7, 819–38.

Mulkay, M. (1988). *On Humour: Its Nature and Its Place in Modern Society*. Oxford: Blackwell.

Mulligan, J. and Barber, P. (2001). 'The client–consultant relationship', in P. Sadler (ed.), *Management Consultancy—A Handbook for Best Practice*, 2nd edn. London: Kogan Page.

Muzio, D., Ackroyd, S., and Chanlat, J.-F. (eds.) (2008). *Redirections in the Study of Expert Labour*. Basingstoke: Palgrave.

National Audit Office (2006). *Central Government's Use of Consultants*. London: The Stationery Office.

Nikolova, N. (2007). *The Client–Consultant Relationship in Professional Business Service Firms*. Cologne: Kolner Wissenschaftsverlag.

Nippert-Eng, C. (2003). 'Drawing the line—organisations and the boundary work of "home" and "work"', in N. Paulsen and T. Hernes (eds.), *Managing Boundaries in Organizations—Multiple Perspectives*. Houndmills: Palgrave/Macmillan.

Nonaka, I. (1994). 'A dynamic theory of organizational knowledge creation'. *Organization Science*, 5, 1, 14–37.

——and Takeuchi, H. (1995). *The Knowledge Creating Company*. Oxford: Oxford University Press.

Nooteboom, B. (2000). 'Learning by interaction: absorptive capacity, cognitive distance and governance'. *Journal of Management and Governance*, 4, 69–92.

——(2004). *Inter-Firm Collaboration, Learning and Networks*. London: Routledge.

——Van Haverbeke, W., Duysters, G., Gilsing, V., and van den Oord, A. (2007). 'Optimal cognitive distance and absorptive capacity'. *Research Policy*, 36, 7, 1016–34.

Norrick, N. R. (1993). *Conversational Joking: Humour in Everyday Talk*. Indianapolis: Indiana University Press.

——(1994). 'Involvement and joking in conversation'. *Journal of Pragmatics*, 22, 409–30.

O'Farrell, P. N. and Moffat, L. A. R. (1991). 'An interaction model of business service production and consumption'. *British Journal of Management*, 2, 205–21.

O'Neil, H. M., Pouder, R. W., and Buchholtz, A. K. (1998). 'Patterns in the diffusion of strategies across organizations: insights from the innovation diffusion literature'. *Academy of Management Review*, 23, 1, 98–114.

O'Mahoney, J. (2007). 'Disrupting identity: trust and angst in management consulting', in S. Bolton (ed.), *Searching for the H in Human Resource Management*. London: Sage.

O'Shea, J. and Madigan, C. (1997). *Dangerous Company: The Consulting Powerhouses and the Businesses They Save and Ruin*. London: Nicholas Brealey.

Orlikowski, W. (2002). 'Knowing in practice: enacting a collective capability in distributed organizing'. *Organization Science*, 13, 3, 249–73.

Parker, M. (1995). 'Working together, working apart: management culture in a manufacturing firm'. *Sociological Review*, 43, 3, 518–47.

Paulsen, N. (2003). ' "Who are we now?" Group identity, boundaries and the (re)organizing process', in N. Paulsen and T. Hernes (eds.), *Managing Boundaries in Organizations—Multiple Perspectives*. Houndmills: Palgrave/Macmillan.

Pettigrew, A. M. (1985). *The Awakening Giant*. Oxford: Basil Blackwell.

Phills, J. A. (1996). 'Tensions in the client–consultant relationship'. *Academy of Management Conference Paper*.

Piaget, J. (1970). 'Piaget's theory', in P. Mussen (ed.), *Handbook of Child Psychology*, 3rd edn. New York: Wiley.

Pinault, L. (2001). *Consulting Demons: Inside the Unscrupulous World of Global Corporate Consulting*. Chichester: John Wiley.

Pollio, H. R., Mers, R., and Lucchesi, W. (1972). 'Humor, laughter, and smiling: some preliminary observations on funny behaviors', in J. H. Goldstein and P. E. McGhee (eds.), *The Psychology of Humor*. New York: Academic Press, pp. 211–39.

Portes, A. (1998). 'Social capital: its origins and applications in modern sociology'. *Annual Review of Sociology*, 24, 1, 1–24.

Raskin, V. (1985). *Semantic Mechanisms of Humour*. Boston: Reidel.

Reason, P. (ed.) (1988). *Human Inquiry in Action*. London: Sage.

Robertson, M. and Swan, J. (2003). 'Control—what control? Culture and ambiguity within a knowledge intensive firm'. *Journal of Management Studies*, 40, 4, 831–58.

——Scarbrough, H., and Swan, J. (2003). 'Knowledge creation in professional service firms—institutional effects'. *Organization Studies*, 24, 6, 831–58.

Robson, C. (1993). *Real World Research*. Oxford: Blackwell.

Rogers, E. M. (1995). *Diffusion of Innovations*, 4th edn. New York: Free Press.

Sadler, P. (ed.) (2001). *Management Consultancy—A Handbook for Best Practice*, 2nd edn. London: Kogan Page.

Sahlin-Andersson, K. and Engwall, L. (eds.) (2002a). *The Expansion of Management Knowledge: Carriers, Ideas and Circulation*. Stanford University Press.

————(2002b). 'Carriers, flows and sources of management knowledge', in K. Sahlin-Andersson and L. Engwall (eds.), *The Expansion of Management Knowledge: Carriers, Ideas and Circulation*. Stanford University Press.

Saint-Martin, D. (2000). *Building the New Managerialist State: Consultants and the Politics of Public Sector Reform in Comparative Perspective*. Oxford University Press.

Santos, F. and Eisenhardt, K. M. (2005). 'Organizational boundaries and theories of organization'. *Organization Science*, 16, 491–508.

Sarvary, M. (1999). 'Knowledge management and competition in the consulting industry'. *California Management Review*, 41, 2, 95–107.

Scarbrough, H. (ed.) (2008). *The Evolution of Business Knowledge*. Oxford: Oxford University Press.

——Bresnen, M., Edelman, L., Laurent, S., Newell, S. L., and Swan, J. (2004). 'The processes of project-based learning: an exploratory study'. *Management Learning*, 35, 4, 491–506.

Schein, E. H. (1969, 1988). *Process Consultation: Its Role in Organization Development*, 2nd edn. Reading, MA: Addison-Wesley.

——(1987). *Process Consultation: Lessons for Managers and Consultants*. Reading, MA: Addison-Wesley.

——(1997). 'The concept of "client" from a process consultation perspective: a guide for change agents'. *Journal of Organizational Change Management*, 10, 3, 202–16.

Schindler, M. and Eppler, M. J. (2003). 'Harvesting project knowledge: a review of project learning methods and success factors'. *International Journal of Project Management*, 21, 219–28.

Schön, D. (1983). *The Reflective Practitioner: How Professionals Think in Action*. New York: Basic Books.

Schwartzman, H. B. (1986). 'The meeting as a neglected social form in organizational studies'. *Research in Organizational Behavior*, 8, 233–58.

Scott, J. (2000). *Social Network Analysis: A Handbook*. London: Sage.

Semadeni, M. (2001). 'Towards a theory of knowledge arbitrage: examining management consultants as knowledge arbiters and arbitragers', in A. F. Buono (ed.), *Current Trends in Management Consulting*, Vol. 1. *Research in Management Consulting*, Vol. 1. Greenwich, CN: Information Age Publishing, pp. 43–67.

Sennett, R. (2006). *The Culture of the New Capitalism*. London: Yale University Press.

Simmel, G. (1950). 'The Stranger' (originally, 1908), in K. Wolff (ed.), *The Sociology of George Simmel*. Glencoe, IL: Free Press, pp. 402–8.

Smith, C. and Meiksins, P. (1995). 'System, society and dominance effects in cross-national organisational analysis'. *Work, Employment and Society*, 9, 2, 241–67.

Smith, I. S. (2008). 'Management consulting in action—value creation and ambiguity in client–consultant relations'. PhD Thesis, Series 4, Copenhagen Business School.

Sorenson, O., Rivkin, J. W., and Fleming, L. (2006). 'Complexity, networks and knowledge flow'. *Research Policy*, 35, 7, 994–1017.

Sorge, A. and Van Witteloostuijn, A. (2004). 'The (non)sense of organizational change'. *Organization Studies*, 25, 7, 1205–31.

Stake, R. E. (1995). *The Art of Case Study Research*. Thousand Oaks, CA: Sage.

Star, S. L. (1989). 'The structure of ill-structured solutions: boundary objects and heterogeneous distributed problem solving', in L. Gasser and M. Huhns (eds.), *Distributed Artificial Intelligence*, Vol. II, London: Pitman, pp. 37–54.

Starbuck, W. H. (1992). Learning by knowledge-intensive firms. *Journal of Management Studies*, 29, 6, 713–40.

Sturdy, A. J. (1997a). 'The consultancy process—an insecure business?' *Journal of Management Studies*, 34, 3, 389–413.

——(1997b). 'The dialectics of consultancy'. *Critical Perspectives on Accounting*, 8, 5, 511–35.

——(2001). 'The global diffusion of customer service—a critique of cultural and institutional perspectives'. *Asia Pacific Business Review*, 7, 3, 73–87.

——(2004). 'The adoption of management ideas and practices—theoretical perspectives and possibilities'. *Management Learning*, 35, 2, 155–79.

——(2009). 'Popular consultancy critiques and a politics of management learning?' *Management Learning*, forthcoming.

——and Wright, C. (2008). 'A consulting diaspora? Enterprising selves as agents of enterprise'. *Organization*, 15, 3, 427–44.

——Schwarz, M., and Spicer, A. (2006). 'Guess who's coming to dinner? Structures and uses of liminality in strategic management consultancy'. *Human Relations*, 59, 7, 929–60.

——Clark, T., Fincham, R., and Handley, K. (2007). 'Management consultancy and emotion: humour in action and contexts', in S. Fineman (ed.), *The Emotional Organisation*. Oxford: Blackwell.

——————(2008). 'Re-thinking the role of management consultants as disseminators of business knowledge—knowledge flows, directions and conditions in consulting projects', in H. Scarbrough (ed.), *The Evolution of Business Knowledge*. Oxford: Oxford University Press.

Sturdy, A. J., Clark, T., Fineham, R., and Handley, K. (2004). 'Silence, procrustes and colonization—a response to Clegg et al.'s "Noise, parasites and translation—theory and practice in management consultancy". *Management Learning*, 35, 3, 337–40.

——————(2009). 'Between innovation and legitimation: boundaries and knowledge flow in management consulting'. *Organization* (forthcoming).

Suddaby, R. and Greenwood, R. (2001). 'Colonizing knowledge—commodification as a dynamic of jurisdictional expansion in professional service firms'. *Human Relations*, 54, 7, 933–53.

Sweller, J. (1988). 'Cognitive load during problem-solving—effects on learning'. *Cognitive Science*, 12, 257–85.

Sydow, J., Lindkvist, L., and DeFillippi, R. (2004). 'Project-based organizations, embeddedness and repositories of knowledge: editorial'. *Organization Studies*, 25, 9, 1475–90.

Szulanski, G. (2003). *Sticky Knowledge—Barriers to Knowing in the Firm*. London: Sage.

Tagliaventi, M. R. and Mattarelli, E. (2006). 'The role of networks of practice, value sharing, and operational proximity in knowledge flows between professional groups'. *Human Relations*, 59, 3, 291–319.

Tempest, S. and Starkey, K. (2004). 'The effects of liminality on individual and organizational learning'. *Organization Studies*, 25, 4, 507–27.

Thrift, N. (2005). *Knowing Capitalism*. London: Sage.

Tichy, N. M. (1975). 'How different types of change agents diagnose organizations'. *Human Relations*, 28, 9, 771–99.

Tisdall, P. (1982). *Agents of Change*. London: Heinemann.

Trice, H. M. and Beyer, J. M. (1993). *The Cultures of Work Organizations*. Englewood Cliffs, NJ: Prentice-Hall.

Turner, V. (1977). *The Ritual Process*. Ithaca, NY: Cornell University Press.

——(1984). 'Liminality and the performative genres', in J. J. MacAloon (ed.), *Rite, Drama, Festival, Spectacle: Rehearsals Toward a Theory of Cultural Performance*. Philadelphia: Institute for the Study of Human Issues, pp. 19–41.

——(1987). 'Betwixt and between: the liminal period in rites of passage' in L. Mahdi, S. Foster, and M. Little (eds.), *Betwixt and Between: Patterns of Masculine and Feminine Initiation*. La Salle, IL: Open Court, pp. 3–19.

Tushman, M. L. and Scanlan, T. J. (1981). 'Boundary spanning individuals: their role in information transfer and their antecedents'. *Academy of Management Journal*, 24, 2, 289–305.

Uzzi, B. (1997). 'Social structure and competition in interfirm networks—the paradox of embeddedness'. *Administrative Science Quarterly*, 42, 1, 35–67.

Van Gennep, A. (1909). *The Rites of Passage*. London: Routledge & Kegan Paul.

Warner, M. (1991). 'How Chinese managers learn'. *Journal of General Management*, 16, 4, 66–84.

Webb, J. (2004). 'Organizations, self-identities and the new economy'. *Sociology*, 38, 4, 719–38.

Weber, M. (1968/1922). *Economy and Society*. Berkeley: University of California Press.

Wenger, E. (1998). *Communities of Practice: Learning, Meaning, and Identity*. Cambridge: University of Cambridge Press.

Werr, A. (1999). 'The Language of Change: The Roles of Methods in the Work of Management Consultants'. Stockholm School of Economics, Doctoral Thesis.

—— and Pemer, F. (2007). 'Purchasing management consulting services: from management autonomy to purchasing involvement'. *Journal of Purchasing and Supply Management*, 13, 98–112.

—— and Stjernberg, T. (2003). 'Exploring management consulting firms as knowledge systems'. *Organizational Studies*, 24, 6, 881–908.

—— and Styhre, A. (2003). 'Management consultants—friend or foe? Understanding the ambiguous client–consultant relationship'. *International Studies of Management and Organization*, 32, 4, 43–66.

—— Stjernberg, T., and Docherty, P. (1997). 'The functions of methods of change in management consulting'. *Journal of Organizational Change Management*, 10, 4, 288–307.

Whittington, R. (1992). 'Putting giddens into action'. *Journal of Management Studies*, 29, 4, 693–712.

Whittle, A. (2005). 'Preaching and practising "flexibility": implications for theories of subjectivity at work'. *Human Relations*, 58, 10, 1301–22.

—— (2008). 'From flexibility to work–life balance: exploring the changing discourses of management consultants'. *Organization*, 15, 4, 513–34.

Wilkinson, B. (1996). 'Culture, institutions and business in E Asia'. *Organization Studies*, 17, 3, 421–47.

Williams, K. and Savage, M. (eds.) (2008). *Remembering Elites*. Oxford: Blackwell/Sociological Review.

Willmott, H. (1993). 'Breaking the paradigm mentality'. *Organization Studies*, 14, 681–720.

Wilson, J. M., O'Leary, M. B., Metiu, A., and Jett, Q. R. (2008). 'Perceived proximity in virtual work: explaining the paradox of far-but-close'. *Organization Studies*, 29, 7, 979–1002.

Wood, P. (ed.) (2001). *Consultancy and Innovation (in Europe)*. London: Routledge.

Wood, G. (1998). 'Projects as Communities: consultants, knowledge and power'. *Impact Assessment and Project Appraisal*, 16, 1, 54–64.

Wright, C. (2008). 'Inside out? Organizational membership, ambiguity and the ambivalent identity of the internal consultant'. *British Journal of Management* (forthcoming).

—— and Kwon, S.-H. (2006). 'Business crisis and management fashion: Korean companies, restructuring and consulting advice'. *Asia Pacific Business Review*, 12, 3, 199–214.

Wright, C. and Sturdy, A. J. (2008). 'Both client and consultant: managers as gatekeepers, knowledge brokers and partners'. Paper presented at 24th EGOS Colloquium, 10–12 July 2008, Amsterdam.

Zabusky, S. E. and Barley, S. R. (1997). ' "You can't be a stone if you're cement": reevaluating the emic identities of scientists in organizations'. *Research in Organizational Behaviour*, 19, 361–404.

Zucker, L. G. (1986). 'Production of trust: institutional sources of economic structure, 1840–1920', in B. M. Staw and L. L. Cummings (eds.), *Research in Organizational Behavior*, Vol. 8. Greenwich, CT: JAI Press, pp. 53–111.

Author Index

Subject Index

Note: Bold entries refer to tables.

Printed and bound by CPI Group (UK) Ltd, Croydon, CR0 4YY